ADAM PASCARELLA

Adam Pascarella is the founder and CEO of Second Order Capital Management, an investment management firm in New York City. Earlier, he was a litigator at Baker McKenzie, one of the world's largest commercial law firms. Adam graduated from the University of Michigan and University of Pennsylvania Carey Law School.

REVERSED IN PART

15 Law School Grads on Pursuing Non-Traditional Careers

Adam Pascarella

Editing by The Pro Book Editor

Typesetting and cover design by Arjan van Woensel

eBook ISBN: 979-8-9855004-1-7

Paperback ISBN: 979-8-9855004-0-0

1. Main category –LAW / Legal Profession

2. Other category – BUSINESS & ECONOMICS / Careers / General

First Edition

To my wife Leah:

For always inspiring me to take chances,

be bold, and live life to the fullest.

TABLE OF CONTENTS

CHAPTER 1 —»» *page 1*
Traveling Off the Beaten Path

CHAPTER 2 —»» *page 12*
Keith Rabois – Operator and Venture Capitalist

CHAPTER 3 —»» *page 36*
Tiffany Duong – Writer, Explorer, and Inspirational Speaker

CHAPTER 4 —»» *page 59*
Daron K. Roberts – Former NFL Assistant Coach
and University Lecturer

CHAPTER 5 —»» *page 80*
Jessica Medina – Accredited Financial Counselor

CHAPTER 6 —»» *page 104*
Anthony Scaramucci – Entrepreneur and
Former White House Communications Director

CHAPTER 7 —»» *page 117*
Melinda Snodgrass – Author and Screenwriter

CHAPTER 8 —»» *page 139*
Richard Hsu – Legal Recruiter

CHAPTER 9 —»» *page 161*
Diahann Billings-Burford – Nonprofit CEO

CHAPTER 10 —» *page 184*
Jay Bilas – College Basketball Analyst and Sports Personality

CHAPTER 11 —» *page 205*
Ayelette Robinson – Actress and Entrepreneur

CHAPTER 12 —» *page 230*
Sander Daniels – Entrepreneur

CHAPTER 13 —» *page 248*
Nelly Baksht – Artist

CHAPTER 14 —» *page 263*
David Hornik – Venture Capitalist and Educator

CHAPTER 15 —» *page 287*
Angela Saverice-Rohan – Management Consultant
and Privacy Expert

CHAPTER 16 —» *page 308*
Mia Dell – Policy Director

CHAPTER 17 —» *page 328*
Twenty-Five Key Takeaways

Acknowledgements —» *page 353*

About the Author —» *page 354*

CHAPTER 1

Traveling Off the Beaten Path

I never saw myself writing this type of book.

I was always attracted to having a "tracked" career in the legal field. You likely know what I'm talking about—especially if you were (or are) interested in becoming a lawyer.

The path to career success starts by doing well in high school. Great grades and standardized test scores are a must. It's also important to join interesting extracurriculars, obtain stellar letters of recommendation, and write a great personal statement. Once you get to college, there's even more pressure to perform well. In fact, if you're thinking of attending law school, you may strategically select your courses so that you can graduate with a higher GPA. Regardless, you do well in your college courses, score well on the LSAT, and go to law school. In law school, you again focus on getting the best possible grades, recommendations, and summer internships so that you can get your dream job after graduation. As if that wasn't enough, the bar exam stands in your way. Only when you pass the bar exam does your professional career as a lawyer truly begin.

As a newly minted lawyer, it is all too easy to remain on a track. For instance, if you decide to work at a Big Law[1] firm, you will follow a well-defined track to partnership. Among many other things, you will need to bill a certain number of hours per year and sell yourself within your firm. The track may not be easy, but the path to partnership is there

---

1   In this book, you may see me or others reference the term "Big Law." If you are unfamiliar with the term, a Big Law firm is a large commercial law firm with offices in many large cities. These law firms have a variety of practice areas and often have corporations or wealthy individuals as clients. While incoming associates are paid handsomely, Big Law firms are generally known for long hours and demanding work.

if you want to pursue it. Even outside the narrow world of Big Law, it's relatively easy to find a tracked path in your specific practice area.

Ultimately, a tracked career is straightforward. It's a long road, yet a paved road. The track is appealing for so many reasons, but one of the most compelling is that so many others have done it. Sure, there are risks. Just because a track exists doesn't mean you will successfully navigate it. Nonetheless, a tracked career path can be comforting because it offers a clear way of achieving a "successful" career. Whether you define success as a hefty paycheck, working in a prestigious profession, giving back to your community, or something else, a tracked career path can get you much closer to your goals.

Like many others, I was attracted to a tracked career in law. In high school, I was interested in politics, history, and policy. I even attended summer school with the Junior State of America, where I took college-level government courses and participated in formal debates with my classmates. It seemed natural to attend a good law school and have some sort of practicing career (the idea of becoming an assistant district attorney seemed especially appealing). If the timing was right, I would later pursue some sort of elected office. After all, plenty of law school graduates are in politics, right?

As you may suspect, the reality has been different. I followed the track to a certain point. After majoring in political science at the University of Michigan, I attended the University of Pennsylvania Law School (now called the University of Pennsylvania Carey Law School). I became a litigation associate at Baker McKenzie in New York City. After practicing for several years, I decided to leave the firm (and legal practice entirely) to pursue a more entrepreneurial career. While that entrepreneurial career naturally had some twists and turns, it led me to start an investment management firm called Second Order Capital Management.

Tracks are appealing, but they often involve major assumptions. I was guilty of falling for those assumptions—even as I proceeded down my track. For one thing, I didn't consider if I would actually *enjoy* legal practice. As a political science major, I assumed my interests in politics and policy would easily dovetail with life as a practicing lawyer. While I found law school and certain elements of legal practice interesting, I quickly discovered that I wanted to do something different. Before my 1L internship, I hadn't had any real, day-to-day exposure in the legal field.

What I assumed legal practice would be and what it actually was didn't match.

Then, my interests changed. Don't get me wrong. There were certain elements of legal practice that I enjoyed. All my colleagues were intelligent, hardworking, and driven. It was energizing to work on complex matters with extremely talented and collegial colleagues. Nonetheless, I wanted to take my career in another direction. Looking back, the one constant in my life was finance. Even in law school, I was more interested in my corporate finance course and other elective courses at the Wharton School than many of my law school courses. When I was supposed to be studying for exams, I was learning corporate valuation frameworks and studying the strategies and thought processes of legendary investors. That passion for finance grew as I became a practicing lawyer. I focused on educating myself on nights and weekends, but I never knew where this interest would lead.

Even considering my interest in finance, I kept feeling the pull of the tracked career. In law school, there was this subtle, yet real pressure to get on law journal and participate in the on-campus interviewing process. Big Law became a more appealing option. Not only was it difficult to ignore the potential compensation, but many of my classmates followed this path. I certainly take ownership over my entire career. Nonetheless, working at a large, commercial law firm felt like an easy and attractive path to follow.

The pull of the track also existed in my life as a practicing lawyer. While I knew I had these strong interests, getting off the track was a separate question. No one forced me to stay on the track, but it wasn't easy to leave. Clearly, there were the practical consequences of leaving. From financial planning to determining my end date, I needed to bypass several roadblocks before making the leap.

But along with this, I felt the fear and uncertainty that many of us experience when making a substantial career change. As you'll read in these pages, there are plenty of seemingly appealing reasons why we shouldn't make a dramatic career move. It took some time to overcome those daunting mental roadblocks. There were some sleepless nights. Even on my last day of legal practice, I felt slightly nervous about my future career.

However, looking back, I can confidently say that leaving legal practice was right for me. I took a calculated risk. While my story hasn't yet been fully written, I can't wait to see how it plays out.

Going Back in Time

What follows in these pages is the book I would have wanted in the early days of my career journey.

When I started law school, I wasn't sure that I wanted to veer from the track of "practicing lawyer." As time progressed, I knew I wanted something different, but getting from point A to point B was a different story. I was looking for some inspiration and tactical guidance.

Sure, I spoke with friends, family members, and mentors about doing something different with my legal background. But at the same time, I searched for input from people who had actually done it. "You can do anything with a law degree" is a well-known trope, yet I wanted to hear from individuals who had gone to law school, perhaps practiced for a few years, and then successfully built a career outside of legal practice. Plenty of successful ex-lawyers are out there, so I wanted some perspective from those who had done something different, whether it involved startups, finance, art, politics, or something else.

Let's back up for a moment. It is important to be clear about what this book *is not*. In this book, I am not:

- Telling you to leave your legal job right now.

- Saying that legal practice isn't rewarding.

- Encouraging every law student or attorney to focus on the negative aspects of legal practice rather than the positive aspects.

- Arguing that you shouldn't pursue a career in legal practice because you aren't passionate about the work.

- Offering tactical and personalized solutions on things like how to best handle your law school debt.

• Declaring that, all else being equal, a career outside the legal industry is better than a career inside the legal industry.

The legal field offers plenty of opportunities for growth—no matter your objectives. Are you looking for a great way to make a difference in the world? You'll certainly find opportunities as a practicing lawyer. What about an intellectually challenging career path? You're in the right place. And what about a way to take on interesting work and achieve financial security? While they aren't the easiest positions to get, there are plenty of opportunities out there.

There are certainly positives to being a practicing lawyer. You shouldn't ignore them. Having said that, you are reading this book. You probably *aren't* looking for a career that involves plain-vanilla legal practice. You want to do something different—even if that involves more risk. In other words, you aren't looking to be shoehorned into a specific practicing role for most of your career. You are searching for an alternate path.

Right now, you may be practicing at a large commercial law firm. You worked really hard to get to this point, but your long-term career interests may lie outside of the law. You may be a law student thinking of what your early career will look like after law school. Even though you are considering a job in legal practice, you are open to other ideas. You may even be a prospective law student contemplating what life will look like after law school. While it is debatable whether you should go to law school to pursue a career outside the law, you want to consider all your options before pulling the trigger.

Whatever your current circumstances, you are in—or about to enter—a field that has experienced an acceleration of secular trends. Law school, which has always been expensive, is getting even more costly. According to data from Law School Transparency, nominal tuition averages for ABA-approved law schools have been on a steady climb upward. For instance, in 1985, private law school tuition averaged around $7,526 per year. In 2019, that figure was a little more than $49,000 per year (over two-and-a-half times more than 1985 private law school tuition *after* adjusting for inflation). As ranked by *U.S. News & World Report*, some of the top law schools charge approximately $60,000 to $70,000 per year.

These are eye-popping numbers. Law school is extremely expensive, and because of this, most law students finance their education through student loans. A *Wall Street Journal* article titled "Law School Loses

Luster as Debts Mount and Salaries Stagnate" presented stark data on the financial burdens that law school grads and new attorneys face.[2] Among other things, the *Journal* looked at the salaries of individuals that were two years out of law school. Out of this cohort, only twelve law schools (out of around two hundred) have graduates earning annual salaries that are more than their debt. While there are ways to tackle that debt, the simple fact is that many law school graduates enter legal practice with substantial financial liabilities.

Even those law school graduates who find the highest-paying jobs (typically at Big Law firms) quickly discover some good and bad news. The good news is that compensation is increasing. First-year associates are getting paid north of $200,000 in salary alone. Law firms are distributing special bonuses, and some senior associates lateraling to different Big Law firms are obtaining six-figure signing bonuses. The bad news is that a challenging job is getting even more challenging. Big Law associates and partners are working more than they ever have before. A *Bloomberg* report stated that law firm associates in 2021 were set to bill approximately 1,817 hours on average, which is ten percent higher than 2020. Perhaps in response to these tougher conditions, there has been an increase in attrition at large commercial law firms.

Making any career move requires a sober look at your goals, finances, growth opportunities, and location. After some introspection, you may discover that the best time to make a substantial move may not be right this second. It may be in the next few months or years. On the flip side, you may read this book and discover that the time to make a major career move is *tomorrow*. No matter what you decide, I hope this book inspires and helps you think about the type of career you want to create.

What You'll Find Inside

In these pages, you will hear the stories of eight women and seven men who graduated from law school but went on to develop outstanding careers outside of day-to-day legal practice. While some may have practiced for many years, all have leveraged their legal skills and experiences in different domains. In fact, this behavior inspired the title of the book.

---

2   You can find the entire article here: https://www.wsj.com/articles/law-school-student-debt-low-salaries-university-miami-11627991855

I'd argue that these fifteen individuals did not totally repudiate their legal education and professional experiences. Even though they may not be practicing every day, they took the softer skills of being a lawyer—of which there are many—and used them to achieve major success outside the legal profession.

The individuals that you will meet in this book are:

- **Keith Rabois** — venture capitalist and operator; member of the "PayPal Mafia."

- **Tiffany Duong** — journalist, activist, and environmentalist.

- **Daron K. Roberts** — former NFL assistant coach and a university lecturer.

- **Jessica Medina** — Accredited Financial Counselor.

- **Anthony Scaramucci** — founder of SkyBridge Capital and former White House Communications Director.

- **Melinda Snodgrass** — bestselling fiction writer and screenwriter.

- **Richard Hsu** — legal recruiter at Major, Lindsey & Africa.

- **Diahann Billings-Burford** — CEO of RISE, a nonprofit that empowers the sports community to promote social justice and improve race relations.

- **Jay Bilas** — ESPN college basketball analyst and of counsel at Moore & Van Allen.

- **Ayelette Robinson** — actress and founder of ActorsGuru.

- **Sander Daniels** — cofounder and COO of Thumbtack, a local services marketplace.

- **Nelly Baksht** — artist in the nascent field of cryptoart.

- **David Hornik** — venture capitalist and founding partner at Lobby Capital.

- **Angela Saverice-Rohan** — management consultant and privacy expert at a Big Four consulting firm.

- **Mia Dell** — policy director at SEIU.

I tried to collect as many diverse experiences as possible. For example, you will hear from some individuals who loved law school and others who didn't particularly enjoy it. Some thoroughly enjoyed legal practice while others didn't practice one day after leaving law school. Then, there are some in this book who haven't completely left the law.

I also wanted to speak with impressive individuals in a whole host of industries and sectors. Quite obviously, outside of legal practice, there are so many different directions you can go. While it's impossible to cover every path, I wanted to touch on some more popular and interesting areas. Even if you want to use your legal education and experience in an area not mentioned in these pages, there are plenty of wise words here to guide and inspire you.

You may be wondering why I chose a question-and-answer format for this book. I think the format offers plenty of benefits.[3] Primarily, you get to hear all fifteen individuals discuss their stories in their own words. Career stories are inherently personal, so I wanted to give each individual an opportunity to express their complete thoughts, reflections, and insights on the page. While I'm not a journalist, I wanted to ask a series of questions that would be most insightful to you, the reader. I hope I have accomplished that task.

The Question of Career Advice

In a book like this, I wouldn't presume to give any type of hyper-personalized career advice. While many lawyers and law students encounter

---

3   My main inspiration was Jack Schwager's *Hedge Fund Market Wizards*. In *Hedge Fund Market Wizards* (and other books in Schwager's *Market Wizards* series), Schwager sits down with successful investors to discuss their backgrounds and investing processes. These conversations are published in a question-and-answer format.

similar career challenges, the specifics inevitably vary. Leaving the law may not be as scary to you as to another person in your position. That said, another potential obstacle—like being financially prepared to make the switch—may be more challenging to you compared to that same person.

All hope isn't lost, however. I do think that you can rely on certain principles when navigating the highs and lows of a career inside or outside the law. You can find those principles sprinkled throughout these interviews. If you are looking for a shortcut, feel free to head to the final chapter, as I provide twenty-five general principles and insights from these conversations. Nonetheless, I highly encourage you to spend time reading these interviews. Context is important, and you'll get all of it by reading the individual discussions.

Along with general principles and insights, there is power in inspiration. All fifteen of these individuals have incredible stories. From Sander Daniels working on Thumbtack at Yale Law School to Jessica Medina transforming her hobby of financial planning into a career as an Accredited Financial Counselor, these individuals have created fascinating careers outside the law. Nothing was given to them. Their aggression, hard work, and grit are qualities we can emulate in our careers. While it's impossible to precisely replicate their paths, seeing how they navigated challenges in their legal and post-legal lives can help you better chart your course.

Sure, a book like this has its flaws. One of those flaws involves survivorship bias. For several reasons, it can be difficult for lawyers and law school grads to build careers outside the law. Not only do we incur career opportunity costs when attending law school, but we must deal with the financial consequences of our decisions. Incurring hundreds of thousands of dollars of debt, it can be much more difficult to take a lower-paying job outside of the legal industry (even if we are extremely passionate about that job). In other words, if we deeply dislike legal practice or deeply want to pursue some gig outside the law, our law school debt may be an obstacle that non-lawyers won't encounter.

But as you'll read, the individuals I interviewed overcame many challenges when leaving legal practice. There was no guarantee they would succeed. Yes, they are talented and ambitious individuals. You'll read how driven that they are. However, I'm sure they would admit that some semblance of luck was involved. There are certainly other individuals who tried to leave legal practice for a non-traditional career yet chose to return to legal practice. Survivorship bias makes it easier for us to ignore their stories.

Having said this, I believe that there is power in hearing these individuals' stories. They show that it *is* possible to take your legal education and experience and use it in a different way. The path isn't easy or straightforward. Setbacks are common. Patience is required. But if you want to leave legal practice or do something different with your law degree, these interviews can give you some practical and emotional support. They can provide light in a tunnel full of anxiety, fear, or doubt.

Marrying Inspiration and Action

This book is a meditation on an important subject. Leaving any sort of job for a dramatically different career is a big deal. It's especially true if you've invested at least three years of your life and hundreds of thousands of dollars. It goes without saying, but you don't want to make this decision lightly.

I hope this book inspires you on your career journey. In a book like this, one statement or takeaway can be monumental. It might provide some new perspective on a decision you've grappled with for months or years. When we're pondering a major career decision (like dropping out of law school or leaving legal practice), it's easy to get stuck in our heads. As lawyers, we are more analytical than the average person. At the same time, we may be evaluating our decision from the same perspective. We may go over the same factors and variables, hoping they provide a little more clarity before we make a decision.

This is one of the many reasons I encourage you to read each interview in this book. For instance, even if you have no interest in becoming a sports broadcaster, legal recruiter, or artist, you may discover that those interviews resonate with you. They might provide a unique lens or perspective to help you evaluate your decision in a different way. The only way to know is to venture beyond your circle of competence and read those discussions.

With all of that said, inspiration isn't enough. We must be proactive and take ownership of our careers. As you'll read in these pages, all fifteen individuals weren't passive. They didn't sit back and wait for things to happen. When they saw a compelling opportunity or felt dissatisfied with their current work, they took action. If they failed, they course-corrected.

They took real-world data, learned from their mistakes, and advanced toward their goals.

Simultaneously, doing something non-traditional is scary. You need to evaluate whether the potential rewards are worth the risks. While many of these fifteen individuals felt some nerves before making their career switch, they didn't let those nerves hold them back. They used the information they had and made a decision. Like Teddy Roosevelt said in one of his most famous speeches, they entered the arena. At worst, if they failed, they would not "be with those cold and timid souls who neither know victory nor defeat."

Whether you stay within the legal field or do something outside of legal practice, I encourage you to construct a career on your terms. Make sure that when you look back on your career, you are—at the very least—content with the choices you made.

Success isn't guaranteed. However, we can control our effort. We can do our diligence and speak with individuals in a sector or industry that interests us. We can take a deep dive into our finances to determine whether we can afford to make a move right now. We can work on our inner selves and develop the confidence to pursue our career goals. In the end, we have much more control than we might think.

CHAPTER 2

Keith Rabois

Operator and Venture Capitalist

It goes without saying, but a legal career can be immensely satisfying and rewarding. In the thick of our working lives, it can be easy to forget about those soaring platitudes that we heard during our law school graduation ceremonies and bar admission ceremonies. As much as the public likes to criticize lawyers, we play an important role in our society. The rewards in the legal profession can also be great, whether they come in the form of pursuing justice, defending an innocent client, or achieving financial security for your family.

However, this book is about traveling off the beaten path and doing something non-traditional with your legal degree. It's about leveraging your law degree or legal experience outside of traditional legal practice. No matter the direction you travel, there is career risk with your decision. It is a big decision. You shouldn't take it lightly. Opportunity costs are a real thing, and every door you open closes doors in other interesting areas.

Consequently, before making a major career move, you must look inward. In some situations, the right decision may be to stay within the legal profession. But if you are certain you want to leave legal practice, it is important to evaluate your skills. As you will read, attorneys bring plenty of skills to the table even if they aren't in the courtroom or representing a client at the negotiating table.

There are plenty of ways to analyze a new gig or career path outside of legal practice. However, no matter the industry or sector you consider, one framework can help clarify things.

Can I be one of the best in the world at this?

One former attorney who used that framework to achieve major success is Keith Rabois (pronounced RA-BOY). If you are familiar with the tech startup world, you may have already heard of Keith. A former Sullivan & Cromwell litigation associate, Keith was a member of the

PayPal Mafia, one of the most famous groups of collaborators in Silicon Valley history. Working with other tech rock stars like Elon Musk, Peter Thiel, Reid Hoffman, and Max Levchin, Keith helped create the first widespread digital payments system—all in an era where it was thought to be crazy to exchange real money with strangers over the internet. In the early days of PayPal, Keith was the head of business development, focusing on devising a competitive strategy against competitors like eBay, Visa, and Mastercard. His efforts paid off, as eBay acquired PayPal for $1.5 billion in July 2002.

With that sort of achievement, many would rest on their laurels and seek early retirement, but Keith and his colleagues didn't stop there. They founded, operated, or invested in a murderer's row of Silicon Valley companies like Tesla, LinkedIn, SpaceX, Facebook, Yelp, and YouTube.[1] Simply put, the PayPal Mafia has created many billions of dollars of value and redefined how we work, play, and communicate.

After the eBay acquisition, Keith worked at some of Silicon Valley's most promising startups. He joined Reid Hoffman to become Vice President of Business & Corporate Development at LinkedIn. He worked with Max Levchin at Slide, taking a strategy and business development role. He then joined Jack Dorsey at Square, becoming COO when there were only twenty employees at the company. He may be one of the best-connected players in the startup world.

Keith has extensive experience in having scaled scrappy startups into publicly-held corporations. His operating experience has also made him a preeminent startup investor. After leaving Square, he became a general partner at Khosla Ventures and is now at Founders Fund in Miami. In his career as a venture capitalist, he has led investments in companies like Stripe, Affirm, and ThoughtSpot. As if he wasn't busy enough, Keith has also embraced the founder role, cofounding the well-known real estate marketplace, Opendoor, which began trading on Nasdaq in December 2020.

Keith has built a celebrated career as an operator, technologist, and investor. Many of his public profiles and news clippings pay more attention to his successes in the startup world and less attention to his

---

1   For a comprehensive list of companies that PayPal Mafia members have either founded, led, or invested in, see Fleximize's Ventures of the PayPal Mafia, which you can find here: https://fleximize.com/paypal-mafia/.

early years in law and politics. As he told me, he had long-held ambitions to become an attorney and enter politics. Traveling to Silicon Valley and working with startups was certainly not part of his long-term plan. Content with his legal and political career, he was a rising litigation associate at Sullivan & Cromwell, one of the preeminent Big Law firms in the country. He received accolades for his legal work, including recognition by the Chief Justice of the United States Supreme Court.

So why did he make the jump from Sullivan & Cromwell into the world of startups? One reason was that he had members of his strong professional and personal circle helping him take that risk. As he told me, one particular friend gave him the confidence to make a move because she said he could be world-class in this new world of internet startups. After a short stint working with the Quayle campaign and a political tech startup, he joined Peter Thiel (another Sullivan & Cromwell alum) and others at PayPal. The rest is history.

Keith is plugged into the tech startup ecosystem. Combined with his prior experiences as a lawyer, he has a wealth of knowledge about attorneys leaving legal practice to do something else. While the stereotype of lawyers as risk averse, conservative, and poor entrepreneurs exists, Keith says that lawyers often develop certain advantages that can serve them well in startups. From there, it's about recognizing those advantages and leveraging them in your new career.

* * *

I'd like to start by asking you about your decision to go to law school. You're at Stanford University and you're involved with extracurriculars like the *Stanford Review*.[2] You're undoubtedly thinking about your career options as well. Did you become serious about law school after starting at Stanford or were you always thinking about going to law school?

2　Keith was an opinion editor of the *Stanford Review*, an independent newspaper at Stanford that is often associated with conservative and libertarian viewpoints. One of the Review cofounders was Peter Thiel, who Rabois later joined at PayPal.

I pretty much planned and decided to become a lawyer and get involved in law and politics since roughly sixth grade. I kind of put myself on that classic trajectory. I went to Stanford, studied political science, majored in political science, and optimized by GPA. I became involved in a lot of activities—some of which were ideological. But otherwise, I was consciously aware that I was creating an application for a top-tier law school. So yes, it was a very long-term objective.

What was it specifically about law school that intrigued you? Did you think you'd leverage your law degree to run for office or work behind the scenes in the political world?

I felt like I'd be involved behind the scenes (primarily on the policy side). Perhaps a bit of speech writing or appointed roles at some point. I don't think I ever totally envisioned running for office directly.

At that point, you weren't really thinking about practicing yourself. Rather, you were you going to use your law degree in a different way.

Yeah, if I could. I mean, obviously, the roles in policy and politics are limited. There's more scale in the actual legal profession. I liked both to some extent, but I figured I'd have wanted a more traditional mixing and matching of legal practice in politics that one sees in the D.C. political and legal worlds. Essentially, it would involve going in and out of practice, government, and policy.

You went to Harvard Law School. It seems self-evident, but why Harvard? There is certainly the prestige and all of the benefits that come with that.

Certainly, back then (and as far as I can tell today), law is still a very credentialist industry. It's really critical. "Where did you go to college? Where'd you go to law school? Where did you clerk? What law firms did you work at?" There's a hierarchy. You can bypass some of that, but fundamentally, those are the tools that clients and other potential people assess you by. So I was definitely focused on the prestige and the brand and things of that sort.

Looking back at law school, I think graduates have a pretty positive or negative view of it. Where would you say you come out on that spectrum? Do you remember it fondly? Or were there tougher times?

Directionally, I was pretty positive. It was certainly more academically challenging than undergrad. Undergrad at Stanford was very easy for me. In law school, I enjoyed most of the classes (virtually all of the classes). I liked thinking in terms of concepts and ideas. Obviously, law school is made for that.

I didn't love the weather in Boston. It was really cold and chilly (even abnormally cold). Actually, one other observation I remember was that at Stanford, people are taller than average. Harvard Law people are shorter than average, so I felt like I grew taller. At five foot eleven, I was shorter at Stanford and taller at Harvard. But I generally liked law school. You know, there are parts that you can edit a bit. For example, the process of getting a clerkship was very disorganized, very ad hoc, and expensive at the time. I think that's improved.

My only critique of law school was that three years is too long. The opportunity cost is too large. You hit diminishing marginal returns—certainly significant diminishing marginal returns of learning—after your first year. There's no reason that law school should be more than two years.

It also seems like at least some 1Ls question whether law school was the right decision entirely. Did that happen to you?

No, not at all. During my first year, I learned an immense amount about the world. It broadened my thinking, refined it, and made it more precise. I think my intellectual framework improved, rather than decayed, during law school. I think that's true of most people who have gone to law school. I think the rigor and quality of their thinking improves. The structure of their thinking improves. So no, I actually think it was a solid investment. I would actually recommend law school for non-lawyers if it were more like an eighteen to twenty-four-month program, not thirty-six.

Can you elaborate on that a little more? That's an interesting idea.

Yeah. I do think that the rigor of thinking—the quality of thinking that law school develops—is very valuable in almost any profession. But the opportunity cost of three years and the expenses associated with it is too hard to really justify for someone. But if it was one-and-a-half to two years, I would highly recommend it.

Similarly, society (for better or for worse) is so infused in law and regulation today that even if you want to operate a business in different fields, having a sound foundation in law can be very helpful. Again, that's a very difficult thing to justify in three years, but at one to two, it would certainly be better than going to business school.

If tuition could be lowered, it would be a more attractive option as well.

Yeah, that's relevant. But I think the opportunity cost for three years is even more devastating.

Going back to your law school experience, did you have a specific class or professor that you really enjoyed?

Yeah, there are a few. Constitutional Law was a favorite. Corporate Finance Theory (which isn't a law school class) was actually quite useful in my subsequent career. I enjoyed, of all things, Evidence. I actually found it fascinating and quite compelling. So there were some favorites, but they were mostly driven by the quality of the teaching and the professors—not necessarily the substance. I think all of the topics were moderately to very interesting. Probably the only one I didn't like was my Legal Writing class because it was kind of a gimmick.

It seems like law students at least consider positions at large commercial law firms for several reasons, but it primarily comes down to financial reasons. Law firm associates receive a hefty paycheck and most graduating law students need that money to pay off their loans. You worked in Big Law—specifically at Sullivan and Cromwell. But you also clerked with the Fifth Circuit Court of Appeals. Can you discuss your motivation behind those choices, especially due to your early interest in entering the political world?

Sure. So I think the reason why people wind up in large commercial law firms is partially economic, but I also think it's the path of least resistance. In other words, there's this recruiting apparatus and machine, especially at a top-tier law school like Harvard, that just shows up. The process of getting a summer associate job and a full-time job offer is so much easier than the process of getting a political or policy-oriented position where you have to do all the hard work yourself.

So I think that's what causes it to be the default. It's "Wow, all of these people are recruiting me" versus "I have to go take on all of this inertia and find an opportunity." Along with this, obviously, is that the compensation is significantly higher on an average basis for a first-year associate than it would be in some other field.

For the appellate court route, that's a very conventional way to go for people who have aspirations in politics. Obviously, a lot of people are interested in the issues of the day. For better or for worse, over the last half-century at least (if not the full century), many issues have been affected by the judiciary. So a lot of people who have political and policy preferences and interests want to work as an appellate court clerk.

I think it's an amazing job. On my first day as a law clerk, the judge called all three of us into her chambers, sat us down, and said, "I have some good news and some bad news for you. The good news is, basically, this is going to be the best legal job you ever have." She was right about that. The bad news part (which I guess I should have learned from that speech) was, "Wow, I should get the hell out of law pretty quickly."

But I loved it. Being a law clerk was incredibly rewarding, challenging, invigorating, and intellectually stimulating. Everything about it was outstanding. It was very different than the practice of law as a second-year associate (which was really my next job).

Which judge did you clerk for?

Edith H. Jones in the U.S. Court of Appeals for the Fifth Circuit.[3]

Okay. What sort of skills did you pick up from that experience?

---

3   In 1985, the U.S. Senate confirmed President Reagan's nomination of Judge Jones to the Fifth Circuit Court of Appeals. She served as chief judge of the court from 2006 to 2012.

Well, obviously, you learn the substantive parts. You learn how the court system really works, what makes an outstanding brief or a good advocate versus a mediocre one, and how to frame arguments in a way that's going to resonate with decision-makers. That's all valuable for someone who aspires to be a *litigator*. Secondly, it's a heavily writing-oriented position. I do think the quality and caliber of your writing improve just by doing it every day. Your writing improves by getting strong feedback from your colleagues, your peers, your judge's clerks, and the judges in other chambers that are commenting and editing your work. It's a great way to learn to become a better writer.

Finally, it's a thinking job. Most of the more, let's say, contentious cases before a circuit court have arguments on both sides. So rigorous thinking from a first-principles basis, like the foundation for a decision, is a very challenging intellectual exercise. I think it makes you sharper.

Right. Generally speaking, would you recommend that law students think about clerking even if they don't want to be litigators?

Yeah, absolutely. Unfortunately, if they do it, it would be the best job they have in the legal profession for a very long time. That is, other than the compensation. The compensation obviously has been raised since my day, but it is clearly going to be less than other opportunities.

Then from the Fifth Circuit, you make your way to Sullivan & Cromwell. What was it about that firm that made you choose it over others?

Well obviously, I talked about the hierarchical nature of law firms and the credential brand halo of how the profession works. Sullivan & Cromwell, for probably a century, has been at the forefront of the legal profession. That definitely resonated with me.

Somewhat as a traditionalist, conservative person, I appreciated the foundations of the firm (which were still pretty conventional). For example, we wore suits and ties to work. We had secretaries and did things "by the book" in the way that the practice of law (for the most part) was in the 1950s.

Maybe this is irrelevant these days and to your book, but Sullivan & Cromwell's reputation and brand had always been somewhat as a "business lawyer." This meant it was widely encouraged for litigators, corporate transactional associates, and partners to understand business problems and to be a business counselor and consiglieri to the client. So it would be normal and expected to be reading the *Wall Street Journal*, *BusinessWeek*, *Fortune*, or *Forbes* as part of your job. Having a broader business context was considered part of our brand.

Then, there were two more things that differentiated Sullivan & Cromwell. One (legally specific) was that I liked the flexibility. I worked primarily during my four years there at the Washington, D.C. office. I liked the flexibility of working in Washington but for a New York firm. I had the prestige, the compensation, and the client base of a New York firm. By being able to live in Washington, D.C. and live in a culture where I could meet political people and be involved in political things, I felt like I was getting the best of both worlds.

The second thing that differentiated Sullivan & Cromwell was that its brand was (and still is) about being a perfectionist. The firm goes through all kinds of hoops and hurdles to have everything perfect—every brief and every document. That resonated with me as well. It was painful because I spent a lot of hours improving something from eighty percent to ninety percent to the ninety-third percentile to ninety-nine to ninety-nine point nine. A lot of sacrifice was involved, but I am sort of a perfectionist.

How did you discover that the firm fit your personality? Were you a summer associate there or did you hear about it from other people?

I was a summer associate before clerking.

Got it. So you were at Sullivan & Cromwell for four years. Was your plan to stay longer than that?

My ideal plan was to stay and try to become a partner there. When I left, I was just beginning as a fifth-year associate. I was on the right trajectory. And back then (I don't know what the current timeline is), it was roughly an eight-year partnership track. That was my default plan. It was stay there, try to become a partner, and then maybe with the security of a partnership, jump into politics. It would be a little easier to go back and forth to an appointed position in an administration as a partner.

Oh, interesting. That was still in the back of your mind and you thought partnership would lead you there?

Yes, that was certainly my aspiration. Obviously, it was very rare. Especially on the litigation side, one associate per class would be selected partner in the model that they were employing.

So what prompted you to leave as a rising fifth-year associate? You were getting relatively close to a potential partnership, but you decided to take a chance on something else.

A couple of things. Mostly, I was persuaded that I should enter the business world and this internet revolution by friends from Stanford during the late nineties. They would constantly try to recruit me out of the legal profession. I was kind of happy, so it was a pretty significant burden for them. But at the height of the internet bubble in February 2000, they were able to persuade me. So that was the most important: I was persuaded to try something different. But I resisted it for a while because I actually did like my trajectory and the challenges with it.

There were two things I didn't love that made me perhaps more amenable. Particularly at Sullivan & Cromwell, we were all expected to be generalists. I didn't specialize. One of the things that I did really well was write briefs. I was very successful in filing motions to dismiss and other appellate court documents. I'm sure the quality of my brief writing was definitely at the higher end within the firm. I was kind of doing very well by developing highly-framed legal arguments (even somewhat difficult arguments) to make them attractive to judges.

But the only way to be really successful at S&C—at least back then in the nineties—was to be very well-rounded. There wasn't a way to specialize. I wasn't thrilled about that and I probably wasn't as good at all at taking depositions or defending depositions as I was at getting motions to dismiss granted. So if I could have specialized, I would have been happier and would have been more likely to stay.

Secondly (and I think this is still roughly true), the progression was very hierarchical. The firm had a very lockstep model. You were a second-year associate, third-year associate, fourth, fifth, et cetera. And that really defines your identity—regardless of the performance. More importantly (perhaps more tangibly) is that it defines your compensation. All fifth-year associates basically got paid the same. I think that led to some resentment among the top ten or twenty percent of associates in any class. For example, many corporate associates would opt out and become investment bankers. They would go to Goldman Sachs or Morgan Stanley. For me, my way of opting out was to jump into the startup world. The compensation varies by orders of magnitude. So from my perspective, I think the compensation felt too socialist in some ways.

Ultimately, in thinking about why I really left the firm, it also probably wasn't accidental that in January 2000, my last month at the firm, I actually billed three hundred sixty-four hours.

Did you really?

Yeah. In my defense, I was probably a little bit more open-minded to a recruiting pitch. But that conclusion related to that in a little bit more of a serious sense (that's probably more apocryphal). One of the ways you had to compete in the legal profession and become a partner at a place like S&C was by pure hours. There was just no way around pure hours being a brute force input into your performance. I didn't want to compete just on the basis of pure hours. I need a lot of sleep. I get drained when I don't have a lot of sleep. I felt that it was a bad idea to compete on that basis. There really was no way to go from fifth-year associate to partner without sleepless nights.

Right. You were kind of looking for something more scalable, right? Instead of putting in your time, you wanted to have the time work for you.

Yeah, I mean, I'm an advocate for high-quality work ethic and things of that sort. I wasn't looking for an easier job in any way. But I was looking for something where the dimension you were assessed on had less to do with input time and more to do with output. I felt like I needed eight hours of sleep to be sharp and effective. The only way to really be successful entailed some significant sleep sacrifice.

Notwithstanding the lockstep compensation, did you have any sense of the golden handcuffs or any feelings of risk aversion that gave you pause before leaving?

A bit. As you know, at the height of the legal profession, there is this ladder. Once you jump off the ladder, you're kind of off the ladder. That may not be obvious externally. I definitely had some risk aversion in terms of knowing I was probably sacrificing a career at a top ten or so law firm by pulling the trigger and jumping to the internet. It wasn't as much of an economic issue. This is going to sound crazy low, but back then, I probably went from something like $185,000 per year to $120,000 per year. But after adjusting for taxes and stuff, that's not that big of a difference.

Right.

It wasn't a massive economic risk as much as a career trajectory risk. The biggest risk that I was particularly focused on at the time was that I was doing very well as an attorney. I was recognized as one of the top lawyers under thirty in the United States by the Chief Justice of the U.S. Supreme Court. I was on a good path. It wasn't perfect, but it was a good path.

What I was concerned about was that I jumped onto this new career trajectory. I was sure I could be competent. That didn't scare me. But could I be truly world-class at it? I had no idea. That was a big source of hesitation. So what I did is I actually called up one or two of my friends from Stanford who had been very successful in the first internet generation. And I remember asking one in particular. I asked her, "Is it possible I can be the best in the world at this?" She said, "Absolutely." And I said, "Okay, I'll do it." If she said anything else, I wouldn't have done it.

Interesting. So that was your litmus test before you proceeded.

Yes. "Did I have the potential to be in the top one percent" was critical because I wouldn't have been willing to forego the legal trajectory unless there was some belief that I might be able to be excellent at this new thing. I had no way of knowing, so the only way I could figure it out was to find people that were in the top one percent that knew me well enough and ask, "Is it possible" or "Is this is a bad idea." That helped persuade me that there were a lot of reasons why I would like this. But could I be extraordinarily successful at it? That was less obvious to me.

It's tough to give general career advice. However, would you recommend something to that extent if a Big Law associate is thinking of

leaving to try something that they've never tried before? Essentially, should they canvass their friends and see whether they can be really great at it?

Yeah. There's also what your expectations are. Obviously, I was ambitious. It was important to me that if I jumped into a new profession or a new field, I would have much upside potential.

When you left Sullivan & Cromwell, you actually took some time to work in the political work. Specifically, you joined Dan Quayle's presidential campaign in 2000. How did you find that opportunity?

Well, as I mentioned, the virtue of being in a D.C. office at a law firm was that I got to meet some pretty interesting folks. This included a very senior partner at Williams & Connolly named John Vardaman. He basically started the firm and was one of the old school partners that had been a longtime friend and counselor to the Vice President of the United States, Dan Quayle. I was able to meet John through some connections. I wound up doing some research for him and a group of others that were considering supporting Dan Quayle's presidential run in 1996. I think I did some good work on some of those simpler projects. They kept asking me to do more complicated analysis and preparation as part of my free time (similar to pro bono work).

One of the things I did was help prepare the Vice President for an appearance on CBS's *Face the Nation*. He did very well. He did an amazingly great job and people noticed. His friends and former colleagues and potential donors were like, "Wow, he was really sharp." So for better or for worse (and not necessarily meritocratically, but fundamentally), I got all the credit for that. People were very happy. That led to some opportunities to do more things like speech drafting. I got closer to him and to the people around him. That presented some opportunities when he decided to run for president going into the 2000 election cycle.

So working for a startup was still in your mind, but you decided to work for Quayle during the election season and then proceed from there.

Yeah, exactly. That was good because there are some commonalities between a campaign and a startup. They are very different from law firms. As I said, I had a secretary and all the support structure at Sullivan & Cromwell. But when you go into a startup, you don't have that support structure. Often, you don't have your own office. You certainly don't have your secretary. So going into a campaign (an underdog campaign to some extent) was a great way to prepare me to go back to working with my hands, doing things myself, and having to worry about the cost of things. That was a good cultural transition in terms of preparing me to be effective at a startup.

It sounds like you heavily relied on your drafting strength and ability in the campaign to make a name for yourself.

Yeah. What I was able to do that I think people noticed was, first, because I like to read, I read more broadly than most people in politics. I, therefore, was able to come up with and develop anecdotes, stories, and even some policy ideas that were a little different. If you just read the same things, you tend to have the same stories, anecdotes, and data points. I was able to constantly develop fresh ideas on the fly. I think that stood out.

What also helped me was combining this skill with political instincts (essentially a sense of how something would resonate with real people). I think one of the challenges lawyers have is that they're very smart and top one percent IQ types, but they don't really have a barometer for how things resonate. To be effective in most political roles, you need to have both. I think that the policy types or polling types that worked with the communication types felt like I had a pretty good filter for that. They didn't think of me as a smart, egghead lawyer. They actually liked my ideas and felt that they were relevant in the political framework.

That's interesting.

That was a skill that I developed due to political curiosity over the years. But I think that's what allowed me to sort of get ahead.

I've worked with people who've gone on to do amazing things. Our pollster was Kellyanne Conway. John McConnell was our chief speechwriter. He has been a speechwriter for every Republican president for basically most of my lifetime. Jon M. Baron was a very good communications director (like top of the field).

I was able to work with some incredible people. But they also seemed to like my work product, which was a gauge because they don't suffer fools at all. Their future depends on the work product. So I got to become the policy director and be in charge of policy for the campaign.

From there, you transitioned into startups. Your career in the start-up world is extraordinary to say the least. You're a member of the PayPal Mafia. You had instrumental roles at LinkedIn, Slide, and Square. You're also a founder and a venture capitalist at Khosla Ventures and now at Founders Fund. But like we discussed, before you entered the startup world, you were a litigator. I think it's interesting because one stereotype is that litigators find it difficult to make the switch from law to opportunities on the "business side," so to speak, whether that's a general counsel role or something else. How were you able to make that switch and pitch yourself when making that switch?

Yeah, it's a great question. I agree with you generally that litigators are less prepared and less able to make the transition to a set of business roles. There are a couple of things that may have been relevant for me. One is I decided to do it cold turkey. I immediately jumped into a purely business role. I didn't do the "I'm going to be an associate general counsel" or "I'm going to work in corporate development." It was like, "If I'm going to do business, I'm going to do business" and I don't want to be a half-lawyer.

So I jumped. I was able to jump because the person who hired me had confidence in me. He knew me from college and thought that he could teach me. I didn't know about technology, business development and technology, or marketing and technology. It was good that I had a mentor to teach me. One reason I was comfortable making the jump was I also felt the same: he had the right skills and experiences to quickly teach me what I needed to know.

Third is that one of the areas of law where I had experience was antitrust litigation. So at least in antitrust litigation, you use some business frameworks and some business vocabulary. Things like market share and market power are concepts that you have to understand. There was some slight transferability there.

So those were quite powerful. They propelled me forward. I got lucky in the sense that at the height of the internet bubble, there were so many companies being founded and funded. There was so much demand for talent that you couldn't just hire experienced people. That's why I got my job to some extent. Companies needed smart, talented people that they thought they could train because they couldn't just go get the other people who had been doing it before. They were all taken.

And then for the political experience, the first startup I worked with was heavily involved in politics as a business. My domain expertise from the campaign was considered relevant. So that little bit of expertise from politics actually made it slightly easier for people to justify hiring me (which was important).

Would you say that the environment is similar today? Say there's a practicing lawyer out there that wants to transition into technology (either in a practicing or non-practicing role). Would you give them similar advice as you would give back in the internet bubble or would there be something different?

Yeah, there's definitely a shortage of talent. Every one of our companies is famished for talent. So I think there's some flexibility there and some willingness to be creative about the source of talent.

That said, the key formula for me was I had context with this person who was willing to hire me. Without that relationship, it would have been difficult. Basically, someone was taking a bet on me that, based upon his experiences with me, I could learn fast and that I had the upside potential to compensate for the risk of working with someone who had less experience. If you're going to hire someone less experienced, you have to believe that they can actually be better. You have to believe that they might, if things work out, be better than what you could hire with experience. It doesn't mean it's going to be true in practice, but you want some upside potential to compensate for the risk you're taking.

So those were all really important foundations. And then, finding someone who can teach you how you are going to bridge the gap between your level of business sophistication and your current knowledge base as fast as possible. Obviously, this is because you're at risk of making mistakes and not being effective until you bridge that gap.

But I would definitely recommend that people who really want to get out of law to get out of law. Now, in practice, people may not have the option. Some people may have to take an interim role that is a hybrid (like a corporate development role). But I think if the goal of leaving the practice of law is to become an effective business executive and leader, then I would start learning business and leadership as fast as possible, not as slowly as possible.

And learning business and leadership is just finding a role with someone that trusts you and can mentor you?

Yeah. I think it's important. That's a foundational skill. That's the advice I give to everybody (not just the lawyers). The best way to take an opportunity is to pick your boss. Pick the best possible boss you can find that can teach you the most, that can put you on the steepest, fastest learning curve, and that has potential in their own career so that they can take you with them as they succeed.

Generally speaking, do you think attorneys struggle to make it as entrepreneurs or operators in the startup world? I guess the argument goes that attorneys are risk-averse. They look at the downside rather than the upside and don't act quickly. Do you agree with that?

I think there are some challenges. If you think about how you are trained in law school, you're fundamentally trained around issue spotting. That's how you're rated on almost all law school exams. So by definition, your brain tends to identify the things that could go wrong because it's how you're assessed. It's how you're graded.

I think the startup world (entrepreneurial endeavors particularly) is mostly about the upside. It is about looking to "right" and how valuable or important something can be if things go right versus "where are all the things that can go wrong." An entrepreneurial endeavor, by definition, is like an irrational, heroic exercise. You're basically saying, "There's some part of the world, some vertical in the world, that I'm going to totally transform and revolutionize from my proverbial garage." In some ways, it's ridiculous, but it's actually possible and it happens enough that it's plausible. So to some extent, focusing on all the things that can go wrong isn't that helpful. Because, of course, there are lots of things that can go wrong. The question is: can you chart a course to make it work? I think that's a hard translation.

Measuring yourself in terms of output instead of input can be challenging. For example, in law, you bill by the hour. I remember (certainly in my first year or so) having this natural tendency to record everything I was doing. I felt like if I didn't write it down, it didn't count so to speak. You have to counter that a bit.

So yes, figuring out how to go from risk-averse to risk-seeking in some ways is a big challenge. I had a good friend of mine in college observe the irony of my career trajectory. He said to me, "Rabois, you used to be the most risk-averse person I knew in college and now you're like the most risk-loving. What happened to you?" He was probably making the observation over a three or four-year period of time.

I remember thinking of when I knew I'd be successful in business. At first, everybody sort of somehow knew that I was an ex-lawyer when I would attend meetings. Then, there was a period of time (this was before LinkedIn, so it was pretty hard to look up someone's background unless they were super famous) where they would somehow guess I went to law school. And then, there was that period of time when it switched and people would find out that I went to law school. They would say, "No way. Oh my God. I never would have believed that." As soon as that happened, I thought to myself, "I think this actually might work."

You definitely have to change your framework. I think that can be a major challenge. It's a major challenge even for some general counsel as they navigate from a corporate environment to an entrepreneurial venture. But it's certainly a challenge for a lawyer becoming a business-person.

Do you change that framework through experience? That's the only way, right?

I think so. Maybe some people have a natural intuition about risk and reward. Maybe it can be taught or articulated in a kind of logical sense or through a case study sense. Maybe. I don't really know.

On the opposite side, what benefits did your law degree and legal experience provide when you were at PayPal, LinkedIn, and even now in venture capital?

Yeah, I think there are two. One is that some areas where I've had the most success are fields that are heavily regulated—like financial services, or these days, healthcare. I think it's because I don't have to depend on lawyers as a black box. I can kind of navigate myself and have a strong perspective on the probabilities that something can work from a legal or regulatory perspective. Therefore, I'm not outsourcing the judgment call to someone else.

I sometimes use a metaphor: even if you've never practiced medicine but you went to medical school, if you go to the doctor and the doctor says, "This is what's wrong with you, et cetera," you'll ask just sharper, smarter questions than someone who has never been to medical school. I think that has been very helpful. I, therefore, look for companies that sort of have legal or regulatory risks because I think I have a comparative or competitive advantage *vis-a-vis* other investors that I compete with.

Secondly, the other area where it's really helpful is in basically trading legal risks versus business risks. In negotiations with counterparties, I can trade some legal risk or legal provisions in, let's say a contract, for economic terms because I understand the value of both.

So for example, let's say you wanted me to bear the liability for X, Y, and Z. In a traditional decision-making process, the lawyers sort of decide and fight back and forth about the liability shifts. Whereas I'll be like, "Sure, I'll take the liability shift if you give me ten basis points." The ability to do that on the fly can lead to a better outcome either because you can make a deal happen that might have otherwise gotten blocked due to bureaucratic inertia or you can get better net terms because you sort of have asymmetric information about the legal risks and you're getting compensated for it. But generally, if someone has only grown up in one domain, they can't make those tradeoffs. They can't even communicate with their colleagues precisely and clearly enough for the teamwork to be effective.

That's really interesting. Let's say that a Big Law attorney wants to start a company instead of taking a general counsel role or something else. They're pitching potential team members (or even venture capitalists like yourself) and they're talking about their team, market size, and other things like that. When you're evaluating an attorney-founder or an attorney who is on the founding team, what are some things that you want to hear?

Well, it would really depend and vary on what market they were conquering or attacking. I would want to almost surely hear that there's some rational reason why a legal background is an advantage. I would certainly want to understand their ability to connect the dots between risk and reward (along the lines of the discussion we just had). Third is related to recruiting. The other thing about the legal profession is you're generally not managing a lot of people (if anybody). Company building is definitely much more about people and putting people in the right roles, aligning them, replacing them, or editing the team. It's not something lawyers generally learn how to do very well. So some complement to this legal founder who has some of that DNA or some proven aptitude to do this stuff would be quite important.

Would it matter if that lawyer-founder is pitching something that isn't legal-related? Say some consumer app or product.

Yes, absolutely. They would need to have a very good and very compelling reason why they have some differentiated advantage there.

Whether that's personal experience or just different insights about the market?

Yeah. It could be personal experience or it could be that the consumer app has a lot of legal risk associated with it for a variety of reasons (and they can help navigate that successfully).

Got it. If I can make it a bit broader here. Let's say there are current law students that perhaps had an internship they didn't like and now don't know what to do. What are some things that you would recommend that they think about?

Well, I think sometimes you have to try different things to know what you're really going to be excellent at and really enjoy. Like obviously, I spent a lot of time in financial services. I've been involved in at least three public companies in financial services and probably have a few more on the way. I didn't know I was going to do anything related to payments and financial services. Until you try it and experience it, it's hard to have a correct opinion of what you really should be doing with it your life.

So I think it can help to try a diversity of roles and verticals before deciding where you have a competitive advantage and where you have excitement. It's hard to forecast that just at a theoretical level.

If readers think that they may want to take a risk like you did, yet fear or risk aversion is holding them back (whether they're at a Big Law firm, in government, or something else), do you have any advice for them? How can they break through those mental barriers and take a risk?

It depends. It's not for everybody. For example, I always describe what I do for a living as like a roller coaster ride. The roller coaster goes up and down and terrifies you. Sometimes it's per day, sometimes it's per hour, sometimes it's per week or per month. But some people love riding roller coasters. They actually pay money to scream. Other people hate roller coaster rides and would never pay money to do it. At some point, you have to decide how much you enjoy the terror of a roller coaster.

It's not for everyone.

No. Even though I think entrepreneurial endeavors are wonderful, incredibly impactful, very meritocratic, and extremely important for the future of society, I don't think everybody should join a startup.

But if attorneys do, what kind of skills do you think they should leverage to stand out from the pack?

Yeah. So I think the first thing is to broaden your business thinking. I would read everything from a magazine like Fortune to some very thoughtful business books (and there are a few). I would read occasional business blogs like Stratechery.[4] Get familiar with the vocabulary and the thinking—even while you're practicing law.

I would try to see if you could develop some degree of taste as an amateur (like understanding why some products work and others fail). In

---

4   Stratechery is a blog on the strategy and business side of technology and media. Ben Thompson, a former employee at Apple, Microsoft, and Automattic, is Stratechery's founder and writer.

any field, it's possible to be an informed amateur. For example, I've never done sports for a living, but in some sports, I have a fair amount of knowledge and I can have a reasonable conversation with people who do it for a living. Or I do interior design for my own house. I do it by myself. It's kind of fun, and hopefully, people think it's cool looking. You can develop an amateur level of taste in fields. Then, if you get good as an amateur, you can potentially dedicate your life to it and maybe have a shot at being a really good and excellent professional. But if you can't develop that taste as an amateur, there's a significant gap to bridge.

There are definitely differences between amateur and professional level expertise. But if you try at the amateur level, develop some taste there, and people seem to think you have reasonable taste as an amateur, your likelihood of success is enhanced.

Would you recommend people follow their passion rather than some big opportunity they think may be out there? Is it more about passion?

No. I'm very anti-follow your passion. I think that's silly advice. Passion comes as a result of experience and success, not the other way around. I think you should find a role and a set of challenges where you have a disproportionate ability to be successful. If there are skills you have, you want to leverage those skills vis-a-vis other talented people. And if there are things that you're very bad at and don't want to do, then try to find a role that doesn't require you to be doing that every day. For example, when I talked about being a lawyer, I didn't want to do discovery. If anything, I was good at avoiding discovery assignments.

I think business allows you to specialize more than law does. So find roles where you can thrive because you're leveraging things that you're either very proficient at or things you enjoy doing. That's what develops the passion, not the "Oh, I like this area." I think that's a terrible way to make decisions.

Just two more questions here. When you hear people say they want to go to law school to open up doors or potential options, what do you think about that?

I think it's reasonable subject to my comments about the opportunity cost being quite high for three years (plus your direct costs). I don't think it's a bad idea from a "what would I learn" perspective. I certainly think it's a better idea to do that than go to business school.

Yes. The opportunity cost is pretty large and you have to evaluate that.

Yeah. You know, especially in the technology ecosystem, you can accomplish a lot in your twenties. It's kind of funny. Most of my legal friends and co-clerks are now entering the primes of their careers. And to some extent, I'm getting older in my career. So it's really like top of mind for me. Several of my co-clerks were recently appointed appellate court judges by the president, so they're finally getting to the top of their profession. Whereas with my progression, by the time you're my age, you're actually starting to decay significantly.

It's a different kind of perspective. One anecdote around this is really funny. Maybe a year ago, I was invited to give this talk to the Harvard Law School Alumni Association. I was pretty excited to do it and the week before, they sent out this email to the entire alumni association. You know, "Come see Keith Rabois speak," blah blah blah. And it had my class on it. It said "Keith Rabois, Class of 1994" and I was so mortified. I was like, "Oh my God, I don't think they know how old I am." I thought, "Oh my God, this is the worst thing ever." They were sending it out with my class as a positive and I was like, "Oh my God, this is literally the worst thing that's happened to me in a year."

But anyway, the opportunity cost in your twenties in technology is high. This is because instead of sitting in class all day, you can actually do things that are pretty productive. There isn't a line you have to wait in. Whereas in the law (and to some extent the political world), there is a line to wait in. It is a stark contrast for those who want to do something in technology or the Silicon Valley world.

Would you do anything differently? Whether that's law school, Sullivan & Cromwell, or anything else?

Look, if I knew what I was going to wind up doing with my career, I think law school may still have made sense. However, I would have tried to compress law school (maybe combine it with an MBA). Not that I like MBAs but, you know, I was going down that obvious trajectory looking for the classic credential. I certainly would have left Sullivan & Cromwell earlier just because I think, both in law school and practicing law, you hit diminishing marginal returns in your learning. Those years were pretty expensive years in what I could have been doing in the business world.

I don't know what I would have done. But compressing law school plus clerking plus practicing, I spent roughly eight years of my life practicing law. It was probably too significant of an investment to justify.

I often get asked to give advice to people graduating or who have recently graduated from college. I usually start with a story and anecdote centered on the fact that I spent all my twenties basically studying and practicing law. So I'm like, "By definition, anything you do in your twenties is going to be better off than what I did. Because I kind of wasted my twenties."

Obviously, with hindsight, I'd probably edit my twenties a bit. But that's with a lot of hindsight. As I said, sometimes you don't know what you should be doing until you try different things. So yeah, I'd probably make that one change and probably would have taken advantage of more technical classes while I was at Stanford (where I was too terrified of screwing up my GPA). I did take some, but I was very consciously aware that that wasn't in my sweet spot and could screw up my GPA (which would undermine my ability to be accepted to a law school like Harvard).

CHAPTER 3

Tiffany Duong

Writer, Explorer, and Inspirational Speaker

If you look hard enough, certain moments in life are positive catalysts for change. Some are more obvious than others. While most disappear into our distant memories, others become life-altering moments that turn our dreams into realities.

One of the more obvious catalysts is a firing. Though it may be frustrating—even traumatic—in the moment, being terminated can be one of the more positive things to happen in a career. Take Gerard Butler, for example. While most of us know him for starring in movies like *300* or *Olympus Has Fallen*, Butler's earlier career was in law. As he described to *Esquire* magazine, Butler graduated from law school with honors. As a trainee lawyer at a Scottish law firm, he was less interested in legal practice and more interested in acting. "When I put on a suit and tie," he said, "I became desperately unhappy." A week before he was set to qualify, Butler was fired. Even though he was humiliated, his termination was the catalyst for landing his first role in a Steven Berkoff play. If he *hadn't* been fired, it's likely he wouldn't have become the A-list movie star he is today.

Another underrated catalyst is a major health event. Covid-19 has caused nearly all of us to reassess our current lives and goals. It was a shock to the system and made nearly all of us realize how short and precious life is. As we go further back through history, we can see that individual maladies and illnesses have sparked positive change. Henri Matisse, for instance, passed the bar exam in France and took on work as a law clerk. One year later, he suffered from appendicitis. While on temporary bed rest, his mother gave him some art supplies to pass the time. The rest was history, as Henri decided to leave his nascent law career behind to pursue his new passion for art.

A similar type of catalyst occurred for Tiffany Duong when she went on a scuba diving trip. An unhappy associate at a Big Law firm, she'd been working on a late-night deal when she came across an opportunity to travel to the Galapagos Islands. Tiffany jumped at the chance. As she described, her trip was the galvanizing force leading her away from legal practice and towards a life she loves.

Tiffany is now a writer and journalist, an explorer, and an inspirational speaker. She has tapped into her lifelong passion for the environment and taken on various roles in her post-law life. For instance, Tiffany regularly writes about the environment for the international news source *EcoWatch*. She has also developed a specialty in ocean and scuba diving stories. She shares her gratitude and passion for the ocean by storytelling for the Professional Association of Diving Instructors (PADI), *Scuba Diving* magazine, and *Alert Diver*. In the advocacy arena, she campaigned against harmful swordfish drift gillnets with Turtle Island Restoration Network and was a scientific diver for the Coral Restoration Foundation. Tiffany even worked with Al Gore's Climate Reality Project and became a trained climate reality leader. That experience catalyzed her to teach "Climate Conversations" at the University of Miami's Osher Lifelong Learning Institute and to consult with other schools and companies on their sustainability initiatives. As she describes on her website, her mission is to "involve and inspire others to see our world in an entirely different way—and to want to save it." She is laser-focused on fighting for our planet however she can.

Tiffany's passion for the environment existed well before law school. She even worked in renewable energy law before she left legal practice. If she wanted, she could have remained as a practicing lawyer and worked on environmental projects. However, Tiffany wanted to feel more alive and make a bigger impact. Inspired by her diving trip to the Galapagos, she took a chance and hasn't looked back.

Whether you are thinking of pursuing a non-traditional career immediately out of law school or are contemplating an exit from legal practice, I encourage you to identify potential catalysts in your life. An eye-opening trip, a conversation with a trusted friend or mentor, or even a once-in-a-century pandemic can be just the thing to help you try something new with your career.

* * *

Tiffany, I'm really excited to hear about your legal career and how you built an impressive new career as a writer, explorer, and inspirational speaker. How would you describe your career since you left legal practice? In other words, if someone came up to you on the street and asked you to describe your professional life since you left Sheppard, Mullin, Richter & Hampton, what would you say?

I would say that the time since leaving law has been the journey of my life. It has been challenging, rewarding, exciting, and nourishing to my mind, my body, and my soul. I've tried so many different things and come a little closer each time to figuring out what I want my legacy on this planet to be. With what I am doing now, I feel like this is what I was meant to do. Had I stayed in law, I don't think I would feel that way.

How do you think you discovered that? As far as writing and ocean advocacy, is it something that you thought about or researched in the past? Did you plant these seeds before law school?

I went to law school because I wanted to do something environmental. I knew that in college and way before law school was even a thought. I knew I wanted to do something to help the planet. I went to law school because I wanted to give that thought some legs. I hoped that in the journey of going into law, I would find something to do.

It was a very vague idea. I wanted to give myself a bigger skill set and more ideas because I didn't actually know what doing "something environmental" meant. Then, I was fortunate enough to work in renewable energy law (which would seem pretty aligned with that goal). But I later realized that the Big Law lifestyle just wasn't for me. Equally important, I also learned that while the effect of the work was noble, legal practice wasn't hands-on enough for me. I knew deep down that I needed to be fully immersed in the world I want so desperately to save.

I quit law after a scuba diving trip to the Galapagos Islands. I just decided to start with a clean slate and give myself the freedom to explore different careers—both inside and outside of the environmental space. Through that exploration, this feeling within me grew. Basically, I felt this calling deep within me saying, "Okay, the ocean saved me from a life that I hated. It really did. So I need to dedicate the rest of my life to saving it."

That's kind of the mindset that got me into ocean advocacy. Then, when I started as a scientific diver and an ocean journalist, I felt like I could tell not just my stories about the power and importance of the ocean, but also those of others. Through stories, through connection, we get others to care.

Each job between law and now has been a step that has opened my eyes to different opportunities, skill sets, and people. And it's still changing. I imagine it always will be. I never would have thought this before, but I love how my life no longer has a clear, set path the way that a life in the law does. I love that I can change and will change and that my jobs can shift with me.

Right. As you said, the path is pretty clear when you are a lawyer. In that Big Law environment, for example, you need to hit a certain number of billable hours for a little less than a decade. Then, you're potentially up for becoming a partner (which involves its own track as well). What you are doing is off the beaten path in so many ways. But if I could just go back and ask you about something you said earlier on. You said that before law school, you were interested in environmentalism. You wanted to do something to help the planet and you connected that with law school. Can you further discuss how you connected the two? Did you ever think about becoming an environmental advocate in the legal space or something similar to that?

When people asked me, "What do you want to be when you grow up," I used to draw a picture of myself standing in front of a bulldozer in the Amazon. I never really gave any thought to that until I got to this point in my career, where I dive and replant coral (which is an endangered species and dying). I've also gone to the Amazon to work in a research camp to help scientists there and tell their stories.

I always had that environmental vein in me; I just didn't really pay attention to it. When I graduated college, I didn't know what was next. I thought, "Well, I will basically use law school as a steppingstone to buy myself some more time, to figure out an actual career, and to gain some skills that everyone in society says are super helpful. Like, "Why wouldn't you want to learn how to write better, research better, be diligent, and be a lawyer?"

Interesting. So you ended up going to Penn Law School (I went there as well). Can you discuss why you chose to go there over other schools and what life was like at Penn?

Sure. I was coming from UCLA, which is a huge public school that I loved. So I didn't want to go to a really tiny law school. I wanted to go somewhere middle-sized. For being private, Penn is a pretty large school. I also wanted a new experience. I wanted to go away from California because that's where I'm from. I thought law school was an easy way to hop in and out of a new location and get a different taste.

Beyond that, I loved that Penn offered things like the Toll Public Interest Center and study abroad. I started law school in 2007. When I was there, Penn was just starting to offer environmental classes and climate change classes. That was pretty exciting to me. It felt like, "Okay, this aligns with why I was thinking of going into law."

Right. That is one of the benefits of Penn. Even though you are pursuing a law degree, I found that they really let you embrace a multidisciplinary legal education. It also looks like you took one year off between UCLA and Penn. It's hard giving advice because people's situations are so different, but if a prospective law student came to you and asked whether they should take one or two years off before law school, would you say that's generally a good idea?

Oh, absolutely. I am so glad I took that year off. I wish I had taken more time off.

I think with law school (and really any grad school or higher education after college), you'll do really well if you approach it like a job. You go in there, work hard, but then you don't let it consume your entire existence during that time. With that mindset, you can go back home every day to your life, your family, or other jobs in some cases.

In law school, I saw my classmates who had taken even more time off than me cope with the difficult parts of law school in very healthy ways. They seemed like they were able to create mental and emotional separation from law school. They were able to treat it just as a job. It didn't consume them. For me, I tried to achieve that, but I don't think one year off is enough to shake the mentality of college. College is very all-consuming of your person. I think once you have some time away, you actually can treat law school like a job. You can learn and explore your interests without making it everything. Because if you let it, it will take over everything.

Yeah. I think it's a good idea, too. I took one year off, and I don't regret it whatsoever. I think more prospective law students should do the same. Do you have any general advice for law students that are maybe in the thick of law school? This can be anything from things they should do to succeed on exams to things that can help them have a better and less stressful time.

I would say that you shouldn't let law school consume you. Remember to do things that keep you physically, mentally, and emotionally healthy. Don't stop exercising. Don't stop seeing your friends. Don't stop calling your family. All of that stuff is important.

I would also say that you shouldn't try to reinvent the wheel. If there's an outline bank, use it as a starter and then add your own stuff. Don't try to make your own fresh outline. You just don't have the time. Law school is the beginning of teaching you how to prioritize how you use your time. You just can't do it all. Trying to do it all will just create an additional layer of stress that you don't need.

Finally, there's so much more to law school than just going to class. Make connections with your classmates. If you allow them to be, they will be really great assets in your practice. Especially at a place like Penn, look at joining extracurriculars. I used to volunteer at a local reproductive rights clinic. I helped escort people going in for procedures so that they would get past protesters. I also used to volunteer at a refugee clinic. While I was at Penn, I studied abroad in Rome. All of those things were vital to my experience of law school and helping me get through it.

Yeah, I agree with all of that. From my perspective, I would also add that participating in a clinic can be a great learning experience. You get the hybrid of both learning and doing. It suited my preferences, as I'd rather do the work instead of sitting around in a room and thinking about legal theory. So I really enjoyed my clinic and would recommend that readers look into these opportunities.

Absolutely. I would also say take a lot of different types of classes. Don't only take courses like Evidence, Contracts, and Torts. I think I took a "Films in Law" class where we watched *The Godfather* and examined it through a legal perspective. Those classes did not just get me interested, but they provided a nice way to give legal theory and practice a different lens that I could appreciate. Plus, they were usually awesome and provided such a necessary mental break from "traditional" classes.

As many of us know, law school isn't just about succeeding on exams. While they are important, it is also about getting your first job after graduation. There's a lot of pressure for everyone involved, whether a law student wants to go into Big Law or work at a district attorney's office. Like several others in this book, you decided to enter private practice after law school. Can you speak about why you chose that path? You mentioned it in that you thought you could parlay legal training with your interest in the environment. Can you take us back to that time and explain your thought process?

Of course. So during on-campus interviews (OCI), I still wasn't sure if I wanted to go into Big Law. At least during my time at Penn, it felt like everyone participated in on-campus interviews because they make it really easy to do so. They bring all the firms on campus and "everyone's already doing it." It's a set path—the set path. In the same way that a "sure, why not" mentality and set path had brought me into law school, I was like, "Well, I'll just interview and see what's out there," and, many years later, I found myself stuck in that trajectory.

During OCI, I got really lucky because one of the firms where I received an interview slot had a climate change practice (that's what they called it). When I was speaking with the partner who came out to interview us, he was telling me how they help build really huge wind and solar farms. By doing the contracting and negotiations, they are helping to build the future that we need for energy change. Instead of Brownfield laws (where you're chasing around a bad guy that's already polluted something), they are actually trying to build a healthier planet. When he said that, a lightbulb went off. I was like, "This could be great."

That actually was what prompted me to even try Big Law. I ultimately ended up getting that job and working with that practice group through my entire practice (across three different firms). So I went into Big Law to follow my passion for environmental law because I didn't really have a set idea of what that was. I ended up working in that same practice group throughout my career.

When did this happen?

I graduated from law school in 2010. So I think I interviewed in 2008.

I feel like back then, a climate change practice wasn't common.

Oh, it really wasn't common.

I'm sure it's a lot more prevalent today. But that's great you found the firm with that type of work and that you were able to work there. What did that practice really entail? Can you give the readers a glimpse of your day-to-day work?

It probably was just like any other Big Law transactional junior associate's work. I had to create to-do checklists for deals, sit in on calls, and analyze contracts. They just happened to be environmental contracts or renewable energy contracts.

It's great that you found your niche or focus right away. Did you feel like you had to be pretty assertive to get into that practice group and stay in that practice group? In some circumstances, new Big Law associates are placed into certain categories. They are perhaps shoehorned in a specific practice group after their summer associate experience. It may be difficult to transition out of that practice group. So did you feel like you had to be more assertive in pursuing what you wanted to pursue?

In a different way, yes. I think I did something like eighty-nine interviews for firms—even though I knew I wanted to do environmental work—to get this one job offer that worked out. But because I was hired into this group, I didn't have to fight to do that work once I was hired.

Still, with different presidential administrations or resources available in the world, the work sometimes shifted during those five years. There was a good sector of time where renewable energy projects just weren't being built. To keep my billable hours up during that time, I was forced to do general corporate work, real estate, or (I hated this) oil and gas work. It's the same type of contract, you just remove the word "renewable." So I technically knew how to do that work and they expected me to. But for me, I went into law to do good environmental work, and it killed me to be an oil and gas lawyer.

During those days, I had to hustle in a different way to stay within my group and keep doing only work I believed in. So it was a hustle to find that practice, and it was a hustle to stay true to it through my whole practice.

How did you stay energetic and enthusiastic to get through those eighty-nine interviews?

It was crazy. My on-campus interviewing happened the week that Lehman Brothers crashed. So everything was chaos. It was 2008. Everybody was doing that many interviews because you'd get an offer and then the next day, the firm would be dissolved. Or the firm would say, "Sorry, there's no summer program anymore." So everyone in my class was in a hustle. I think the adrenaline of it kept me going (along with a lot of caffeine).

And grit as well. You have to get the work done, so you just do it. Is there anything you particularly enjoyed or didn't enjoy about Big Law?

I loved working on the really big projects. I'm still proud to say that I helped write the contracts that built the largest solar thermal farm in the world (at that time). I think that's really cool. It's on the road between Los Angeles and Las Vegas. Every time I drive past it with others in the car, I'm like, "Hey, I helped build that." I think that's amazing to be part of.

There was also a lot of great camaraderie and "deal high." I imagine litigators feel something similar during trial. I used to thrive on that high. I thought it was really great to be part of a project that created a discernible end product that made the world better. That's really satisfying on a professional level.

Now, years removed from my legal practice, I can also truly appreciate how many talented, efficient people work in Big Law. When we were on and a deal was closing, it felt like we could literally move mountains together, if we found the right contract precedent. I've not found another work situation where so many people can focus together on one single goal with as much dedication and efficiency.

That makes sense. If you don't mind me asking, you switched between three different firms before you left legal practice. Can you discuss that process of lateraling between different firms? If attorneys are reading this and doing something similar, what are some things that they should think about?

So again, my switch was driven by the practice area and the practice group. I left my first firm after around eight months. This was because my entire practice group moved firms. It was kind of like a group acquisition, and I chose to go with them.

That was why I left so early in my career. I really let my desire to stay in that area of law guide me. We were one of the premier groups in the nation doing this kind of work. I was enjoying it and wanted to keep growing in it.

When I went to my third firm (I believe it was four years after that), I was following a senior associate. She got promoted to partner at the new firm and asked whether I wanted to go with her to support her as she grew our same practice area in the new firm. I enjoyed learning from her and decided to follow her. My transitions were always driven by me following this practice area.

Let's talk about that decision of leaving legal practice to do something else. That decision was galvanized by your trip to the Galapagos. What happened during that experience and what did you learn from it?

When I left law, I was a fifth year. In retrospect, I was pretty unhappy during that time. I used to soldier through my work week. I would live for the two hours after work where I would veg out and watch TV with a bowl of shredded cheese. The same would be for my two days of the weekend (if I had two days) and my two weeks of vacation. I would convince myself, "Okay, there's work Tiff and then the real Tiff is outside of the law." Looking back, I realize how sad it was that I effectively turned myself "off" for so much of my life just to survive it.

I tried a bunch of different, high adrenaline activities during my time off to feel alive again. I felt like I had to do this to contrast the robot-human that was getting through my legal work. One of the things that I picked up was scuba diving. Then, one day, I remember I was working on a deal at 3:00 a.m. in the office by myself. I got this email about a scuba diving trip to the Galapagos. That had been on my bucket list. I was really frustrated with the deal and thought, "You know what? Like, eff it. Let's go." I just signed up at 3:00 a.m. and was like, "Yeah, I'm in."

I went on the trip thinking it was going to be a normal trip. I went by myself, which ended up being such a blessing because no one was meeting me as a lawyer or as anything. It was just like, "Oh, you're another diver." I think that freed me to think of myself differently, too.

I went there and remember I just felt really alive. I slept on the deck. I didn't sleep in my room so that I could watch the stars all night. There was a volcano, and there was bioluminescence in the water. Dolphins were jumping in it. It touched me really deep in my soul. I remember standing at the bow of the boat at 3:00 a.m. crying. I was just thinking, "I haven't felt this alive in ten years. In all of law school and all of practice, I haven't felt this alive and connected to myself, to nature, to the planet, or to really anything." I realized I'd been slowly numbing myself to the world to keep practicing.

It all cut me really deep. Then, I was on a drift dive (it's called a drift dive because you have to drift with the current). It was my first drift dive ever—both on that trip and in my life. I remember we all dropped down, and I was holding onto this rock because I was so scared. I saw everyone leaving. In that moment, I was like, "If you don't let go, you are going to die at the bottom of the ocean."

So I was screaming in my head. I was eventually like, "Okay, Tiff. Just go for it." I let go of the rock and drifted with everyone else. It was a mind-blowing dive. That taught me that I don't have to have control of every situation. I can just let go and trust that life is going to take me somewhere good. I will be okay.

And since then, that's what I've done with my career. I quit without a plan. Basically, when the airplane landed back at LAX, I made myself promise nothing would be the same. I would not forget how I felt on the bow of the boat. I would not go back to just numbing myself. So after that trip, I did all of the work to quit. About three weeks after getting back, I quit without a next step. I focused on putting things into place so that I could allow myself to go with the flow.

That's such a cool story. It's really the physical manifestation of what you were feeling at the time. You needed to physically let go of both the rock and the career that wasn't satisfying you. If that's not a signal, then I guess I don't know what is.

Yeah, it was a huge *aha* moment for me.

I'm sure. Compared to some of the other profiles in this book, your duration of "I want to leave legal practice" to actually leaving practice was rather short. In those three weeks, were you thinking through any of the financial ramifications of that decision? What thoughts were going through your mind at the time?

It manifested in three weeks, but the emotional journey was rather long in the making. On my very first day in Big Law, I was already telling myself that I'd be surprised if I made it one year. I just didn't have that inner feeling that Big Law was for me. It took me five years to get to the mental and emotional point where I allowed myself to quit. It seemed like a quick decision, but there was a five-year buildup.

Throughout my entire practice, I was always telling myself, "Okay, this is kind of cool, but I don't think it's for me for the long term." I couldn't see myself becoming any of my partners. I didn't necessarily want their lives. So I never felt like I really fit in or felt like, "Yes, put me on this conveyor belt towards partner and everything." I did quit on a whim, but there was a big buildup and a lot of mental work to get there.

I did consider finances. I think maybe a year and a half or two years before I quit, I realized that I had fallen into golden handcuffs. I was buying things and experiences and eating out to make myself feel better about how dead I felt during the week. That lifestyle isn't conducive to saving money. I had started lessening those expenses two years before I quit just in case I wanted to quit.

I also had hired a life coach (which I would recommend to anyone). Life coaches have galvanized my life ever since that point. But my first life coach truly helped me quit law by forcing me to think about what I actually wanted for my life. She helped me give myself permission to leave. I realized I was ultimately looking for emotional permission to do it. No one is going to be able to give you that but yourself.

You were definitely setting yourself up. It took years to get to that point, but once you got there, you were ready to roll.

Yes. And then after I quit, I actually ended up selling my house. It helped me keep funding this exploratory period, which led me to this happy place where I am now.

It hasn't been rosy the entire time, either. I want to make sure to say that. I moved home for a spell. I borrowed money from my mom. I have had to do a lot of things that, as a lawyer moving through in her thirties, you don't necessarily want to do. I could've told myself that those things were bad or shameful or whatever, but then I'd still be stuck in that life that I hated. Or I could suck up all those insecurities, trust in the flow, and trust that I'll end up okay. It's important to remember: if somebody is willing to help, and if you're willing to ask for help, you can use that positive force to catapult yourself into something that might be better.

In retrospect, were there any things that you maybe should have considered before leaving?

In hindsight, you can always do better. If I had been mentally and emotionally able, I wish I would have left sooner. I love every day of my life now—even on the worst and crappiest days. It's not always great, but not for one millisecond have I regretted the decision to leave. Each misstep and hop has brought me closer to myself. Knowing that I'm living out that version of me that wanted to be in front of the bulldozer (but just underwater now) feels so great.

I think I also would have spent some time exploring before I left—just to maybe push myself to leave sooner. I could have taken on a side job writing for a newspaper (if that was something that I thought of then). I could have volunteered with an ocean clinic or something like that.

Sure. I think you made a lot of important points there, but especially on the importance of experimentation. I think one of the fears about experimenting is failure. Many lawyers are perfectionists. They want to do things right and perfectly. But that may hurt them in the

end—especially if they are trying to determine what they actually want to do. They have to go out there and fail a couple of times.

Not just a couple of times, many times. Failure is a necessary part of success. But when you're a lawyer trying to leave such a set path, you convince yourself, "I need to know the next set path to jump on." But that's not how the rest of the world works.

I totally fell on the same bandwagon before, too. I was terrified to fail. I was really a perfectionist. I'm a super people pleaser. I had to work through a lot of that to give myself permission to let go and leave without a plan.

There is one thing that really helped me do this (and that I would recommend to anybody). One of my coworkers (who also quit around the same time) showed me a *Planet Money* podcast. It was on dating, and it basically said you shouldn't try to find someone to marry unless you go on fifty dates because you need data. The idea is that by forcing yourself to go on so many different dates, you will learn more about yourself and what you really want in a partner. Hopefully, after the fifty dates, you'll choose more wisely. So you make a spreadsheet and you fill in dates one, two, and three. You write down where you met, how you felt, red flags, things you loved, and other takeaways.

My friend and I then applied this approach to new careers. It helped us realize, "Why are we trying to commit to a new career when leaving the law before we even know what that career is or what we like?" We made a sort of pact to make spreadsheets of fifty potential career data points. Everything we tried was just a data point, not the rest of our lives or careers by any means. This helped take the pressure off of knowing what our next steps would be.

I worked to really embrace this mindset of exploration. I gave myself the freedom to try things and not consider them a failure if I didn't like them. Learning what you don't like is just as important as figuring out what you do like. I still remind myself of this today when I get scared to try new things. I remind myself it's just a data point and add it to my same spreadsheet, which I still keep up!

Totally. So you have this vision of writing, doing environmental work, and exploring the world. How did you go from that point of leaving legal practice to doing the work that you are now? You have done so

many cool things and have traveled to plenty of interesting places. You even worked with Al Gore. How did you find those incremental career opportunities?

They really started off as another data point on this spreadsheet. I still use and update the spreadsheet to this day. I think I have four hundred data points on it now. Each of those jobs, interviews, books read, et cetera started off as a data point of, "Maybe I'll try that. Maybe I'll explore that."

Also, I didn't just pick random things to try. For example, during my year after leaving law, I wanted to try field work. I was thinking, "Maybe I want to go back to school and become a marine biologist so that I can help the ocean."

I really wanted to see if I enjoyed field work. So I went to the Amazon rainforest to join a research camp and immerse myself in field work—even though it wasn't oceans. What that taught me was my upper limit of how much time I can spend being covered in bugs and mud and without a shower is two or three weeks. That wasn't conducive to field life. I was so grateful to have learned that then instead of trying to go back, do my science prerequisites, and then go to school for marine biology.

Everything else I've done and tried has started the same way, with me saying, "Maybe I will like X. Let me try to get a data set point. Let me put myself in a situation to create a data set point on X, test it, and see how I feel afterward. Let me do this instead of following 'the path.'"

Therefore, when I did my first ocean advocacy job, it was with an organization called Turtle Island Restoration Network. I ran a campaign against swordfish drift gillnets because they kill a lot of animals (whales, dolphins, sharks, and all the other things that we love). I thought, "Maybe I'll like this because the transition from law to advocacy makes sense." When I tried it, I was like, "This is so great. I love this and it feels right. I'm excited to do it." That data point told me, "Okay, let's veer that way instead of field work."

Everything cool that I've done (or that I think is cool) has started as a data point in trying to figure out my life.

I think that's a great model. So when you are trying to collect those dots and get those opportunities, is it simply Googling what's out there, seeing what's interesting, and applying to those opportunities? Is it more about relationships? Or is it a combination of both?

Everything. I think especially as a lawyer and someone looking for some certainty, you always think there is one set path. But everyone's life is entirely different. I found that swordfish job on an Indeed.com posting.

I found my next job with Coral Restoration Foundation as a scientific diver. I still wasn't sure if it was ocean field work that I didn't like, so I was like, "Okay, let's give it one more data point." I found that job on Instagram. It was an ad that I saw when following a hashtag.

Then, I found my first journalism job because I was going around town in the Florida Keys (where I live) and the editor of the newspaper overheard me talking to a friend. He was like, "Hey, would you want to write for some money on the side?" I was like, "Yeah, why not?" When I started doing that, I loved it more than anything else I was doing. So I was like, "Let's veer that way now."

Allowing myself to shift like that has been so rewarding. Now, I kind of do a mix of everything.

It's so interesting. Those opportunities were there, but you also had to be open to them. You had to embrace them as they came along. This editor could have offered you some work and you could have been like, "Oh, that's not really related to my career path. It's not how I see my career going." But you were actually open to those opportunities and they served you well.

Exactly.

I was looking at your website. You say that your mission is to "Involve and inspire others to see our world in an entirely different way and to want to save it." It's a great mission statement. How do writing, journalism, and exploration fit into that? How do you connect your overall mission with creating content?

I think that every story is an environmental story and a human story. I think our society has detached the two, and by bringing them back together, we can save the world and ourselves. So I tell stories that connect them and show how we are a part of this bigger thing. We are connected to each other and also to the planet. No one sector can suffer without consequences to everyone else. Therefore, in everything I do, whether it's in my advocacy, writing, or talks that I give, I want to showcase that connection. I also want to help people connect to wild, natural places that they wouldn't necessarily care about (but that they should).

You also started Ocean Rebels, which I understand is a media production organization. Can you speak about why you started Ocean Rebels? At the same time, you became an entrepreneur, so can you also discuss some of your experiences starting something new?

Ocean Rebels started as an effort to film these environmental stories and tell them through video. It has shifted right now to be more encompassing of my advocacy, teaching, and writing work. It happened as different people have come and gone in the organization. It's not a "real" legal organization, but kind of how I organize myself and this effort.

When we started Ocean Rebels, we believed that we needed to do things differently. The idea behind it is disruptive media. I don't necessarily mean that in a Sea Shepherd or PETA, spray-things-with-blood kind of way. Instead, I think how we think about the world is flawed. It needs to change. I want to do whatever it takes in whatever medium to galvanize that change and catapult it further.

Next up, I am thinking of leveraging the Ocean Rebels platform to democratize exploration. I always wanted to be an explorer, but as a first-generation Asian-American from an immigrant family, literally no one I know "explores" for work. I want to change that whole mindset by going on expeditions and creating content that helps people connect to those places. First up, I want to create an ocean-climate TikTok presence.

When you are doing your environmental work, do you use your legal training in any way? Do you even think about your prior life as a lawyer? If so, how do you use it to your benefit?

I didn't think about it. But in retrospect, I can totally see how my legal skill sets have helped me. They are still being applied in my work today. As a journalist, I have to quickly research and distill a lot of information. As a junior associate, that is all you are doing: you're reading and summarizing into one-sentence takeaways. That has helped me so much because I can do that quickly.

My legal training also helped with writing clearly. Legal training taught me that every sentence has a purpose. There's no fluff. That has really helped my writing (in the non-legal sense) become stronger.

There is also organization and time management. I learned to multi-task and compartmentalize by working for different clients. Now, as a freelance writer, I do the same thing to work for many clients while also doing things I love for myself. I even still keep a calendar where I track my time in six-minute increments (even though I don't need to).

Do you really?

Yes. I'm six years out from law and still do it. I realize that it actually helps me get so much done. It's super crazy. I don't know any other ex-lawyer that does it.

I was going to say. You're the only one I know that does that.

It sounds crazy, but it helps me go about my day in a super carefree way. I even calendar things like, "eat the broccoli" or "take your pills." This way, I don't try to remember things anymore. Law taught me to trust my calendar, so now I do 100 percent and I don't worry about whether I'm going to get certain things done. I just calendar it with enough buffer and go through my day, allowing my calendar to guide me. I've been trained through law to follow my calendar so regularly that this now helps me get a ton of things done every day. I feel like I live three lives in the span of one.

I agree. There are so many soft skills that you learn in law school and legal practice. You can then apply them in so many different ways. If you really think about it, it almost becomes a part of you (for better or for worse).

Yeah. You can't forget it. Still, if I'm walking somewhere and see ice on the road, I'm like, "That's a liability." You can't unlearn it.

Exactly. I'm wondering if you have any first principles for law students or lawyers that want to build a career in journalism or advocacy. Perhaps we can start with journalism. You've written for

some cool publications. Let's say that a lawyer wants to make the switch to becoming a full-time journalist. What are some of the first steps they should take?

If you want to go into journalism, start writing. It's hard to make the shift from legal writing to advocacy or journalistic writing because your goal is different. In legal writing, everything is footnoted, cited, and super precise. It doesn't necessarily have the most compelling story. It is the accurate legal story. Journalistic stories are accurate, but they need to be couched in a way that moves people. Start writing and then examine your writing to see how it can improve.

Also, take writing classes for fun. I've taken so many writing classes and I'm so jazzed about each of them. I feel like I'm improving in this craft. These classes, and what I've produced in them, have shown me just how much I love writing. I never would have guessed that leaving the law, but now, it's something I want to do for the rest of my life.

And if you feel like those kinds of classes are too expensive, a mindset shift you can employ is to think, "That's basically your tuition, right?" It's also much cheaper than going back to grad school for writing. Just take some casual classes for data points, see how you like them, and explore.

What kinds of writing classes?

I've taken classes on personal essays, creative nonfiction, opinion writing, service writing, travel writing, cultural critique, and freelance journalism.

These are all online?

Yes. Because of the pandemic, they were all online.

My initial impression of journalism or writing is that you just have to get out there and start writing. You need to start building a portfolio. From there, you try to network and meet people (like when you serendipitously met your editor). The opportunities then compound upon each other. That's my impression. Is that accurate?

It is. There are also things that I've learned in the meantime. If someone is really serious about starting, there are calls for pitches all the time on Twitter. You can search for "freelance" or editors of certain publications.

If you want to get some bylines or writing credits under your name, approach your local paper. That's where I started. I started with my local community paper in the Florida Keys. See if they'll accept something for free. Then, you start getting bylines with your name. You get some practice and that might turn into a column once per month. Then, maybe you are paid. You just work your way up.

My journey in journalism has been two years now. I started with just the community paper. I then ramped up to international publications with millions of views, and now into the biggest dive publications out there. That required me to stay on my grind, be out in the field, and tell good stories.

What about starting a blog? If you're interested in a very esoteric topic, you can maybe start a blog, keep writing about that topic, and then pitch yourself to different publications.

Totally. Show that you know how to finish a product. Show that you know how to create writing that can move people. Blogs are great.

I used to practice writing in a similar way when I was a lawyer. In retrospect, I didn't realize it until later. I used to write Yelp reviews. I needed a creative writing outlet, and I would play games with myself like, "Okay, write ten Yelp reviews before you get back to this contract." I did that throughout my legal career.

I'm sure it has paid off. You never know how something like that is going to help in the future.

Yeah.

As far as advocacy work and exploration, I'm assuming it is somewhat more of an amorphous career track compared to law or journalism. How do you even get started in advocacy or exploring? Is it more actively pursuing opportunities like you were doing or something else?

No. Someone told me something important early on in my journalism career (it also applies to advocacy). Don't sell yourself short and think that you're just a beginner. With a legal career behind you, use that and parlay that. Show that you are sidestepping in as an expert. You're not starting from the bottom and trying to come up.

I can talk about advocacy in the ocean space from having worked in law and policy. If you want to start doing speeches, there are many trainings. Like the Al Gore thing was a training. It's a free climate training that you can apply for and pursue. If accepted, you get trained by Al Gore and his whole team. I've used that to teach at the University of Miami on climate.

I also do presentations around the community. There are lots of different organizations (like libraries and dive groups) that are always looking for speakers because they have monthly series. If you offer your services for free, you can practice your message and skills. You can then get some presentations under your belt.

As far as exploration and joining on expeditions, the same advice can apply. Next year, I will be going to Panama to assist with turtle research, Norway to conduct research on Orcas by snorkeling with them, and Tanzania with a non-profit teaching women financial independence through sustainable, micro-financed businesses. I found two of those opportunities by talking with friends who were doing amazing projects and asking how I can help. I found the other in a Facebook group, where the leader put out a call for women explorers, and I applied saying I was an ex-lawyer, divemaster, journalist, and ocean advocate.

Right. It's really about looking at the skills and knowledge that you have. From there, find those opportunities.

And be willing to put yourself out there. It's scary to be like, "Hey, I'm going to speak" or "I'm going to write this." But put yourself out there. If it sucks, that's okay. Doesn't matter if it's your first try or your fifth try. Keep doing it, and you'll get better.

I was going to ask. How do you get over that fear or anxiety? Is there no other way than just doing it?

There's this quote that has guided me ever since I quit law. It's something like, "If it excites you and scares you at the same time, you should do it." I'm still scared when I write for big publications, when I cover a huge story, or when I speak. I'm still scared, but I allow the excitement in me to override it.

I wasn't scared about the deals I was doing in law. I didn't want to mess it up, but I wasn't invested in the outcome the same way I am here. So I let that guide me. I realize that the fear means that the work means something to me. That alone makes it worth doing.

Now, every time that I am scared, I try to flip the script in my head. If I'm going to cover a big story, instead of being like "Oh my God, I'm worried it's not going to go well," I wake up that day and am like, "Today is a great day to tell that story." I put that in my head and think, "Okay, we're going to do it."

As some people say, fear is just excitement without the breath. The same physiological reaction occurs when you are experiencing both excitement and fear.

That makes sense. I love that.

Are there any mistakes or things that readers should avoid if they want to get into writing, advocacy, or exploration work? These can be mistakes you've made or that you've seen other people make.

I don't think there are mistakes. I think there are learning opportunities. It also depends on what you want to do. My career is like advocacy slash journalism slash writing slash exploring. So I would say treat everything as a data point and don't be afraid of failure. Failures are great. They teach you more than your successes.

With your writing and advocacy, be honest with yourself and your sources. Give people credit. I always make sure to send articles I write about people back to them so that they can help amplify me. If I mention someone in a talk, I send them an email afterwards about how well their work was received by the audience.

A big part of all of this is also learning how to be your own best advocate. They don't teach you that in law. You're a cog in Big Law. Outside of that world, you need to do the opposite. Don't be afraid to be "out there" and really be yourself in the world. Be big and be you because, after law, you already have so many amazing skills. You just need to learn how to use them for your own dream.

Are there any resources (like blogs, books, or articles) that would give readers more insight into becoming a journalist or advocate?

For leaving law, I would highly recommend the podcast *Lessons From a Quitter* and *Former Lawyer*. The hosts of both podcasts were lawyers and they left law. *Former Lawyer* is more about directly leaving and helping you get around the mindset of leaving. *Lessons From a Quitter* is that and even beyond. It flips the script on quitting to be a great thing. We stay too long in careers, relationships, and situations that aren't perfectly aligned for us because we're scared of the unknown. They make us unhappy, but we're too scared to leave. Those two podcasts help tackle all that, imposter syndrome, and so much more. I'd highly recommend those two.

As far as books, I loved *You Are a Badass* by Jen Sincero and *Big Magic* by Liz Gilbert (especially if you want to do something creative). *Finish* by Jon Acuff is also super good.

Finally, I got a lot of help from life coaches. If you're looking to shift, recognize that maybe your mindset also needs some work. Invest in yourself and allow yourself to pay someone professional to help. It's so, so great.

Those are all great recommendations. Finally, what are you the most excited about? This can be anything for the next year, five years, or your entire career.

I'm excited that my life is not a set path anymore. Something that used to scare me so much was not having certainty. Now, I'm so glad that it's not certain. I have built up enough trust and confidence in myself and my skill set that no matter what I choose next, a million options will be available to me. I'll let go and make it worth the ride.

CHAPTER 4

Daron K. Roberts

Former NFL Assistant Coach and University Lecturer

Non-traditional careers can be fascinating. As a society, we certainly tend to celebrate them. While survivorship bias is likely at play, we draw attention to those risk-takers who put all of their chips on the table and come out on top.

Separating ourselves from the social peloton can be exciting and exhilarating, but that adventure doesn't come without costs. Having a non-traditional career involves hard work—a ton of hard work.

Non-traditional careers are difficult because they are simply that: non-traditional. While the potential rewards are great, the sheer amount of sacrifice involved is too much for some people.

Rejection is all too common. If you are trying to create or do something new, the ups and downs can be stomach-churning. Even if you find that perfect gig, job, or opportunity, the work isn't over. It is just beginning. You cannot rest on your laurels. You need to prove yourself every day.

Daron K. Roberts is an excellent example of someone who has chosen a non-traditional career path and has thrived. Even though there were trials and tribulations on his journey, Daron dug deep. He relied on his intelligence, work ethic, and can-do attitude to reach the highest levels in American sports.

I came across Daron's story when I interviewed him for my podcast, *The Power of Bold*. He successfully completed one of the more unique career switches I have ever seen. Daron graduated from Harvard Law School and immediately pursued his dream of becoming a football coach. He didn't want to become just any football coach, however. Daron wanted to become an NFL coach, even though he had virtually no experience as a football coach at any level.

Many of us wouldn't contemplate this sort of career move. Even if the idea of becoming an NFL coach sounded interesting, the odds of successfully pursuing that path would probably seem too slim. Moreover, there are opportunity costs. We all have a finite amount of time in our careers. On the one hand, we have more resources than ever to pursue our dreams. On the other hand, the clock is always ticking. By spending years on a dream that may not necessarily come to fruition, you will undoubtedly miss out on other intriguing opportunities.

Graduating from one of the best law schools in the world, it would have been all too easy for Daron to find a "traditional" job as a law firm associate, assistant district attorney, judicial clerk, or public interest lawyer. Instead, he chose a different path. After graduating from Harvard Law School, he began what he described as a "letter-writing campaign" to get into the NFL. One day, he received a call from Herm Edwards, the then-coach of the Kansas City Chiefs. Ultimately, Edwards offered him an internship with the Chiefs. Even though Daron would receive no pay, no benefits, and take on eighteen-hour workdays, he was all-in. He wanted to give everything he had to this golden opportunity.

The path wasn't easy. At times, Daron slept in the Chiefs' stadium. He had to learn a complex playbook and how to break down film. But through hard work, Daron eventually received a coaching gig with the Chiefs. Not only that, but he parlayed that experience into coaching positions with the Detroit Lions, the West Virginia University Mountaineers, and the Cleveland Browns.

Daron describes his journey from Harvard Law School to the NFL in his book, *Call an Audible*. To get a full sense of his path from Harvard Law School applicant to NFL assistant coach, I encourage you to read the book. While Daron doesn't coach football anymore, he has applied that same work ethic and grit to other opportunities. He is the founding director of the Center for Sports Leadership & Innovation (CSLI) at the University of Texas. Daron is also a partner at Notley Ventures, which provides capital and knowledge for the social impact community. And being a number one LinkedIn Top Voice in Sports, Daron shares his knowledge about sports and life with thousands of LinkedIn users.

Even if you aren't interested in sports, Daron's path shows us that even the most non-traditional careers are possible. While the path can be incredibly rocky, the opportunity is there if you choose to pursue it.

* * *

The story of how you transitioned from Harvard Law School to the NFL is absolutely fascinating. But before getting into that, let's start at the beginning. Can you share your law school origin story?

My earliest thoughts of law school were probably somewhere in my elementary school years. My dad bought me a children's book about Thurgood Marshall. I was enamored with his courage and perseverance. I recognized that the profession was something that people respected. My dad also made it a point that even with nearly twenty uncles and aunts on each side of me, we didn't have any lawyers in the family. Because of this, he suggested that this could be a good profession to enter.

How old were you?

I was around nine. I knew what being a lawyer looked like. I remember seeing *To Kill a Mockingbird* and watching Atticus Finch. But probably like most people who have not been to law school and/or on the other side of the law (i.e., practiced), I'm not sure that I knew what it meant. I'm not sure that I know what it means now. I think it means a lot of different things, right? A lawyer can do a lot and can serve in a lot of different capacities (like corporate or criminal).

That's certainly true. As you grew up, what did your family or friends think about your early goals? As you describe in Call an Audible, your interest in law school and a possible political career seemed to consistently grow in those earlier years.

From my perspective, everyone was supportive. I competed in debate. I was class president all four years during my time in high school. My parents were students of political affairs and we would talk about issues related to politics. So all of the people around me, teachers, and friends seemed to be supportive. They thought it was cool. That's the great thing about the law, right? If you say you want to be a lawyer or a doctor in the United States, then people usually give you the thumbs up.

Now, most of those people don't have any clue what it takes to get to those two positions. Not many people can identify with it, but in our culture, the doctor and the lawyer have maintained prominence in our collective psyche. So people gave me the thumbs up. They were excited. Everyone wanted me to chase my dreams.

Do you have any general advice for people that are thinking about going to law school? Are there certain things they should strongly consider or other things that they should simply ignore?

I get this question one million times per day. For people thinking about law school, I suggest you think about several different things.

One, evaluate why you want to go to law school. *Be very honest.* Is it because it sounds good? Is it because it sounds prestigious? Is it because it is your default answer because you don't know what you want to do and you think it sounds prestigious? You really need to be honest with yourself about the why. Why do you want to go to law school and what did you hope to accomplish with the degree? Period.

Step two: go talk to a lawyer. It doesn't matter what area of practice. Talk to as many different lawyers and in as many different areas of the law as possible. Shadow a lawyer. Watch him or her in their element. This will give you much more experience and data than most undergraduates have when they make the decision to go to law school.

When speaking with a lawyer, what types of questions should prospective students ask? Are there certain questions that are more valuable or insightful than others?

Since I'm not a lawyer, I'm maybe not the best person to answer this question. But these are some questions that I would ask a lawyer:

- What is your day like? Walk me through the beginning and end of your day.

- What types of matters do you work on?

- How much time do you spend with clients and other lawyers in the office?

- How much time do you spend traveling?

- What subject matter do you work on?

- What is the best part of your day? What is the worst part of your day?

- Before you arrived at your firm, were there certain things you thought you would do that you rarely get to do?

- Before you arrived at your firm, were there certain things that you thought you *would not* do that you frequently do as a practicing lawyer?

It would also be great if readers could talk to a first-year attorney, an associate that has three or four years of experience, and a partner. Talk to someone at a nonprofit. Talk to a general counsel. In the best of all worlds, readers would talk with lawyers in all facets of the legal landscape to get as much information as they could.

Like many other prospective law students, Harvard Law School caught your eye. When you were looking at both Harvard and other law schools, what were some of the most prominent variables or factors that you considered?

I cared about reputation and ranking. Period. That's it. For me, I wanted to go to a law school that would give me a lifetime of value in terms of reputation. I wanted to go to a well-respected institution and Harvard fit that bill.

I became enamored with Harvard at a very early age. I can't tell you how. I just knew that it was the best law school in the world. I was just enamored with going to the best law school in the country. Harvard Law School was the place for me and it was really that simple.

As you describe in *Call an Audible*, it took several years for you to get into Harvard Law School. You were waitlisted several times. In the interim, you were at the Harvard Kennedy School and working with Senator Joe Lieberman in Washington, D.C. While these oppor-

tunities were certainly exciting, being on the waitlist for your dream school is never ideal. How did you develop the willpower to keep going and keep applying to Harvard Law School?

This is a really good question. I don't have an answer. I just really wanted to go to Harvard Law School. For me, I was not being rejected. I was being waitlisted, and so I saw some glimmer of hope every time the letter would come back that I had been waitlisted. It felt like I was close—even on attempts number two and three and four. I still felt like I was close and I was confident that I could find a way to get in.

I also relied on my faith. I'm a Christian. I prayed a lot and meditated quite a bit. I also read a lot of stories of people who had found ways to get in, so I just kept the embers of hope burning.

Your persistence absolutely paid off. You received the good news after four attempts. What do you think was the ultimate catalyst for your admission?

I get this question a lot. I don't know the answer. The admissions process for law schools—especially Harvard Law School—is a black box. I have found no reliable data. The admissions office never said, "Hey, we admitted you because of X." All I know is that I received a call from the Harvard Law School admissions office in April 2004. They said they had a spot for me and they asked if I would accept it. I said yes.

So many people have asked me: "What did it take? How did you know? What did you do? What turned the tide?" I wish I had an answer for it. I don't know at all and I don't think I'll ever know. The most important thing is that I realized that if you really want to achieve something that seems difficult, the only way to do it is to keep at it for as long as you possibly can. You need to do it as long as your heart, mind, time, talent, energies and willpower allow you to do it. Who knows when the "no," "wait," or "maybe" becomes a "yes?" So I didn't look at those waitlist letters as a "no." I saw them as a "not yet."

As you imply, there's no secret in getting off of the waitlist at any law school. But do you have any thoughts on what prospective law students can do to tilt the odds in their favor?

It's a common question. In fact, I need to write a book just on this question. I have no clue. I rewrote my personal statement four times and was waitlisted four times. I had 12 different people recommend me for law school and was waitlisted four times. I retook the LSAT and increased my store. Still waitlisted four times. I even visited Harvard Law School's admissions office. I took a flight from Washington, D.C. to Boston and sat in the admissions office corridor. A receptionist kindly told me that they did not take walk-in visits or any visits of that nature. I left a packet of supplemental material (I can't remember what was in it) and walked away. I asked prominent alums to call on my behalf for four years. I was still waitlisted each year.

So I don't know. It's a crapshoot. All I tell people is to get really good grades in undergrad. Try to get the best LSAT score that you can. Write a compelling essay and get some people that can recommend you. Make sure they can speak deeply about your passion for life, your work ethic, and your potential to make a change in the world. From there, let the chips fall where they may.

If I had the answers, I would start a law school admissions company and charge exorbitant amounts of money to help people navigate the process. But to this day, I have no clue.

One decision that prospective law students need to make is whether they should take some time off between college and law school. Where do you come out on that question?

Prospective law students should take some time off. The reason why I say this is if I look back at my classmates, the students that I thought maintained their sanity were the ones who had some distance from college. In other words, they did not graduate in May and then enroll in law school in August. I think having some professional experience or traveling for a year will not impact your law school admissions. If law schools want you now, most of them are going to let you defer for a year.

I also just think life is too short to go straight through to law school. Once that clock starts for law school, it doesn't stop. You will accumulate a lot of debt. You're going to feel the urge to go and work to pay off that debt. Then, the rat race begins.

I am also a firm believer that high school students should take a year off in between high school and undergrad. Undergrads should also take a year or two off. Go travel, go work, go write, or do something else before law school. I think it's a good way to gain perspective and get some distance. I think for me, having worked on Capitol Hill and been in graduate school for two years, I entered Harvard Law School with a relatively low level of angst and anxiety. I was at peace with the law school process.

So if a prospective law student is going to take a year off, should he or she find a position in (or related to) the legal field?

No, no, no, no, no. Take a year off. By that, I mean don't do anything in the legal world.

I think it's the most redundant thing when people go and become a paralegal or legal assistant and then go to law school. If you think you will become a lawyer, you will probably do it for the rest of your life. Please don't spend one year in between undergrad and law school doing anything law-related. Go travel to a country where you don't know the language.

I wouldn't do anything legal-related in an off-year. I actually wouldn't call it an off-year at all.

After those years of persistence and determination, you finally arrived at Harvard Law School. Take us inside those three years at HLS. Is there anything in particular that you enjoyed or didn't enjoy about the experience?

I loved my section (section seven). Some of my best friends in life are from section seven. I had a very good experience with several faculty members—particularly Randall Kennedy[1] and David Wilkins.[2] These two men in particular were mentors to me and helped guide me throughout law school.

---

1   Randall Kennedy is still at Harvard Law School. As the Michael R. Klein Professor of Law, he teaches Contracts, Criminal Law, and the Regulation of Race Relations.

2   David Wilkins is also still at Harvard Law School. Along with being the Vice Dean for Global Initiatives on the Legal Profession, he is the Lester Kissel Professor of Law. He is also the Faculty Director of the Center on the Legal Profession and the Center for Lawyers and the Professional Services Industry.

What did I not enjoy about Harvard Law School? The first-year experience is tense. You take one exam that's worth one hundred percent of your grade and that is it. Because of this, there is so much uncertainty surrounding where you stand as a student. That wasn't very enjoyable at Harvard Law School, but I also don't think many other people enjoy that at other law schools.

Considering the intense competition at Harvard and the pressure that comes with doing well on exams, do you have any best practices for law students that are trying to handle that pressure and competition?

I think that they should have a hobby. Whether it is drawing or playing music, something to get away is helpful. I also think that working out, running, or some kind of physical outlet is good to get some perspective.

For me, meditation worked. Mindfulness and self-compassion are things that we need. These are especially important. Understanding that you aren't isolated in law school. Other people are having this experience and it's going to be okay.

Did you use any time management strategies or frameworks to balance studying and your hobbies?

Here's how you can make it very simple. Thirty minutes per day, five days per week. Period. I think it's as simple as saying, "Here's my class schedule. Here's when my study group will get together. Here's when I'm going to eat. I'm going to spend this thirty-minute block of time Monday through Friday and do some very basic athletic activity."

I think that's it. I think it gets more difficult when you make it complicated. Just do thirty minutes per day, five days per week. The easier it is for you, the more likely that you'll follow through with it.

During your 1L year, what was the career plan? Did it shift as you entered your 2L and 3L years? I'm assuming that you were at least considering some role in the political arena.

During my 1L year, my plan was to graduate from Harvard Law School and practice law in Houston at a major corporate firm for three to four years. From there, I would transition from Houston to my home district in east Texas where I would open up a law office. I would then run for public office (preferably state Senate), become a state senator, and then run for governor and become governor by age forty. That was the plan.

That's quite an ambitious plan. As we'll discuss in a few moments, that plan took a much different turn. But before we get that, I'd like to ask you one thing. If a reader is in law school and thinking that law school isn't really isn't for him or her, do you have any suggestions or things that they should think about?

If you're in law school and you don't think you're in the right place, I would say a couple of things. I think graduating with a law degree is a good thing. There's a lot of social cachet and professional cachet that come along with it. I think that's a good thing. I would say finish.

In terms of what you do *once you finish*, that is up to you. Now, I can't really prescribe that. You need to take an inventory of what you think makes you happy. Try some professions. Maybe go back to the internship phase of your life. Consider some shadowing experiences.

But I'm a big fan of graduating from law school once you're in it. I think that there is value in that. Now, there's the separate question of whether you want to practice later. If it's not for you, make that decision later, but definitely graduate.

After that, I think the world is yours. Go experiment. We don't experiment enough. We view professions and careers from the outside. Instead of that, talk to people who are in your dream profession. Get shadowing experiences, do internships and externships, have coffees, and reach out to people on LinkedIn. Be very vigilant about trying to gather information related to the place where you think you want to go.

Part of your initial career vision was practicing at a large corporate law firm before entering the political arena. Can you take us into your thought process at the time?

I started to seriously consider it during my first year of law school. When I looked at how much debt that would be with me after law school, I thought I should probably go to a place that will pay me an exorbitant amount of money at a very early point after my law school career so I can pay off debt.

You worked at Baker Botts in Washington D.C. for your 1L summer internship and then split your 2L summer between Fulbright & Jaworski[3] and Vinson & Elkins in Houston. What factors were important to you when making these decisions?

I looked at the firms that had prestige in Texas. Those three top firms were Vinson & Elkins, Baker Botts, and Fulbright & Jaworski. So I knew I was going back to my home state because I was going to eventually get into politics. Because of that, my sole goal was to go to a top firm that had a lot of cachet in the state of Texas.

You had an experience unlike many other law students in that you worked at three Big Law firms for two summers. What was your ultimate impression of Big Law life?

I thought that Big Law life was okay. I did not dislike big firm life. I wasn't completely enamored with it. It was just okay. I felt like my satisfaction level was at a flatline when it came to law firms. The work was somewhat interesting but it wasn't like I felt it was riveting work.

That said, I had great experiences at all of my firms. There were really good people there. But I never felt like I was in a place that was fulfilling my ultimate purpose in life. Something was missing for me.

Going to a so-called "Top 14" law school like Harvard, there can be some subtle pressure to pursue a Big Law job. This is because of things like the ease of participating in on-campus interviews and the eye-popping compensation offered to junior associates. These firms obviously provide great opportunities for law students that are interested in them. However, if a reader isn't necessarily interested in or enthused about working at a Big Law firm, how can he or she avoid the inertia or pressure to nonetheless pursue these positions?

---

3   In 2013, Fulbright & Jaworski combined with Norton Rose. The combined firm is now called Norton Rose Fulbright.

I think it's easy. If you don't want to do it, don't do it.

But let's back up a little bit. Before law school, be very honest with yourself. If you are going to rack up this kind of debt to go to law school, how are you going to pay it off? Do you feel pressure to pay it off through a big firm job? If the answer is yes, then just know you're getting into that.

There's no one at your law school graduation ceremony that is putting you into a paddy wagon and shipping you off to Big Law firms. This is a choice and it's a choice that you have to make. There are people who make $50,000 per year in other professions who are able to pay their bills, live a good life, and enjoy their work.

I think we shouldn't give ourselves an out by assuming we have to go to a big firm because we have debt. First of all, be honest about it upfront before you go to law school. Be honest with yourself and ask whether you can realistically avoid that life if you don't want to do it.

Secondly, after you leave, be courageous and creative about your career life after law school. If it's something you don't want to do, the only measure of how much you want to change that outcome is to be vigilant about researching and finding other opportunities. I think a lot of people complain about big firm life, but then they don't explore anything else. They say, "Big firm life is awful" as they walk through the front doors, but they don't consider other opportunities.

Instead, explore. Get out there and talk to people. Get out there and do internships. Stop complaining about it and explore. Otherwise, you deserve every outcome that comes to you from big firm life.

So let's assume a prospective law student takes that advice and is thinking about their career path before enrolling in law school. If he or she asked you what they should know about Big Law life, what would you say?

Well, for one thing, it pays a lot of money. It gives you a lot of experience in terms of different kinds of legal work. But I didn't practice there, so I can't really speak to that too much.

You received full-time job offers from all three of your law firms. Why did you turn them down?

I turned them down because I wanted to coach football. I realized that after working at a football camp the summer before I graduated from law school. That camp took place at the University of South Carolina. I really enjoyed that camp. I knew that I wanted to coach football so I turned down all of my law firm offers.

Why did I do it? Because I know that I only have one life. If I went to the firm right after I left school and made a lot of money and bought the right cars and lived in the right neighborhoods, it would become increasingly difficult for me to shed that life. So I decided to do it early. I also turned down those offers because I knew that if I let them linger, I might take them.

When making your transition, what was missing from your life in the law that you thought you could find in football?

This is where I want to dispel the myth. I did not go to football because I was disgruntled with the law or because I hated the law. There was nothing of that sort. My decision to go to football had less to do with the law and more to do with the fact that I really enjoyed my time coaching football for three days at that camp. I wanted to get more of it.

Makes sense. No matter the career, there is power in role models. The journey can seem more attainable if we can look at others who have done the things that we want to do. Did you try to emulate anyone specific for your transition from law to football?

Yes, I studied people who had made similar transitions. One of them was Rick Neuheisel. He was the head football coach at UCLA (among other places). He had a law degree so I studied his story.

In particular, I reached out to Mike Leach. At the time, he was the head football coach at Texas Tech University. Mike Leach went to Pepperdine Law and then found his way to become a head football coach. After reaching out to him at Texas Tech, I made a visit. I spent two weeks learning from him, talking to him, and getting advice. In terms of things to think about, he was the person that gave me the most guidance. We talked about everything from nuclear proliferation to play calls when you're in the red zone and down by two touchdowns or more. He's an incredibly smart individual and someone who helped quite a bit.

Did you see this transition as a big risk? What was the backup plan (if any)?

I didn't have a backup plan. Was it a big risk? I don't think so. I had a law degree from Harvard, so I didn't think that I was going to starve at any point in my life. I also felt like one of the reasons why I went to Harvard Law School was so I could take huge gambles in life. This, to me, qualified as a big-time gamble. Call it blind optimism or faith but I was very confident that something would work.

Because there was no backup plan, I was going to write to every college team and every NFL team. I was going to find some coach to give me a shot. From there, I would parlay that first experience into the next coaching gig and go on and on until I got to the top. That was my sole ambition.

So I canceled my bar exam test date. I was going to take it in July but did not take it because I had to work at a training camp. There was no backup plan because I did not want an easy out if things got rough.

At this point, you have worked at the football camp in South Carolina. You've spoken with Mike Leach and have studied the paths of other football coaches that made the switch. You're ready to go pursue that dream. At the same time, how did you deal with the expectations of others when you knew you wanted to do something different with your law degree?

You know, Adam, I just really don't give a damn about what other people think. My dad is a Baptist minister. He would take me with him to funerals and weddings and I became acutely aware of the fact that time is a finite resource. At some point in my younger years, I became very content with doing things that people didn't think that I could or should do. I realized that not only could they not live my life, but that I only get one shot at this thing and I'm going to do it my way. The people that were disappointed didn't have to live my life.

I had a lot of support from my family. I also had some mentors that questioned whether or not this was the right decision. But I had to live my life, right? It would be different if I had made a pivot to go and start selling cocaine. I was going to coach football. This was a fairly benign pivot. If anyone wasn't on board with my decision, that was their problem.

So I think it's important for readers. You only get one shot at this thing called life. If you're going to law school because you won a debate tournament back in high school and it just sounds like the right thing to do, you should reevaluate your life. If you're going to work at a law firm because everyone else is trying to get into Big Law, yet you don't like it, you should reevaluate your life. I just think life is too short to be consumed with what other people think. That's been my philosophy for the entirety of my life.

Clearly, you were all in. Looking back, however, would you have taken the transition slower? Say finding a job in the legal world and acquiring some type of football experience on the side?

You know, Adam, I wasn't in a position where I had any latitude to take anything slow. I think this is a very important point when you're trying to transition between two disparate professions. All of my Harvard Law School background had absolutely no value to coaches. They didn't care that I had been to Harvard Law School. They were coaching football. I was in a position to take the best gig that I could and run with it.

I didn't have time to go fast or slow. Once the door was open, all I could do was run as fast as humanly possible through the crack. Period. I wasn't going to turn this into some kind of brief or decision tree. I was going to write to NFL and college teams. Once the best opportunity came my way, I was going to say yes, pack up my things from Cambridge, Massachusetts, and then go wherever I had to go to start coaching football.

In *Call an Audible*, you say you treated your NFL dreams like a political campaign. What do you mean by this?

So when I looked at my assets and compared them with where I wanted to land, I saw that I did not have much football coaching experience. Frankly, I had worked a camp for three days as a volunteer coach, so I could not tout my coaching ability. Because of this, I crafted a letter that expressed that I had worked in the most grueling legal environments on the planet (i.e., Harvard Law School). I had spent countless hours in the library writing briefs and reading cases, and I was going to take that same work ethic to the team where I landed. Even though I would be at the bottom of the totem pole, I was going to do whatever I needed to do to gain experience.

And when I say a political campaign, I went on a letter-writing campaign. I went to the World Wide Web and found the websites for all thirty-two NFL teams and fifty NCAA football teams. I looked at the bios for every assistant coach and every head coach. I tried to find any commonalities that I could express in a letter. From there, I just embarked on a letter-writing campaign. My sole goal was to get as many letters out into the world of football and to hopefully land somewhere. In many ways, I was running a direct mail campaign.

Considering all of that, what are some key takeaways for readers that want to break into an industry where they have little to no experience?

The number one lesson? Regardless of where you are coming from, if you are going to a place where you don't have much experience, it is to your benefit to offer your free services. It doesn't matter if you are a Ph.D. student or have an advanced degree. Your willingness to do whatever it takes—however menial—can be a great inducement to convince the gate-keepers to let you into that new profession. We cannot assume that any sort of clout or respect that one has had in another profession will carry over into the next destination.

Harvard Law School didn't carry much weight with the Kansas City Chiefs. They wanted me to learn how to coach football. So I needed to first just get into the door. This is one of my lessons in *Call an Audible*. Just get in the building. You won't come in at the VP level or some higher senior executive level. Just get in the building, and then from there, you can try to make your mark.

So what did this look like in practice?

I just offered to work for free and do any task. If I needed to clean chalk-boards or clean up trash, I would do it. I offered to restock the kitchen. I took on menial tasks just to build credibility.

In your book, you speak about the sheer amount of sacrifice you had to make to stick around with the Chiefs. This included things like those menial tasks you just mentioned and even choosing to stay at work for days at a time. Do you have any tips for readers on how to

deal with a stressful, uncertain environment? What advice would you give for transitioning lawyers or law students who are facing struggles or challenges in their new field?

In terms of stressful or uncertain environments, I think there are several things. First, having that thirty-minute physical outlet per day is important. Maybe talk to a therapist. I've never had a therapist, but I think it's something that you may want to consider.

I don't have many good answers in this area. But it's helpful to take a real evaluation of your life and determine whether you truly want what's on the other side of your particular challenge. Not all challenges or uncertain environments are good for you. Really be honest to see if you want what's on the other side.

From these menial tasks, however, opportunities started to open up. You started to get some hands-on football experience in the NFL. Was there a steep learning curve? If so, what tactics did you use to make the learning process easier?

Yes. There was a steep learning curve because I didn't know high-level football strategy. Because of this, I read plenty of books about football strategy. I attended as many meetings as I could. I took as many notes as I possibly could. I talked to people about the profession. I tried to gather as much intel as I humanly could about all of these facets. I was just an information gatherer.

If you're going to a place where you need to learn quickly, become a sponge. Watch as many YouTube videos, read as many books about the industry, and talk to as many people who have done it. I did all of that and kept copious notes. With those notes, I tried to find similarities and other things that would help me.

Once again, humility is important. If you're going to a new place, it's more than likely that you'll need to start at the bottom. Forget about where you've been. Be humble enough to start at the bottom and then work your way up.

At any point throughout your coaching journey, did you ever think of making a transition to legal practice? If so, why didn't you?

The short answer is no. Never. I was having too much fun as a coach to think about going back to the law.

If a graduating law student or current lawyer wants to work in sports (either in a practicing or non-practicing role), what advice would you have for them? How can they tilt the odds in their favor?

Okay, let's start with a practicing role. Every team and every league have attorneys and general counsels. I would try to find some way to network with general counsels. If you want to work with a team, maybe go to their industry conferences. Learn more about the profession. On the player side, there are agents. You don't need to be an attorney to be an agent, but it probably helps. So I would talk to agents if that's what you're interested in.

On the business side of sports, I still think it's about talking to people in the profession. I don't think there's a prescribed roadmap. At the beginning, it's helpful to gather information about how your law degree can be used in the sports context. As for a non-practicing role (like a coach), I think my blueprint could be the right one. That is to offer to work for free and see if someone wants to take a gamble on you.

I will say this. Sports is entertainment, which means that there is high demand. The number of positions is very limited. Search for ways to differentiate yourself from others who are looking for those same jobs. Another thing I would say is please don't mention the fact that you love sports. Most of the industrialized world loves sport. Find some way to not depict yourself as the fan. There are enough fans and teams are not looking for fans. When teams are hiring people, they're looking for employees that can add value. They don't need super fans. So please downplay any sort of fandom that you have and stick to the value that you can bring to the organization.

For readers that are about to make the switch into some sort of sports role, what is the most important thing to keep in mind?

I don't know if there is an important thing. If I had to say, however, I think it comes down to humility and information gathering.

Are there any particular advantages that attorneys have when making this type of transition? What about disadvantages?

This is a tough question because there are so many different positions in sports. For example, if you want to become a general counsel and you're an attorney, you're in a good position. The skill set that you need relates to what you have done. Now, if you're a lawyer and want to become a coach, that's tough. People don't care about the law when they're putting together plays for a team.

So it depends on what you're trying to land. I will say there are advantages, though. One advantage is that lawyers learn problem-solving and troubleshooting in law school. That's also what the practice of law is. These problem-solving and troubleshooting skills have value, whether you are a coach trying to determine the best play call on third down or a general manager trying to determine what player to draft. I think the problem-solving skills have a lot of value.

As far as disadvantages, I think that we can sometimes be too smart and overthink things. That can be seen as a disadvantage in the profession.

You took a one-year sabbatical after coaching and then returned to the University of Texas. There, you started the Center for Sports Leadership and Innovation. Why did you do that?

I was at the Cleveland Browns and we were all fired. I went home, scrambled some eggs, and my kid saw me. He asked me whether I ate breakfast. I thought to myself: "Why is he asking me this?" I then realized that I spent so much time with other people's sons. My own son didn't know me.

So I decided to take a sabbatical from coaching. I came back to the University of Texas and the Ray Rice episode unfolded. I started talking with UT's president about ways that we could cultivate leadership and character among our student-athletes. I then proposed a Center for Sports Leadership and Innovation. I teach a course to all freshmen athletes around leadership and financial literacy. The Center also has a program called Captain's Academy. This is where we bring the varsity captains from Austin Independent School District to the University of Texas to teach them leadership traits and skills (like mindfulness, mindset, decision-making, and social media etiquette). We also have a program called I

Lead where we bring in leaders from the sports world. We have had Mia Hamm, Kevin Durant, Shaun White, and others come in and talk about pressing issues in sports.

Similar to your work in the NFL and college football, did you find your law degree or experience helpful in this new chapter of your career?

Yes. Going back to problem solving, I think my legal degree and my experience navigating new terrains have been helpful. The law degree came into play through surveying, issue spotting, and even strategic planning.

If you had to navigate your transition again, is there anything that you would have done differently?

Absolutely nothing. I would still go to law school. I would still go work at that football camp in South Carolina. I would still graduate from law school and would still write letters to all of those teams. It has created in me a very well-rounded approach to life and I would not change any facet of the professional decisions in my life.

For lawyers and law students that are nervous about making a similar transition, do you have any advice to help them overcome their fears?

I just think it's important to be honest. If you are comfortable with living in fear and regret, then stay where you are. I don't think it's for everyone. I think that some people are paralyzed by the fear. If you're comfortable staying there, fine.

For me, I have always been incentivized to take risks because time is a finite resource. I only get one chance to live a life that is meaningful to myself and to the people around me.

Can you recommend a book that has inspired you on your career journey?

Sure, I'll give you a few books. I'd recommend *The Alchemist* by Paulo Coelho, *Narrative of the Life of Frederick Douglass*, and *Steve Jobs* by Walter Isaacson.

Finally, any advice for those lawyers or law students that are in the midst of making that transition into a new sector or industry?

My philosophy on life is this: cast a wide net. If you are trying to break into a new field, there is no blueprint for what will work. Do everything and hope that something sticks.

What does "do everything" mean? Write a letter to every person that can possibly hire you. Try to set up a coffee with anyone that you think could possibly help you. Go to industry conferences that deal with the area where you'd like to transition. If you are looking to work with a particular person, find where he or she is speaking. See if they are going to be at a conference on a panel. Professionally stalk the people that you want to be.

Send emails. Go old school and send faxes. Make phone calls. I just think that when you're trying to break into an area where you don't have any currency or cachet, everything is the right thing (within reason). Of course, I'm not asking you to do anything that's criminal in nature. But with everything you do, try to gain traction.

Exhaust all possibilities. Be relentless in your pursuit of a small opening to the life that you want to live.

CHAPTER 5

Jessica Medina

Accredited Financial Counselor

It is impossible to make any sort of career change without considering the financial consequences of that change. This is true whether you are moving to another company in your industry or are pursuing a gig in a totally different sector. For as much as we may not like it, money plays some part in when (or whether) we grasp certain opportunities in front of us.

This dynamic is even more complex for lawyers. A 2020 survey by the American Bar Association (ABA)[1] shows that more than ninety-five percent of law school graduates took on student loans to attend law school. At the time, more than ninety percent of respondents had at least $65,000 in student loans by the time they graduated (and that's just law school debt). Combined with undergraduate student loan debt and other loans upon graduating from law school, the ABA reported an average student loan amount of a whopping $164,742. While programs like the Public Service Loan Forgiveness Program can forgive some law school graduates' debt, the vast majority of graduates will spend years paying off their debt.

Therein lies the rub for starry-eyed prospective law students. One side of the equation contains their dream jobs in the legal industry. On the other side is the harsh reality of debt, bills, and cash flow. Obviously, it isn't impossible to go to law school and become a human rights lawyer or specialize in constitutional law. However, pursuing those career dreams may lead to some financial challenges, especially if those law students take on hundreds of thousands of dollars of debt.

---

1   You can find the full ABA survey at this link: https://www.americanbar.org/content/dam/aba/administrative/young_lawyers/2020-student-loan-survey.pdf

Current law students and practicing attorneys understand this. Before entering law school, it is easier to spend more time envisioning career possibilities and spend less time considering the financial realities of getting a JD. Those consequences directly affect your early career decisions. Whether seeking a lower-paying legal job while carrying student debt or making a more substantial career transition out of the law, you must sit down and look at the cold, hard numbers. An alternative career is certainly possible, but you must consider the financial consequences of pursuing that non-traditional career.

Jessica Medina is a former practicing attorney who understands this. She is a former Big Law and SEC attorney who became an Accredited Financial Counselor. Accredited Financial Counselors like Jessica help their clients by educating them in sound financial principles, helping them manage debt, helping them achieve financial goals, and more. While Accredited Financial Counselors do not offer advice on investing or tax strategy, they help clients build strong economic foundations and reach financial goals.

Jessica found her new career as an Accredited Financial Counselor by looking at her hobbies. While she enjoyed her earlier years at the SEC Division of Enforcement, she wanted to leave and try something new. A conversation with her now-husband convinced her to marry her hobby of financial planning with a new career helping others better manage their finances.

Jessica's story offers many insights for all types of law students and practicing lawyers. She experienced the financial challenges that many law school graduates face—including student debt in the hundreds of thousands of dollars. Her current job is helping her clients—including lawyers at Big Law firms—think about financial aspects of making a career change. The following conversation will show that having a strong handle on finances can make pursuing a non-traditional career that much easier.

* * *

Jessica, in your legal career, you have navigated both Big Law and the SEC. Now, you are an Accredited Financial Counselor. Through-

out your career as a whole, what accomplishment most stands out to you?

Well, I think that one of my greatest accomplishments is having raised two kind and brave twin boys. I was pregnant as a 2L in law school, so they got one year of law school under their belt. They've been with me ever since. For the majority of my motherhood, I was single. Being able to finish law school on time, secure a job at a prominent Washington, D.C. firm, make the transition to government, and now transition completely out of the law (while also still being able to raise nice and what appear to be happy teenagers) is one of my greatest accomplishments.

I was pretty driven by myself. If I had remained by myself, I think I would've been pretty successful regardless. To have the level of success that I had while also raising a family is really what sets me apart and is one of the things that I'm most proud of.

I'd agree. Your law school experience was starkly different compared to others in this book. It even sounds like your experience in Big Law was substantially different. But before we discuss all of that, what is an Accredited Financial Counselor?

That's a great question. I have to do so much educating of what it is that I do. So the financial industry has a number of professionals that are licensed to do particular things. As an Accredited Financial Counselor, I always like to say I work with money and with people. I am interested both in your numbers and your values (what's important to you and your personality). I do this to ensure that whatever strategies I put together to get you to your financial goals will match up and resonate with you as a person.

Being an Accredited Financial Counselor just means that I have gone through a personal finance curriculum. I have taken an exam to test my knowledge of personal finance—beyond my own personal finance journey and story. It also means that I take continuing education courses and have ethical requirements that I must maintain when working with clients. But Accredited Financial Counselors really focus on daily money management habits, paying down debt, building up credit, making sure you're saving for the future, and how to create all of those good habits that will help you build wealth. That wealth will perhaps one day be managed by an investment advisor or a certified financial planner. But we don't sell any financial products. We don't advise on investing, tax strategies, or insurance products. However, we are familiar enough with the finance world to be able to educate our clients.

When I was leaving the SEC, it was really important to me that I wasn't in the investing world. I wasn't particularly impressed by it. I really wanted to help what seemed to be an underserved segment of the population. These are folks that aren't ready to reallocate their 401(k)s. They're just trying to find more money to stick in their 401(k)s. That's really where we focus.

So it's more about building habits. Perhaps there is more of a short-term focus, but you are also helping your clients build those habits for their long-term financial health.

Exactly. It's also a lot about financial literacy. So it's about making sure people understand different financial concepts like compound interest, be able to compare savings rates, and figure out what they need to be earning to cover all of their financial obligations (not just the day-to-day). I do a lot of educating. I run a lot of trainings and many of them are free. It's about making sure that people who maybe didn't get a good finance education—either at home or in school—have that need filled.

So take me back to law school (or even legal practice). Did you ever envision that you would be doing something like this? Or was it the totality of incremental decisions that you made?

It's so funny. I hated money for so much of my life. I hated having to think about it. I thought it was dirty. I wasn't supposed to talk about it. I grew up in a home where talking about money was rude.

I'm Dominican and Puerto Rican. In many immigrant families, there are all kinds of weird superstitions about money. We were no exception. We never talked about things like retirement savings. Nobody in my family made anything close to what I made when I graduated from law school.

So I didn't have a very good foundation when I went out into the world to become an independent financial person. I really never wanted to think about it. The fact that I ended up at the Securities and Exchange Commission alone shocked me. And that I now basically only deal with money as my entire career? I could have never guessed it in a million years. But it is so perfect and I love it so much. It's probably because money made me so uncomfortable for so many years. If I can change that for other people, that could be the difference between night and day.

Interesting. So much of it comes down to this mission of helping others that were in your position.

Yes. I know what it feels like to not want to talk about it or be embarrassed to talk about it. I think I can serve my clients in a way that really speaks to them as opposed to just being somebody who has always loved money and has always been good with money. That's not my experience.

Well, let's go back to your earlier years—specifically when law school seemed like a good opportunity to you. When was that?

When I was in high school, I wanted to go into musical theater. That was my dream. I was in the choir, theater, and all the things. Right before my senior year, I took government (which was a required class during the summer). That summer, my high school was bringing dogs onto campus to do sniff searches. We had just finished up the civil rights section in my government class. I was just appalled by the entire idea that they were going to bring in dogs for random searches. I was like, "What about unreasonable searches? What's going on? What's the framework? How do we determine what success is?"

So I went and spoke to the school board. I argued against them bringing dogs onto campus. I was so pumped up by the whole thing. Of course, they brought the dogs. It made no difference and the dogs were so cute. Everybody loved them. It was fine. But that really stoked this fire in me. I thought, "Wow, I wonder if law could be exciting?"

I had always done well in school (as many lawyers do). We are typically academically successful. So I was looking for something that would be intellectually challenging. Of course, my only impression of lawyers was from television, so it all seemed very dramatic. I thought, "Oh, I can marry theater and intellectual stimulation in this dream career that will be full of prestige and money. My family would be so proud to have a lawyer in the family."

It all seemed to fit together really well. When I went to college, I knew I was going to go to law school after college. Everything that I did from that moment forward was laser-focused on making sure I got into a good law school and became a lawyer.

Was that during your freshman year of college? Were you picking your courses because you wanted to get good grades so that you could get into those great law schools?

That is exactly right. I sat down with my advisor. Granted, she was in the political science department, which ended up being one of my majors. She was probably a little biased. But I told her, "I'm thinking about sociology because I'm really into society and civil rights and I want to change the world." She told me, "Yeah, the sociology department grades on a B curve. You may not want to go in there if you're trying to get into law school. The political science department is much more generous." Then, I was like, "Okay. Note to self: I'm becoming a political science major."

In retrospect and considering where you are now, would you have chosen sociology?

It's hard, right? I did well in college and I did get many "A's" out of the political science department. I did end up getting into a good law school, so there were all of these things that were built on top of each other.

It's always hard when people ask me this question. I don't know that I'd be where I am if I had done something differently. But I loved my sociology classes. They were hard. They weren't my best grades, but I definitely enjoyed them the most. If I had to go back and decide, "Do I just want to do something because I love it?" that's probably where I would start. Now, granted, would I still have gotten into Columbia? I don't know.

Exactly. You never know. Speaking of that, you attended college at the University of San Diego and then went straight to Columbia Law School. Would you recommend a similar path to others? Say there is a reader that is very interested in law school (like you were). Perhaps they want to go straight from college to law school, but they would obviously miss out on some years of actual work experience.

While the analysis is slightly different for everyone, do you have any thoughts?

I would say that the folks who did not go straight through (like me) did much better. Number one, I think they were more appreciative of the experience because they were coming from the workforce. I went to college in San Diego. My senior year was a cakewalk. Going from that to 1L year was quite the wake-up call in a very uncomfortable way. It was a hard transition.

Also, it's just so much school. It's year after year after year of just academics. You kind of get burned out of just being a student. Whereas my friends who had taken a couple of years off and had been out in the workforce were very motivated to be in law school. They had something to compare it to. They had been working at a job and maybe hadn't been earning what they always hoped that they would be able to earn. That was one of the reasons why they were going to law school. They wanted to better their careers and their earning potential. But they would always tell me, "You have no idea how much easier this is than work. This is wonderful. I want to be a full-time student forever." And I'm like, "No, don't do that. That's what I've done. It's horrible."

Having that comparison and also being able to save some money so you don't have to completely finance your law school career (like I did) is always a better situation. Looking back, I do wish I had taken some time off in between—just to prepare myself and be a little more mature when I went into law school. That being said, I survived, but it was rough.

Well, let's talk about that. You went to Columbia, and as you alluded to a few moments ago, your experience was much different than others' experiences there. Can you take us inside your experiences there and the challenges that you had to overcome?

Yeah. My first year was hard, but great. After a few bumps in the beginning, I was like, "Oh yeah, I really have to study. I can't just cram all this in at the end of the semester." I did pretty well. I really enjoyed my teachers. I do love learning, so I was happy and excited to be learning new things. I was also very challenged, which I had not really been earlier in my academic career. I was no longer the smartest person in the room—by far. I was surrounded by a lot of really smart people. But it also made me feel good that I was surrounded by all of these smart people and that we were all going into the same industry.

In my 2L year, I got pregnant with twins. That year was crazy. Academically, that was my worst year (all with good reason). It's funny: when you have twins, everything happens much sooner just because you get huge really, really fast. Columbia just has two semesters per academic year. For my second semester, I spent half of it on bed rest because I was so large. Columbia has a lot of classrooms that are set up like church pews. I didn't fit in the pews anymore. I had to have people taking notes for me. But I had already developed really strong friendships from my 1L year. I also had family in New Jersey (that's where I'm originally from) so they were able to bring me groceries and things like that.

But I didn't take any time off. I had a conversation with my dean in between the semesters. He asked me if I wanted to take a break at least until after the kids are born. Then I could come back. I was afraid that if I did, I would never come back. So I said, "You know what? I want to finish." The boys were due right around finals, so I figured I could make it. I thought, "Okay, if I could just make it to the end of this year, I'll have the summer to recover. Then, I'll figure out my 3L year." It basically just became "I will figure it out when I get there. Let me just get through this next phase."

I had a lot of support—both from the administration and my community at Columbia. If you asked me, "Do I remember a lot of it?" I would say no. It's all kind of a haze. But I remember I got through it and I did okay. I definitely did better on the finals before the birth. I had one after the boys were born and that one was not as good. But I made it through and finished on time. That was my big motivator.

I think having kids in the middle of law school (especially if you're by yourself) is difficult. I had amazing support systems—both in family and in friends. But it also really, really motivated me to make sure that I was going to get this done. Now, it no longer felt like a choice. It felt like, "I need to do this because this is how I'm going to support my family for the rest of our lives." In terms of motivation, it was ramped up even more than whatever I originally brought with me.

It's such an inspiring story. Because leaving Columbia wasn't an option, you had no choice but to figure it out. While you were extremely motivated, how did you actually find the time to fulfill

all of your academic obligations? Even considering the support that you had from friends, family, and Columbia, you still had to get all of your work done.

I am really driven. I noticed that about myself when looking back at my life. I really get stuff done if you put a bunch of obstacles in front of me. A lot of it came down to time management. 3L year is probably the easiest year where you could be simultaneously raising kids. But it was crazy. There were other law students who did have kids during law school. I actually ended up meeting a lot of moms who said, "Oh, this is the best time. I get to pick my schedule. I don't have class every day." We would have little playgroups with our babies. That was really nice.

It was more about managing energy. I wasn't sleeping for the first six months. Nobody was sleeping in the house. It was about managing that with the studying and getting things done. During that 3L year, I also tried to take some easier classes. For example, courses that required an essay at the end, rather than a final. I joined a clinic. Those things were very flexible and helpful.

As you're studying and doing all of these things, you are also looking for a job after graduation. Did you participate in on-campus interviews when you were pregnant? How did it go?

Law school is crazy. After your 1L year, you basically have to pick what could be the job you have for the rest of your life. For summer on-campus interviewing (OCI), I might have been pregnant. I'm not sure if I knew. I was doing my first-round interviews with a bunch of firms that would have offered me a summer associate role between my 2L and 3L year.

So I interviewed with a bunch of firms. I had done very well in my first year. I had good grades so they were very excited to have me. I ended up choosing Arnold & Porter in Washington, D.C. During the second round of interviews, I did know that I was pregnant. I knew in my head to be asking particular types of questions. I was on the lookout for firms that were going to make my life easier versus firms that were going to be completely non-hospitable to someone in my situation.

I had that information and they didn't. I was able to start feeling things out. I will say that I spent many years at Arnold & Porter. Beyond my personal reasons, the firm really was one of the most family-friendly Big

Law firms that you can find. They were one of the first to have a daycare on-site. They had flexible working schedules. They had part-time partners. They had all of these things that at least gave the appearance that, as Big Law goes, this might be the best deal you're going to get.

I also just really loved the firm. I loved the people that I met there. They were all quirky in their own way. I thought, "Okay, there is no traditional Arnold & Porter lawyer. That means I don't have to be a traditional kind of lawyer."

You could be yourself.

Exactly. That's what I was looking for. So I accepted the summer associate position. I called them before I was supposed to show up and told them, "I'm due to give birth right at the beginning of the summer associateship. I won't be able to make it because I'll be in labor. When do I need to show up so I can secure a job?" They were understanding, but they are also still a firm. Giving me a slot wasn't a guarantee.

I took six weeks after giving birth to recover and get to know my children. Then, I was commuting between Washington, D.C. and New York so that I could fulfill my summer associateship. So that's how I spent my 2L summer. I was making sure that I secured my job after graduation.

The fact that you did all of that with newborn twins is extremely impressive. You must have had absolutely no downtime.

That's who I was. I was the summer associate who was late to the program because she had just given birth. Everyone in the firm knew me from day one. I was infamous, which was great and not great. I also did a lot of work that summer. I had excellent reviews and I don't want to downplay my own work ethic. But I do think I made a good impression on people. I think they were just impressed that I had the grit to go through that, show up, and still put in a full effort and get to the end of the road.

I got an offer, so I didn't have to worry about it during my 3L year. I knew where I was going. I just had to get through the next phase.

At the same time, at a school like Columbia, there is a strong pull to work at a commercial law firm. The opportunities are certainly there. The recruiters come to you. They make it very easy. People

that may have been interested in government or policy work end up taking a closer look at these opportunities. One thing leads to another and you're a junior associate. Did you feel that pull at the time? I think I read on your website that you wanted to become a federal prosecutor. In law school, were you feeling that conflict? If so, how did you manage that?

Yeah. I even remember during my 1L year. It wasn't for the first semester, but for the spring semester, we started to be invited to firm parties. They would host us at places like the Russian Tea Room and the Ritz Carlton. They would have these cocktail parties because they just wanted you to interview during OCI. They wanted to show their firm and show off what life would be like if you worked with them. It was just a totally foreign environment to me.

I had come from humble beginnings. I was from San Diego, where we didn't really have this kind of practice. I was then in the heart of New York City being wooed by these really, really fancy firms. Yes, I wanted to go into government when I started law school. But Big Law firms were enticing. When I heard what summer associates made for the summer, I was like, "Well, I'm obviously going to do that. Even if I don't go there, why would I not make money for the summer that I can then use later?"

So I think there's absolutely a pull toward these positions. Columbia has a very, very high placement rate into those large law firms. It's one of the best schools if you want to go into Big Law because they place people well there. But that also means that there's a really big focus on that being the path. For a lot of folks that go to Columbia, that is their path. So there is a lot of pressure. As you said, there is a lot of inertia to keep moving toward that goal.

If my situation had been different, I wonder whether I would have immediately ended up at a firm. Would I have just done my summer associateship and then gone to work at a DA's office? A lot of the government doesn't take new attorneys because there is too much training involved. It's too expensive and they don't know anything. They want people with some law firm experience under their belt because it saves them some heartache. But I totally would have done one of those internship programs where you just go straight to the government and you start learning. My life turned out differently, however. I had people to support and had hundreds of thousands of dollars of student loans to pay back. I didn't really see another option for myself. I certainly didn't spend any time examining it. I had an offer and I was like, "Why would I not take this? This is too easy and I have enough things that are not easy in my life right now."

Right. That makes total sense considering the situation that you were in. So for others that are considering Big Law (whether or not they are not pregnant), they should obviously think hard about why they are entering Big Law. Perhaps they should even write down the pros and cons before making their decision. Is there anything specific that you would recommend?

I think it has been interesting. Sadly, we have now been through a couple of recessions since I graduated from law school. At least during the 2008 recession, I was already at my firm. But I remember that they basically delayed graduating law students from starting at the firm for at least nine months or one year. All of the firms were kind of like, "Pump the brakes. I don't know if we can take on more people. Hold on and let's see if we can keep the ones we have."

They were offered a little stipend. Like, "Please go work somewhere else for a while. We can't afford to take you on yet, but there will be a space for you one year later." So people took fellowships. Maybe they did a clerkship that they hadn't originally considered doing. Perhaps they went to work for a humanitarian agency. They took this stipend, spread it out the year, and got to do something that really was fulfilling for them. Many of them never showed up again. They decided, "You know what? I don't think that was the right path for me. I'm going to go somewhere else."

But it's very hard to make that decision when you're in the middle of school. You're already stressed. Do I suggest people take a year off to explore (like a gap year) from law school? No, because I don't know what the ramifications of that would be. But if you're going into Big Law and you don't plan on staying there, be very careful about how long you plan to be there. Make a plan for yourself. Think about what you're going there to get. Stay focused on that and where you're going next because otherwise, just like law school, you'll get sucked into the default mode of everyone around you. You'll forget what you were meaning to do when you got started on this journey.

**Definitely. I think that's all wise advice. I also think part of the prob-
lem is that law students hear about these firms and have some vague
notions of the work involved. But they really don't know. Even if they
are summer associates, they are there for six to eight weeks. Maybe
the tasks they are given are representative of the work that they will
be doing, but even still, it's difficult to gauge what the work is like.
My understanding of your career is that you were in the litigation
department at Arnold & Porter. For readers that are prospective law
students or even current law students, can you provide a sense of
what your day-to-day work was like?**

Yes. Most lawyers at law firms go into a litigation group of some sort. They
are mostly the largest groups at firms. They basically churn through associates for good reason. As a junior associate, my experience completely rose or fell by which partners I was working with and what kinds of
matters I was working on.

There are really huge matters. Arnold & Porter had a number of them
because the firm kind of specialized in class actions. Those matters could
have hundreds of people on them. That means that you're a bit of a cog in
a system, right? You're one piece of a very large puzzle. You're definitely not the one making any decisions. You'll be given your assignments.
Maybe you're doing research, document review, or a mix of both. There
really isn't much more for junior associates to do on those larger matters.

But I also worked with partners that came out of the government and
liked a lean team. They liked to have their hands in everything. They also
liked their associates to really take responsibility for things. So when I was
working on those smaller matters, I was helping prepare for depositions,
summarizing evidence for the partner, and drafting correspondence for
the client or to the court. If there was litigation that we were actively
involved in, I was attending co-counsel calls. All of that was much more
hands-on and felt like legal work. It felt like I was actually representing
a real client that I knew. Whereas on some of the larger matters, it was
much more of "I am low on this totem pole. There is a lot of grunt work
that must be done and I am definitely one of the grunts."

Then, there was my pro bono work. I absolutely suggest it for any
junior associates who can get their hands on it. That's how I took my first
deposition. That's how I argued my first motion in court. It's how I filed
my first summary judgment motion. These were the experiences that I

never would have gotten on my billable matters until way further in my career. To the extent that you can pick up that kind of work, I absolutely suggest it. For Arnold & Porter, they treated those hours just like billable hours.

Yes, it's important to see if your firm lets you count pro bono hours as billable hours. Many firms do, but it's important to double-check. I think that to some extent, all junior associates experience that cog-in-the-wheel feeling. But similar to what you did, it's important to actively pursue more autonomy. So how can readers actually do that? It is more about creating those relationships with one or two partners and building trust that way?

So I think a lot of it has to do with creating relationships with partners. Law firms are basically one hundred fifty mini businesses. Every partner has their own book of business. They run their matters the way that they want to. As a junior associate (especially as a first-year), I took full advantage of my new lawyer status and would email any partner in my firm who seemed like they did interesting work. I wanted to hear more about it. I would invite them to coffee or ask them to drop by and chat with them about their work.

First of all, everyone loves talking about themselves, right? That's easy. That's not going to be hard. If they see you, you seem interested in what they do, and you make yourself available to help (even when you're busy), that will be helpful. Of course, we all have a lot of work. But if you want to find the good work, you're probably going to have to work at one hundred ten percent so that the extra ten percent then becomes more of what you normally do.

But I absolutely suggest that people seek out partners who are doing interesting work. Go talk to them about that work and see how you can be helpful. Then, make yourself helpful. If you can, make yourself indispensable. I think especially in large firms, junior associates tend to get this feeling that they are so removed from everyone and there's no way to start a conversation with someone. "What am I going to talk to that partner about? We don't have anything in common."

I will say one of the things that made it very easy for me to chat with partners was the fact that I had children. I wasn't really into sports or golf or some of the other things that might typically come up in conversation. But we could chat about how crazy our toddlers were. It was just this point of connection that made it easy for me to have a ten-minute normal-sounding conversation with someone that wasn't just about work. It made them remember me. I mean, I was pretty memorable in a general sense because I was the summer associate who showed up with twins.

But also getting involved in firm committees was helpful. You can meet people not just on their matters and because you have been assigned to them, but because they have chosen to spend time with you (or you have chosen to spend time with them). I think building those relationships is so important if you really want to get work that you enjoy.

Right. If we could, let's talk about your transition to the SEC Division of Enforcement. Can you discuss what prompted that transition and how that opportunity actually emerged?

So I had always wanted to go to the government. It took me eight years to get there. It was a long and winding road. Part of it was that the 2008 recession occurred when I was a mid-level associate. Even if I had been thinking about leaving (which I had), everything froze. There were hiring freezes across the government. No law firms were hiring. No companies were hiring. As the economy was concerned, the entire country was just at a standstill.

All of my friends and I were stuck where we were—at least for a couple more years. In that time, I transitioned from general litigation work to primarily SEC enforcement work on the defense side.

How many years were you at your firm?

I was there for eight years. For the first four to five, I was pretty much all litigation. I had done a couple of SEC enforcement matters very early in my career, but then I really went all-in on litigation.

Then, I kind of switched gears. We had some new partners come in who had government experience. They were doing a lot of Foreign Corrupt Practices Act investigations. I thought it seemed interesting and they seemed interested in developing senior associates. I grabbed onto them and got a ton of work. I had never done FCPA work before and it was interesting and exciting. I got to go to Hong Kong and London. These were things that I had never really done with my litigation work. It was interesting, but it is really like a 24-hour kind of thing. Government investigations are happening and we were doing internal investigations for our clients. It was a lot of work, stress, and travel (which was really hard on my family).

So I didn't think that I wanted to do that for the rest of my life at a law firm. However, I still wanted to go to the government. It basically came down to whether I was up or out. I needed to decide whether I wanted to put myself up for partner. I literally got asked by the managing partner, "Are you going to put yourself up for partner?" I was in a very good position. People knew me at the firm. I had done very well. I was working for a group that had really great matters.

I like to think I could have made it if I had stayed. Maybe the partners would say something different. But I really was in one of the top tiers in terms of what they tell you. But when I thought about it, I thought, "I can't possibly do this for another three years." My kids were turning eight. They are as old as my law career. You can't become a partner and then not stay for a couple of years. First of all, in terms of your compensation, you have to get your buyback reimbursed. Then, you have to partner for a little while.

I thought to myself, "I'm going to miss my kids' entire childhood. By the time I get out, they're going to be teenagers. They're not going to want to talk to me. I need to leave now." That really was the deciding factor. I said, "My kids are not at the age where I can afford to spend three more years ignoring them and not being there. These are the years where they're going to make the friends that are going to decide whether they're going to be nice people or not nice people. I want to be there for that."

So I decided to leave. At that point, I was like, "Thank goodness the hiring freezes are thawing." Things were starting to open up. Because I had been doing so much enforcement work on the defense side, I knew folks at the SEC. They had been the investigators on the very matters that I had been working on. A lot of the partners that I had been working with were former SEC staff.

I completed my application and I had good people on both sides speaking well of me. I am sure that made a difference in my application. I think there were one thousand people applying for something like eight open slots the year that I went in. They had just opened back up and I got a slot. So when I was deciding between taking that offer and putting myself up for partner, I was like, "I'm just going to take this job at the SEC."

And look: going to the SEC, it's almost like a lateral move to a firm. They look at you and they're just like, "Well, you'll be back. When you come back, you'll definitely be partnership material." So it still felt like a very natural move other than, "Oh, you could have made partner." I could do an entire chapter on my feelings about all of that. But making this move didn't sound strange to anyone. It seemed like a good move for me. It wasn't hard from the external perspective, but it was hard from the internal perspective because I really didn't want to be a lawyer.

Interesting. But you still did it. That desire to satisfy that younger desire to work in government was still there.

Yeah, exactly. I thought, "Maybe it's not that I don't like law. Maybe it's that I just don't like where I am. If I change where I am, I'm going to have all of that motivation again. I'm going to get back all of that vigor I had when I was a young lawyer and I'll be ready to take on the world." And I did. I had it for like one minute when I was at the SEC. I was super excited to be there, but also super freaked out because this was all that I was doing. I used to be a litigator and now I was just going to be doing securities enforcement. It's a specialized area.

I'm sure you had to learn quickly.

You have to because it's all you're doing. But also, the SEC is great in terms of providing resources. The staff there is amazing. Everyone is so nice, which also makes it very hard to leave. It's just such a lovely place to be. I miss my people and still talk to them.

Can you then discuss why you decided to leave? If it was so great, the opportunity to become an Accredited Financial Counselor must have seemed even greater.

I know, right? It's crazy. Why did I leave this perfectly wonderful situation? I was unhappy. I was still in enforcement, so I was doing investigations and prosecuting people. I am not an adversarial person by nature. I don't know exactly how I got into litigation and all of this stuff, but I basically had spent the past 13 years fighting with people and convincing liars to stop lying. That tore at my soul.

I am a very collegial person. I love bringing people together. I love creating communities and I didn't get to use any of that energy in my day-to-day work. Now, granted, I sat on committees. I did cross-agency efforts. I put all of these programs together, but that was my side gig.

My day-to-day was very adversarial and it was all about conflict. After many years of pretending to be really interested and excited by conflict, I just couldn't put up with it anymore. I thought I was going to leave and start a Subway or something. I was really at the end of my rope. I did not know what to do because I only knew law. I didn't really understand what else lawyers did other than go in-house. I would troll job listings. I was like, "Oh, I want to go work at Hershey. I could eat chocolate all day. I have to review contracts, though. But that's all of law. That's your in-house practice."

I knew that I wanted to leave. I just had to figure out what I wanted to do. This is where my now-husband comes into the story. I met him while I was at the SEC because it was the first time in my life where I had extra time and could go do things. So that was wonderful. We met through competitive karaoke. That's one of my hobbies. I met my husband and he was in the process of retiring from the military. He had served in the Army for twenty-six years.

Part of the military retirement process is getting veterans very prepared for the world. They have a year of trainings that they have to take. This includes things like job readiness, getting their resumés in shape, making sure that they can afford their life once they leave the Army, and managing their bills and financial obligations. All of them are required to meet with an Accredited Financial Counselor. I had never heard of this before. I went to the SEC and we just dealt with investment advisors, stockbrokers, and insurance agents.

At that point, I had already started my own financial independence journey. I wanted out of the law completely. I was like, "If I can figure out a way that I don't have to make a lawyer's salary, then I can do it." I was in the middle of that journey and I had been running spreadsheets and projections. I was figuring out how long it would take me to pay off my student loans, fulfill my retirement, pay for the boys' college, and all of these things.

So he went to the meeting with the Accredited Financial Counselor. He brought my spreadsheets with him. The Accredited Financial Counselor looked at them and said, "Oh, you should definitely use your wife's spreadsheets because these are way better than the ones I have. Has she thought about doing this? Because it looks like she would be really good at it."

He came home and told me this story and I was like, "Oh, could I do this as a job? Because this is my hobby. This is what I have been doing for myself for at least two years as I was planning to get out."

Wow, who could have guessed that this hobby would have been a natural way for you to transition out of the law?

Right? When I was at the SEC, I really came to the realization that it was the law. It wasn't where I was. I still had the same feelings about the law, even though this was the perfect environment. There were wonderful people, wonderful benefits, excellent pay, and a really nice building. All of those things were there and I was still unhappy.

That turning point for me led me down the financial independence movement. I realized that if I can figure out a way to still afford to live my life but not have to be paid a lawyer's salary, I could do something else. It didn't have to be law-related. So I started running all of these scenarios and running projections. I started figuring out how much I needed to have paid down on my student loans, how much to have saved for retirement, and how much in reserves to handle any transition period that I may have. Essentially, what am I going to need to earn to support my lifestyle after I leave the SEC?

I had done all of that work and we were in the middle of that journey when my husband sat down with the Accredited Financial Counselor. I realized what I had been doing for myself is something that I would love to be able to do for other people. But I didn't want to deal with the investment side or the estate planning side. I didn't want to be selling insurance or any of those kinds of things. But you don't need to do that for what I was doing. I was basically just making sure that the cost of my lifestyle was going to match up with what I had to earn in the future. It wouldn't necessarily have to be law-related. So that's how all of that came together.

That's a great story. You just never know what will emerge from a hobby or some type of side project. But you have to at least try.

People kept telling me, "Oh, well just think about what you like doing." I was like, "I don't like doing anything other than karaoke. I don't think I can be a professional karaoke singer." Well, maybe I could. But this thing was different. On the weekends, I would look at my financial spreadsheets just for fun. I would run new projections and do all of these things to squeeze out another $200 per month. Now, I do that for my clients.

For the lawyers and law students reading this book, what should they do to put themselves in the best financial situation if they want to make a transition like yours? In other words, what types of habits should they build?

I think lawyers have to understand that their careers are very, very long. Sometimes, we have a tendency to think of things in black and white. If we're not doing something one hundred percent, then we're not doing it at all. One of the things that I bring up with my own clients is thinking through the different phases of their lives.

When you are a new lawyer, if you happen to be married, have small children, have a mortgage, and/or have a student loan payment, all of that can feel very oppressive. That's because it is. It might not feel like you're making very much money—no matter what you're bringing in—because you have all of these obligations. The hope is that over the lifetime of your career, those obligations will lessen year by year. Your children will get older (which is one of the biggest things). You will age out of daycare and you will basically get a mortgage payment back every month. But figure out where you can capture either increases in income or reductions in expenses and make sure that you're using that money for your future as opposed to using it for your current lifestyle. That's a basic practice and a habit. If you can build that, you will have a much easier road—no matter what you want to do.

Granted, I generally work with lawyers and law firms. That's my experience. Many of them are in Big Law. If you're planning on making a transition out, I think the career trajectory is completely backward. You earn more in the first phase of your career than you may ever earn again. This means that you should plan for that accordingly. Make sure that you are front-loading your long-term savings, knowing that you might not have all of this excess to be catching up on retirement contributions later in life.

Student loans are important. There are all kinds of strategies for dealing with them and I discuss them with my clients. It really depends on how much you have. Are they federal or private? How much are you earning? What's your career trajectory? There are roughly sixteen factors that need to be accounted for before we can figure out the right repayment strategy for you. It's different for everyone.

Paying them off immediately is not the best strategy for everyone. It is for some, but not for most. But if that is your situation, you don't just want to focus on paying down student loans to the detriment of every other financial goal that you may have. You could find yourself at the end of this road of golden opportunity and all you have done is pay off your student loans and have nothing else to show for it. It is a wonderful thing, but that just means that your Big Law career just paid for your degree. That's all it did. You just graduated from law school, but you're older. Yeah, you have some years of experience under your belt, but you don't have very much else to show for it.

I always want people to be thinking about the long road that they have ahead of them. I want them to think of what kinds of things they can tackle now and still be able to live their lives and be comfortable. We don't go to law school and kill ourselves to be uncomfortable all the time. But it's also about thinking through, "What am I going to do ten or fifteen years from now? What is my life going to look like?" We start thinking along those lines so we can plan for those changes and take advantage of them.

So it's about striking this balance. You have to follow a schedule to pay back your student loans, but at the same time, you should be thinking about those long-term financial goals. I think you made a really important point in that many Big Law associates don't realize that they could be at the height of their earning potential right now. They need to take advantage of that in whatever way that they can.

Yes. I do not give investment advice, but I am allowed to do math. One of the things that I like to point out to my clients is if you spend ten years maxing out your 401(k) and never contribute another dime to it after those first ten years, you will have over $2.5 million in your retirement account come retirement. This is from not having done anything for thirty-five years.

When you're thinking about it in those terms, student loans can actually be financed with all kinds of creative strategies. Funding retirement? Not so much. You miss out on contributions; you can't go back. You can't say, "Gosh, I want to max out my contributions for 2016. I have some extra money now. Let me go back and do that." There are some barriers that are impossible to overcome. Those are some of the things that I like people to be thinking about when they are newer attorneys and at the beginning of their careers.

Then, for those that are a bit further along, you have already made some financial decisions. You are now just trying to deal with the ramifications of them. When you're thinking about a transition, I want you to think really creatively about what your life will cost after you make that transition. It probably won't cost the same amount as it does while you're working where you currently are.

That shift can really open up possibilities. Think about how much you spend to just do your job. This includes commuting, transportation costs, dry cleaning, wardrobe, and eating out for lunch every day. You may think you have to eat out every day because you work at a firm and there's no other way that you could feed yourself. You may also have spending just related to the stress of having a Big Law job. We all spend money to make ourselves happier when we are unhappy in our job. That is money well spent, but you might not need to be spending that money when you're really happy with what you do.

So I always want my clients to go through that exercise. I want them to really take a good look. How much are you spending just to be unhappy in your job? Because that money will be recouped. You won't have to cover those expenses when you're happier in a new job. Many of those expenses might just go away. You won't have to support the same type of lifestyle, which means you might not need to have the same type of income. This then opens up so many other possibilities. But that's really hard to imagine when you're in the middle of it.

For sure. That's all very good advice. Generally speaking, I enjoy studying the mistakes of others so that I don't have to make those same mistakes in my own life. I'm trying to incorporate this idea into

this book as well. Hopefully, by studying other people's mistakes, readers can have an easier or better transition. So from your perspective, what are some of the bigger financial mistakes that you see from lawyers or law students that are in the profession or trying to leave the profession?

Well, I think anybody who isn't paying attention to where all of their money is going is probably losing out on a bit of it. I know that it's hard, right? We're busy. Nobody wants to be tracking things all the time. But figure out a system where you can apply some flexible controls so that you can have some visibility and control over what's going on.

I can't tell you the number of clients that come to me and their number one complaint is, "I have no idea where my money goes by the end of the month. I don't understand how I can spend it all, but I do. The idea of going back and checking all the time is nauseating." So it's really important to figure out a system that gives you that clarity but also gives you that control.

I have my own financial mistakes. Now, my children are of college-age. They're both seventeen. One of my biggest issues when I was a young associate was making sure that I was funding my kid's college education. It was really important that I helped them with that. So I prioritized saving in a 529 plan because I didn't know what else to do for college. Now, I have a bunch of money in a 529. I've got one kid who wants to take a gap year and might not go to college at all. And I can tell you: I could have used that money for something else. It will be used for education expenses. We have grandchildren coming so that will be fine.

But I think having a better understanding of what all of your options are and not simply doing what the finance book tells you you're supposed to do or following somebody else's life formula is really important. You don't know what's going to happen. Generally, when you have a better understanding of the financial world, you can be much more flexible with the choices you make. You can create circumstances that allow you to be much more nimble when things don't go according to plan. Believe me, I thought I would have two four-year degrees coming out of these boys when they were done. I don't know if that's going to happen.

Ultimately, it seems like there are simple things that lawyers can do to better their financial health. This includes everything from

401(k) matching to perhaps working with a robo-advisor. The idea of "paying yourself first" is also important in this context.

Yes, I think as lawyers, anything that we can get off our plates is a bonus.

Do you have any personal finance resources that you would recommend to readers of this book? Specifically, I'm thinking of books, articles, or blogs.

Yes. So I don't give investment advice, but I am allowed to give resources for all of my clients who want to learn more. I love *The Simple Path to Wealth* by JL Collins. I actually have my teenagers reading it right now. That's a great beginner's guide to investing. I also enjoyed Ramit Sethi's *I Will Teach You to Be Rich*. I think there are a lot of good principles in there and it is written for a generation that has grown up with everything being automated. So I think a lot of the principles very easily apply to most new lawyers in particular, but experienced lawyers as well.

One resource that I always go over with my own clients is my favorite personal finance book, which is *All Your Worth: The Ultimate Lifetime Money Plan* by Elizabeth Warren and her daughter Amelia Warren. It's from 2005. It's an oldie, but a goodie. All the principles still apply. It's a book that not only teaches you how to be better about your finances, but it teaches you how to make changes on some really structural financial issues that you might be experiencing. So instead of telling you to spend less money on coffee, it teaches you how to renegotiate your car insurance. It teaches you how to make those really big changes on those monthly recurring bills that have a material impact on your overall financial situation. That's one of the things I really liked. Yes, little things are important, but the big things need to be your focus.

For lawyers, we are the best people to be negotiating, right? If somebody is going to get a better rate from a service provider, it's us. We need to use our powers for our own financial benefit. Slash where you can because that's just free money. So I really love her book and some of the balanced budget principles that she lays out there. To this day, I use it with my clients. People are blown away by the simplicity and common sense approach.

Chapter 6

Anthony Scaramucci

Entrepreneur and Former White House Communications Director

No matter what we are trying to do with our careers and lives, it's generally true that we care about what others think of us. After all, we are all social creatures. Since our earliest days on the planet, we have relied on group inclusion to stay safe from predators. Even though the probability of being eaten alive on any given day is virtually nil, we naturally seek acceptance from others even if we don't personally know them. If we do something that veers from their expectations, fear and anxiety bubble to the surface.

This is certainly true for law students and practicing attorneys. A great example comes from our 1L courses. The Socratic Method is partly predicated on the assumption that we will complete our reading to avoid an embarrassing moment in front of our peers. We don't want to appear uninformed or lazy, so we put in the hours to prepare for a potential grilling from our professors.

In legal practice, we certainly want to represent our clients to the best of our abilities. In some situations, we may be defending clients that could lose their liberty. That is certainly motivation to do our best possible work. Nonetheless, some of our motivation may come from the fear of what others may think of us, whether that is our clients, colleagues, judges, or other counsel. Most of us care about our reputations. Shoddy work reflects poorly on us and limits potential opportunities down the road.

In and of itself, caring about what others think isn't a bad thing. It can give us extra drive to perform at our best levels. It can even help us fight off fatigue in the late evenings. That said, caring about others' impressions of us can be a net negative when contemplating—or making—major career moves. It's especially true when discouraging or negative opinions come from people we love. We certainly don't want to let them down, but at the same time, *we* have to live with the consequences of our career decisions. If we can make more independent decisions—or tune out the crowd when necessary—we can get much closer to what we truly want to do.

I would argue that Anthony Scaramucci belongs to this latter camp. The average American knows Anthony from his short stint as the White House Communications Director for President Trump. Before that, Anthony built a notorious career on Wall Street. Along with working at Goldman Sachs (on two separate occasions), Anthony started and built two businesses in the financial services sector. His first business (Oscar Capital Management) was sold to Neuberger Berman in 2001. His second business, which he continues to head today, is SkyBridge Capital. SkyBridge is an alternative asset firm that manages funds, digital asset offerings, an opportunity zone real estate investment trust (REIT), and more. Along with managing billions of dollars, Anthony and his colleagues host the SkyBridge Alternatives (SALT) Conference, bringing together leaders in geopolitics, finance, and technology.

Speaking with him at the Skybridge Capital offices in New York City, Anthony discussed a part of his story that isn't well-known. Before starting a Wall Street investment firm or working in the White House, Anthony wanted to be a corporate lawyer. As he wrote in one of his books, *Goodbye Gordon Gekko*, Anthony was looking for a job in the legal field the summer before he started at Harvard Law School. He eventually found a gig at a Big Law firm, but he found the job boring and repetitive. While the job lasted sixty days, Anthony wrote that "it felt like six years."

Although he didn't see himself as a lawyer, Anthony still attended Harvard Law School. He thought about dropping out several times throughout his journey, but his parents encouraged him to stick with it. Anthony did graduate, but instead of practicing, he used his 3L year to look for jobs at financial institutions. After participating in several rounds of interviews, Anthony landed at Goldman Sachs. While he would eventually be fired and rehired at Goldman, his early days at the storied investment bank would lay the foundation for his decades-long career in finance.

As Anthony describes it, he lives in his own "bubble of reality." He doesn't have the "embarrassed gene." He is willing to fail and fail publicly. Moreover, he can take big risks and think for himself when making momentous career decisions. When he thought about dropping out of law school, his parents' opinions influenced his decision. Yet while his fellow law students found practicing roles they may not have necessarily liked, Anthony followed his interests and forged a non-traditional path. That non-traditional path has led Anthony to start two businesses, work in the White House, and even open a restaurant in midtown Manhattan.

No matter your politics, Anthony's story shows us the power of being yourself. Life is short, and we can't spend time worrying about what others think of us. Anthony can tune out the unnecessary noise in a world where it is all too easy to let others' opinions dictate our behaviors. Even though we may not have thick skin like Anthony, we can emulate his willingness to take risks, deal with the consequences of those risks, and move toward our goals.

* * *

I'd like to start by going back to your time at Harvard Law School. My understanding is that you had some professional experiences in the legal field, but you later thought a job in finance would be much more appealing. Can you take us back to that time?

So you have to understand that I was so naive. I had such limited world experience. From zero to eighteen, I'm coming from a blue-collar family in a suburban environment. My dad worked at a construction site about four miles from the house where I was living.

There was a very affluent school, thank God. It had a good public school system. I got good grades so I was able to get into a good college. But even at college, I had very limited resources. It wasn't like I was traveling all over the world and blah, blah, blah.

So here I am. I didn't really have a breakout moment in my life until after I left law school. I had all of this sheltered limited knowledge base in terms of making my decision to go to law school. I went to law school because my parents used to glorify lawyers. My mother always wanted me to be a judge. I asked Antonin Scalia (may his soul rest in peace), "What's up with these Italian mothers? Why do they always want you to be a judge?" Justice Scalia then said to me, "Anthony, you have to understand something. The Italian mothers think that the priests and the judges are the only two people not on the take. If you're the mayor, you're obviously corrupt and on the take. But if you are a judge and it's a lifetime appointment, you're not doing something illegal. That's why mothers want you to be a judge."

I thought it was really funny. Justice Scalia obviously had a great sense of humor. So for me, I had this very narrow bandwidth. My parents wanted me to get educated. They're glorifying lawyers and glorifying judges. So lo and behold, I said, "Okay, great. I'll go to law school." And then I find out they're actually paying people to be a lawyer, right? I read this article in *Time* magazine that they're paying lawyers at Cravath, Swaine & Moore more than $65,000 a year. I'm like, "That's $25,000 more than my dad is making. I'm going to be a lawyer."

So I go and take the LSAT. I scored very high on the LSAT. I had really good grades. I applied to seven law schools. I got rejected from Yale, but I was accepted to the other six. I ended up going to Harvard.

Now, I'm in the admissions office at Harvard.[1] I've got a $250 check. I took all of my money out of the ATM and it was a cashier's check. When I'm in the admissions office, I asked for a copy of the alumni directory and a copy of the recruitment directory. They are these two big phone books. It's 1986 and I'm going to be a Wall Street lawyer, so I'm leafing through the phone books.

I'm looking up all of the firms that are on Wall Street. I started at 1 Wall Street and I literally cold-called fifteen firms. I've got fifteen names of Harvard Law School graduates that worked at the fifteen firms that are actually addressed on Wall Street.

I hit the jackpot on the first one. I went up the elevator at 1 Wall Street. I figure that's where I'm going to start. I went to Hughes Hubbard & Reed on the twenty-eighth-floor. That's Charles Evans Hughes. If you remember, he was the head of the Supreme Court. I think he ran for president at one time, too. So it is a big, prestigious, white-shoe law firm. I met a Harvard Law School graduate. He's in the corporate department and hired me as a paralegal.

My life started as a "lawyer working on legal things," but I hated it. I hated every minute of it. I felt like I was in a dungeon. I'm in a twenty-eighth floor dungeon and every day is like Bill Murray in *Groundhog*

---

1   As he describes in *Goodbye Gordon Gekko*, Anthony was looking for a summer job before
    starting his 1L year at Harvard Law School.

Day. You're in the library. You're looking up this thing and you're looking up that thing. You're in Carmody Wait. We had Westlaw back then and you have Google today.

There's still Westlaw.

Right, there's still Westlaw. But it was like, "Oh my God, I'm ready to commit suicide. This sucks."

So I had no idea my interests were more in sales, marketing, communication, and being an entrepreneur. I used to hustle newspapers as a kid. I had two or three jobs. I have always had a little bit of dough since the age of 11. My parents said that I had to make money if I wanted to have spending money.

I returned to that mentality. When I got to law school, my parents were like, "You have to finish." I really was thinking about dropping out, but I decided to finish. So I started looking at jobs at Harvard Business School. I went into their resource center. I interviewed at McKinsey, First Boston, Goldman Sachs, Lehman Brothers, and a whole group of different places. I hit it off with a couple of people at Goldman. Then, I went into the stratosphere and got a job offer at Goldman.

Now there, I took the job offer in investment banking. I absolutely suck at investment banking. I don't know anything about it. I'm good at math, but I'm not great at math. I'm not going to say I'm good or bad at spreadsheets like Excel because I never did any. So now I'm trying to learn all this stuff. I'm trying to get up to speed on corporate finance and I suck. We went through the recession of 1990 and the Gulf War crisis. Goldman is letting go one-third of the department. Since I'm in the bottom third in terms of my performance—even though I'm likable and I'm a hard worker—they fire my ass.

It was very humiliating. It was eighteen months after I left Harvard. I had six figures plus of school debt. Now, I'm in a panic. I got fired on a Friday (it was February 1, 1991). I went home and I'm miserable. I went out jogging and realized that the good news is that this job really sucked. I'm free at least.

At that point, do you think about going back to the law?

I think about going back into law. I'm thinking about starting a business. I'm in a fucking panic. Just in a full-blown panic. I have my loans and I'm married. I borrowed some money for my first wife's medical school tuition. So I'm in a panic.

I get a roll of quarters (because there are no cell phones) and take the train back into the city. Now, I'm hustling. I'm punching quarters into the phones. I'm on the street looking for a job and I have my resumé ready. I get on the phone with one of my buddies and he says, "Hey, man. I have a great job idea for you. There's a job opening at Goldman Sachs." I said, "Goldman Sachs, you have to be kidding me. I just got fired from Goldman Sachs." My buddy says, "Yeah, but it's in a different area. It's in the sales area. It's in the equities area. They had a couple of people leave them quickly."

This is learning lesson number one. Don't burn any bridges. So the guy that fired me was actually a great guy. He felt really bad about firing me. It wasn't his fault. I sucked and we were going into a recession. So I went to the guy that fired me and said, "Hey, Mike, you've got to help me. There's a job upstairs on the twenty-ninth floor. I'm working on the seventeenth floor. Are you going to help me? I think I'd be good at this sales job." He then said, "I'll go upstairs, talk to that partner, and see if I can get you the interview. I'll put in a good word for you."

So I went up there and did the interview. On March 28th, 1991, I got rehired. Now, I'm back at Goldman and I'm hustling there. I do very well at that job. It fits my skill set. The starting salary for that job was $56,000. This is a very big lesson for young people. I went from $110,000 to $56,000. You would think from a monetary perspective, that's a disaster. But it was literally the greatest thing that ever happened to me. Now, I'm slotted into a job that I'm actually good at. I'm going to make way more money as a result of that. Does that make sense?

Yes. I think that's why a lot of lawyers at larger commercial law firms don't leave to try something else.

The golden handcuffs.

Yeah. Exactly.

The money is good. They have anxiety. I directly benefited from the lack of money that my parents had. The attitude was, "Hey, if I'm making more than my parents, I'm doing well. God bless." So I was able to take a tremendous amount of risk in my life.

I didn't have that fear and that anxiety. A lot of times when you come from a wealthy family, you go to a top-notch school. You don't want to blow anything. You don't want to be embarrassed. You've probably figured out from my career that I don't have the embarrassed gene. I don't give a shit. People want to fire me from the White House after eleven days? No problem. I don't have the embarrassed gene, so it's fine. That's good for entrepreneurs. You can't be embarrassed and you can't be self-conscious when you're an entrepreneur.

If readers grew up in that sort of environment where it was harder for them to take risks, how can they develop that risk-taking muscle? How can they be more amenable to taking risks, not being embarrassed about things, or even taking a salary cut to do something that they want?

It's a good question. I'm not really sure of the answer. For me, it was born out of necessity because I got fired. But I think that you probably have to be more reflective than me. Hopefully, they'll pick up your book and they'll read it and it'll cause some level of reflection. They may start to think, "Okay, how am I going to live the arc of my true life?"

If you want to live the arc of your true life, you have to take risks. Because you have to imagine your life like this: "What would I do or what would I want to do, if I knew with one hundred percent certainty, that I was going to be successful? What would I do? I don't care about failure." If you live your life like that, you're going to have a fucking great life.

I remember a great line from my grandfather. He said you get the face that you deserve at fifty. Have you heard that expression?

I haven't heard it, but I like it.

You get the face you deserve at fifty. If you're scowling all the time and you're a miserable fuck, you're going to have a miserable face with lines on it a certain way. You're going to look like a douchebag. But if you're smiling and you're living your true life, you're going to be young your whole life. You get the face you deserve.

Going back, let's say that someone is in law school right now and wants to move into finance. Maybe they don't have a background in it at all. They didn't study it in college or have little to no work experience in finance. What would you recommend to that person?

I would recommend three or four things. One, you're going to have to take a course in finance. Either take it online, buy a book, go to a local school, or do it at night. Find somewhere in your city or suburb where you can learn something about finance. I don't think you can just go cold turkey from law school, without any finance, into finance. What ends up happening is there's a language in finance—just the same way there's a language in the law and a language in medicine. So buy the Barron's *Dictionary of Finance and Investment Terms* and read *The Wall Street Journal*.

Learn accounting?

Yeah, learn a little bit of accounting. That was very helpful to me. You have to do all of these things. If you don't, what ends up happening is you'll probably still get the job anyway. People are impressed with lawyers. People are impressed with a legal education. But you'll be behind the eight ball of your peer group. It will take you a while to catch up.

How would you pitch yourself if you're the lawyer trying to work in finance? What skills do lawyers or law students have that are strengths in the financial world?

To me, it's like what F. Scott Fitzgerald said. The brightest minds are the ones that can take two opposing ideas, two conflicts, and synthesize those conflicts in their brain in a way where they could make sense of both sides of the argument. They can think in a concise, analytical, and objective way, which can really help them in their decision-making. So that's where I think a good legal education and good legal training helps people.

Every business is loaded up with decision-making. Obviously, the investment world is based on good decision-making. You're applying your intellectual capital to the marketplace and you're trying to make really good decisions. So those are the things that I would say you get out of a law education.

The other thing you get out of law (which I have directly benefited from) is that I'm not intimidated by lawyers. I also know how to read a law bill and call bullshit on people. I know when they're pressing a button in a word processor and shit is just coming up and I know when they're actually doing work.

So when you're looking at contracts, you're looking at the fine print and negotiating the details.

Yeah. I can understand the conditions precedent. I can understand the language of the transaction, so that's very helpful. But look, I've also got a lot of friends that I met through school and the network. It was a great education. You went to the University of Pennsylvania and I ended up going to Harvard and you see that these are great law schools. They fortify you with a network. They fortify you with an imprimatur slash brand. That helps you get through the door. It helps you get your foot established in your career.

Beyond your prior work at Goldman, you're also an entrepreneur. You've started many businesses. I think Oscar Capital was your first business, right?

Yeah. I sold that to Neuberger Berman in 2001.

And you even started a restaurant called the Hunt & Fish Club in New York City.

I started the Hunt & Fish Club from scratch. We raised the money and made the chef an equity holder. I had an ice cream store out on Long Island that went bankrupt. We couldn't make the rent. So I've had some failures too. I don't just want to talk about my successes.

The point is that I love the journey more than the destination. I accidentally slipped into politics. An entrepreneur I know decided to run for president. I was actually backing other presidential candidates. He lives two blocks from here and we had a good relationship. He asked me to help him and I said I would. And then, I ended up fighting with Reince

Priebus and Steve Bannon. I was offered the Office of Public Liaison job by the President and those two guys did a number on me. Most people don't remember that. Those two guys figured out a way to block it.

That's a learning lesson for your book. Don't let your pride and your ego get in the way of your decision-making. Once your pride and ego are in decision-making, you make really stupid mistakes. I got my pride and ego in there, I turned the chainsaw on, put the hockey mask on, and went after those two guys.

When you were White House Communications Director, right?

Yeah. I probably shouldn't have started my first day in the White House with a chainsaw and a hockey mask. Probably not, right?

What can we learn from that experience? For one thing, I'm sure you have some great takeaways on handling conflict or handling strong personalities.

Well, one, don't put your ego in it. Number two, it wasn't the right job for me. I made the same mistake that I made coming out of school. I wanted the job because I thought I was excited by the idea of the job. But it was a bad fit for me, which was exactly like my first job. I went into investment banking when I should have gone into sales. I shouldn't have been in politics. I could have been very good in the President's Public Liaison position. I wasn't going to be good at the comms job because I didn't really understand the way the swamp works. I didn't really understand the way the press works inside the swamp. I understand it now.

But that's life. I made a mistake and I'm accountable for the mistake. And by the way, the mistake cost me my job. It wasn't the first time I was fired, though. I got fired from Goldman. But I've also done it as an entrepreneur. Unfortunately, I've sat in this room and have had to fire people. Firing people is a brutal thing. I've been fired twice. I probably fired fifteen people in my career. So I've been on both sides of it. Neither side is pretty. But having said that, I lost my job. I'm accountable.

I think the big lessons you can learn from my experience there are not in the eleven days, but the twelfth day. I'm talking about the metaphorical twelfth day when you've gotten your living ass kicked, when you've been put through a woodchipper, and when you've been lit up in the international media, cable news channels, and the gossip world. How do you handle it? I'm like fucking Mayhem from the Allstate commercials. That's something you should learn yourself. No matter what the fuck happens, as long as you have your health and you have a sense of humor, you're going to be just fine.

Well, how can people learn that? Do you think that's more built into some people than others?

No, I think that's learnable. You have to practice it. It's mental conditioning. It's like going to the gym and preparing your body for an athletic competition. You can prepare your brain for the sport of entrepreneurship. You're going to be constantly reading entrepreneurship and reading about self-improvement and keeping yourself well-versed in what's out there as it relates to building your self-esteem. How old are you?

I'm thirty.

Yeah, I didn't have it at thirty. But I have it at fifty-four. What other people think of you is none of your business. You have to think like that. If you can think like that, you can have a great life. I'm in my own bubble of reality. Some people hate me and others don't. Who cares?

What do you think about this argument about lawyers being poor entrepreneurs? There is this argument that lawyers are too analytical, too risk-averse, and too slow-moving.

Some lawyers do. Some lawyers don't. Let me tell you something. I believe that the law is a vocation. The word *vocare* from Latin means a calling. It is a vocation. You need to have a calling for the law. My buddies that were called into the law have done phenomenally well. I didn't have a calling for the law. I had financial anxiety about where I was in life.

You've started all kinds of businesses in your career. Generally speaking, what factors do you consider when starting a business?

You have to dream. If you think about all the things that can go wrong, you're never going to start the business. You can't overly think it though. I wrote about that in *Hopping Over the Rabbit Hole.*[2]

Is there anything you'd say to the law student or lawyer that wants to quit and try something new but is nervous about what could happen? What would be the one thing that you tell them to do?

Not to sound cliché, but you have a short life. I would say go look at Steve Jobs' commencement address from Stanford. And remember what Mel Brooks once said: "Relax. None of us are getting out of here alive." Just relax. So read that statement and watch the Jobs commencement address on YouTube. Live your life with no fear and live your life with gusto. Also, don't be focused on money. Be focused on the process.

An entrepreneur is a capital artist. This business is my canvas. I'm painting on this canvas all day. Now, I was going to put this piece of art up for sale, but the President asked me to go serve the country. I love my country and my life could never have happened in any other country. It has been such an improbable and amazing life. So for me, the President of the United States asked me to go do something for him. I even went to put my company up for sale. That's how *stunad* I am. These other guys are keeping their companies. They have all of these conflicts and all of this other stuff. I was trying to do the right thing.

The good news is that I got my company back. I'm back here. The way that I could describe my political odyssey is like being in the alternative universe of *It's a Wonderful Life* when Jimmy Stewart's car crashes on the bridge. Now, he's temporarily living in an alternative universe. The guardian angel snaps him back to his regular life. All of the sudden, he realizes how great his regular life was and how appreciative he should be (or should have been about his regular life). That's an episode that happened to me.

Another thing that happened was that I realized how dispensable I am. I built a nice company and these people are doing fine without me.

---

2   In *Hopping Over the Rabbit Hole,* Anthony discusses his entrepreneurial journey and lessons learned. He speaks about the challenges in setting up the first SALT Conference, his thoughts on regret, and why we need to "put our egos on the floor, get outside of our comfort zones, and push ourselves, while maintaining some level of gracious audacity."

Charles de Gaulle once said that there's a graveyard filled with men who once thought they were indispensable. I got to learn in my lifetime how dispensable I am, which I think is very useful.

Going forward, how does that impact your goals and the way that you work?

I'm very energized. I want to double the size of the company. I want to hire the best people and do everything I can to make this a fun place to work.

CHAPTER 7

Melinda Snodgrass

Author and Screenwriter

When you look at any list of alternative careers for law school graduates, one career that you will regularly see is author. This is for good reason, as there are plenty of outstanding authors who trace their professional backgrounds to the legal industry.

The quintessential example is John Grisham. After practicing law for around ten years, Grisham started a journey that would lead him to become one of the most successful fiction authors in modern history. That said, most don't realize *how* Grisham became a world-famous author.

After practicing criminal defense and personal injury litigation for a decade, Grisham was elected to the Mississippi House of Representatives. One day, he visited a courthouse in DeSoto County, Mississippi, when he heard the testimony of a young rape victim. Moved by the testimony, he thought of the young girl's father. Because it was such a heinous crime, Grisham visualized what it would look like if the girl's father sought vengeance and murdered the assailants.

As the legend goes, Grisham woke up at 5:00 a.m. to write a book based on this idea. Although busy with his day job as an elected representative, Grisham devoted several hours per day to finish his novel. After three years, Grisham completed *A Time to Kill*. After experiencing some initial rejection, Grisham became a published author in June of 1988. His next novel was *The Firm*, which spent less than one year on the *New York Times* bestseller list. What started as a hobby turned into an opportunity of a lifetime.

Some may argue that, compared to other professions, lawyers have a *slightly* easier time becoming full-time authors. Generally speaking, our writing skills are strong (even if we follow a formulaic legal writing paradigm). Strong writing skills aren't enough, however. Whether writing fiction or nonfiction, you need to be a great storyteller, develop a thick skin, have the discipline to fight through writer's block, and more.

It's difficult to find all of these qualities in one person. Some former attorneys, however, have the entire package. Melinda Snodgrass is one of those former attorneys. She is a bestselling science fiction and fantasy author behind classics like the *Circuit* trilogy, the *Imperials* series, and the *Wild Cards* series (which she created with George R.R. Martin). With Martin's encouragement, Melinda later ventured into the world of screenwriting. She wrote a spec script called "The Measure of a Man" for *Star Trek: The Next Generation*, which was nominated for the Writer's Guild Award for outstanding writing in a drama series. Melinda then obtained writing roles on shows like *Reasonable Doubts, Profiler*, and *The Antagonists*.

Before publishing celebrated novels and arriving in Hollywood, Melinda was an attorney in New Mexico. She worked at Sandia National Laboratories and then moved to a corporate law firm. Ultimately, however, she decided to take the leap and pursue full-time writing. While making the switch is difficult for many attorneys, Melinda relied on her grit, the guidance of friends and mentors, and wise words from a *Star Wars* hero to thrive in her new career.

As we spoke, I could tell Melinda was meant to write stories. She has a true passion for her work and constantly thinks of new themes and characters to share with the world. Regardless of whether you want to become a full-time writer, you can learn many things from Melinda's career experiences.

* * *

Melinda, I'm excited to dig into the details of your career and how you became a full-time author. But to start off, if you were meeting someone new and had to describe yourself and the work that you do, what would you say?

I would say that I was a girl who couldn't figure out what she wanted to be when she grew up. But then I found writing and it was my passion. I literally can't not write. If I go through a day and, because of other things,

I'm not able to sit down and put words down, I get very antsy. I don't know how else to describe it.

I even write for fun. I do the work for which I am paid. This is my "real work." But I also periodically commit fan fiction. I allow myself to write some fan fiction (like *Star Wars* and *Mass Effect*) in the evenings after I'm done with my real work.

I think that's the real key for a writer. If you don't feel that drive, then this may not be the career for you. It's lonely. Unless you are in a writer's room in Hollywood, you are by yourself. It's a grind. It takes me about one year to write a novel that I'm happy with. Also, the money isn't great, so you really have to do it out of passion.

I was looking at your website before our conversation and I loved a quote that you included there. You said, "Above all else, you write because that's just what you have to do." You just described the meaning of it right there. It's almost like you can't help yourself. You have to do it every single day. On the other hand, it's easy to hear about writers that stumble upon writer's block or can't really get the words from their minds onto the page. You're much different.

I have this cosmic cheering section in my head. All of these characters are nudging me and going, "Hey, don't you want to write about me?"

I live on ten acres on the side of a cliff outside Santa Fe. I haven't really been that lonely. Yes, I have my horse and I go to the barn and do that. But I never feel totally alone because of the cosmic cheering section.

So what really excites you most about writing? Is it the fact that you're getting those thoughts and ideas into the written word? Is the motivation more internal rather than external?

I just gave a speech at a virtual convention over the past weekend. The thing that's the key to writing is that the writer has to agree to be seen. You have to be willing to put yourself, your soul, your feelings, and your emotions on the page. They are channeled through the characters you create. But ultimately, you're the one that's becoming obvious to the people out there in reader-land, television-land, or wherever it is that you're writing.

I'm trying to remember which author said this, but it is about the human heart in conflict with itself. It's about what you can say about the human condition that matters and speaks to people. It is giving them that opportunity to say, "I remember what that was like when I fell in love" or "Watching this character go through the grieving process is helping me as I'm going through it now."

Ultimately, plot is far less important than theme. I had this other saying, which is "Plot is the shit that happens. The theme is why it matters." I'm most interested in the theme and how it impacts the people that I've created.

Did your interest in theme evolve over time? And to just zoom out from there, was writing something that you did when you were a child?

Ironically, I did and then sort of forgot it. My mother reminded me that when I was a little girl, I wrote plays for the neighborhood kids to perform in. Of course, in high school, I wrote some really bad poetry (like everybody in high school does) and a few short stories. But then I just moved on.

I had other interests. I was a singer and studied opera in Vienna, Austria. I realized that it wasn't going to work for me. I'm not exactly built for it and I didn't have that one-tenth of one percent voice that was going to make it. My father desperately wanted me to go to law school. That was tremendously important to him. So when I realized I wasn't going to make it as an opera star, I came back to the United States. I finished my degree in history and music and went on to law school.

I did it more for him and I found the study of law fascinating. But I realized at the end of the first semester, I had made a terrible mistake.

Really?

I was good at it. I kept passing the tests and then I passed the bar exam. Then you're like, "Oh my gosh. I'm trapped now."

If I can take us back to a little bit earlier. As you said, your father was a key influence in your decision to go to law school. What were your thoughts about what you would do after graduation? Did you have

any specific ideas or where you would practice or how your legal career would turn out?

I think I didn't. Even my professors knew that I wasn't committed to this in a really fundamental way. I was singing with the Civic Light Opera and singing Guinevere in *Camelot*—all while I was in law school. They kept going, "You must focus more completely on school."

In law school, I loved Constitutional Law. That was my passion. Looking back all these years later, I thought, "I probably should have just gone to work for the ACLU." If I had, I might have remained a lawyer. But I didn't. That was probably a mistake because I don't think I really had thought it through. I was just like, "I'm doing this for him. I'm going to grit my teeth and get through it. I'll take the bar." Then, I passed, and I was like, "Oh my gosh, I passed. What do I do now?"

I ended up first working for the government at Sandia Laboratories. Another young gentleman lawyer and I oversaw the purchasing department and, oh my God, that was boring. I thought the science they were doing was fascinating because I've been a science fiction nerd since I was a tiny little girl.

I left Sandia Laboratories and ended up going to work for a corporate law firm. But then, I was like, "I cannot do this." *Star Wars* inspired me to get the heck out of it.

Star Wars? Really?

Yeah. It was with my best friend at the time. He encouraged me to write— at the time—novels. We always went to see *Star Wars* movies together on opening night. That was our deal. I was watching *The Empire Strikes Back* and Yoda said to Luke, "Do or do not. There is no try."

I had been wrestling with it. I was like, "That's it." I walked into the law firm the next morning, typed out my letter of registration, packed up my stuff, laid it on my boss's desk, and walked out. I was going to try this writing thing.

That's an outstanding origin story for your post-legal career. But if I could quickly go back to your law school experience. Why did you choose the University of New Mexico?

It was about location and money. It looked like I was going to get accepted at William & Mary and my dad said to me, "That's going to be a little
hard for us if we have to send you there." Also, U of M had a really good
reputation. It was a highly rated law school.

I always come home to New Mexico. I was raised here. There's something about this place that's magical in a way I can't describe. So the
thought of going away was a little bit hard. Even when I work in Hollywood, I have never given up my New Mexico house. I always come home.

I've never been before.

This is the best place in the world. Art, music, food, and natural beauty.
It's an amazing place.

**You said a few moments ago that when you were in law school, you
were questioning your decision. This even happened during your
first semester. You stuck with it, however. You graduated, took the
bar exam, and had a career in the legal field before starting your
writing career. What do you think made you stick around and overcome the challenges and stress of law school and legal practice?**

Well for me, it was my love for my father. I could not bring myself to
disappoint him. He had always given me so many opportunities. He sent
me off to Europe to study opera when I was eighteen and said I wanted to
do that. He had always supported me in everything and I felt like I didn't
want to disappoint him.

He actually died shortly after I finished the bar exam. He was dying
while I was taking the bar exam. That made it doubly hard to get through
it. But there was also that realization that "I can't disappoint him anymore.
If I leave, I've left and it isn't going to break his heart."

I think my dad also had this very romantic version of the law. His
idea was that it was sort of like being Atticus Finch. That was mine, too.
I went into law school with that sort of attitude. That was not the reality.
Especially when I ended up at a corporate law firm, it really was not the
reality. I just didn't want any part of it.

**But in the meantime, your father is almost your "why." As you said,
you didn't want to disappoint him. I'm assuming that during those**

tough moments, you thought about him and his expectations for you, which helped you get through those tough moments.

It also turned out that I was good at this. I graduated in the upper part of my glass. I kept going, "Oh, I hate this, but why am I good at it?" I mean, you feel stupid if you're quitting because when you're doing really well, you're like, "Well, maybe this is kind of foolish."

Right. The thinking may go, "Maybe I'm good at this. Maybe this is meant to be." A lot of law students focus on their courses. They want to do their best because they are thinking about their first job after graduation. In your case, you worked at Sandia National Laboratories in New Mexico. Why did you think that opportunity was more attractive than others that were in front of you? How did you get that opportunity in the first place?

One of my dad's friends had connections and got me an interview. It was partly because I knew I didn't really like the practice of law. I liked the study of law a great deal, but I didn't like the practice.

I was trying to avoid going into a firm. Friends of mine who had gone into the big firms in Albuquerque were putting in eighty-hour weeks. I was like, "Yeah, but I still want to sing with the Civic Light Opera and take my ballet classes. I really don't want that life."

So this was an eight to five job. The work itself was boring, but the work that we were supporting was fascinating. It's a cutting-edge scientific research laboratory. It had been totally devoted to weapons in the old days, but it transitioned into green energy and all these other things. So periodically, I would escape from my office and go behind the fence and go visit the scientists. I would ask, "You need how many gallons of ultra pure oil in order to test for fusion? Okay." They were cool and the ultimate work was cool.

Right. Your interests were slightly elsewhere, but you still had this legal training. You took the bar exam. I'm sure you were making good money as well. Can you take us back to that time and your impressions of your career? Because you did end up going to another corporate law firm before becoming a writer full-time.

Well, it was actually one of my bosses at Sandia who said to me, "I've had this happen a lot. You really don't want to spend the rest of your life here." He just chuckled and said, "This is not the place for you." I think he knew I had a wild spirit or something and that this wasn't the right place. He said, "You need to move on."

Then, I tried the law firm. I hated it. Every day was a burden. I couldn't wait until 5:00 came so I could flee and go to my ballet class, jazz class, or rehearsal. I also think part of it is that I have always had a very hard time being told, "I have to occupy a particular space for X many hours per day." I prefer to be in my own space and set my own hours and schedule. So I think that was adding to it.

Also, at the time, I went to a mass autographing that my best friend was in. He was the one that would go to *Star Wars* movies with me. Famous science fiction writers like Roger Zelazny[1] and Fred Saberhagen[2] were there. After the signing ended, my friend Vic Milán[3] took me to a barbeque at Saberhagen's house. I sort of wandered through the house listening to these conversations and they were the most fascinating people that I had ever, ever, met.

When we got out, I grabbed Vic by the lapels and said, "I want to be part of this world." He told me, "You're very artistic. You've been a singer, a dancer, and all this other stuff. If you want to try writing, I'll help you. You can bring me your pages and I'll give you advice." So that's what we did. I started writing in secret.

You were writing when you were at your corporate law firm? Essentially, you were moonlighting?

A little. Yeah. I couldn't do as much. But when I quit, I could really apply myself and crank out pages. I was working on a science fiction series about a federal court judge riding circuit in outer space. I had read a biography of John Marshall riding circuit. I thought that was fun.

---

1   Roger Zelazny was a well-known science fiction and fantasy writer. Some of his most celebrated works were in a novel series called *The Chronicles of Amber*.

2   Fred Saberhagen is another celebrated science fiction author. He is well-known for the *Berserker* and the *Dracula* series.

3   Milán is another well-known science fiction and fantasy writer who authored stories like *Cybernetic Samurai* and *Cybernetic Shogun*. He passed away in 2018.

But when I quit, I also had to make a living. So while I was still working on the big science fiction trilogy, I wrote romance novels under pseudonyms. I could write one in two months and get paid. The advantage is that they taught me how to finish something. You sit down and do the work. You get it done and then you send in the manuscript. Then, you do the next one.

An awful lot of writers make the mistake of waiting for the muse to speak. You can't. This morning, before you and I were talking, I was working on revising a novel that we're about to get back into print again. You do the work whether you feel like it or not.

Right now, I'm reading *The War of Art* by Steven Pressfield. One of the main insights in the book is that writers (and other types of creators) need to act as professionals. Professionals don't take days off—even when they feel like it. They concentrate and get the work done. You seem to be articulating a similar thought. So at the time, you were speaking with your friend Victor Milán. You're thinking of leaving your firm. You see *Star Wars* and you're ready to go. But you still actually have to do it. Can you take us to that time and how you decided to leave your firm?

It was Yoda. What can I say? Do or do not. There is no try. I actually was a Jedi master's padawan. At that moment, I went, "Okay, I quit." I mean, I literally quit the next morning. I didn't even give them two weeks' notice. I just quit. That's how much I hated the job.

I never looked back. I started writing. Then, into my life came George R.R. Martin. He moved down to New Mexico and became part of our group. He was the one that got me into Hollywood.

The path that you've taken from the moment you quit your law firm job to where you are now is really fascinating. What happened during that first year after you quit your job? Some readers who want to follow in your footsteps may be thinking, "Okay, I'm ready to leave my firm. I want to become a full-time writer." What does that first year really look like?

I knew I had a story I wanted to tell with my judge riding circuit in outer space. But I also knew I had to make a living. I always tell writers to never do this. However, the romance market still outsells every other genre by like a mile.

Really?

That is the biggest selling market of any type of book. At the time, romance was even bigger. It was huge and they were desperate for product. I normally tell people, "Only write what you love and what you're passionate about," because if you are inauthentic, it will show. I didn't particularly love romance, but they were hungry enough that they were buying.

Vic helped me negotiate the market and he introduced me to his agent. She was selling my romance proposals. At the time, you could write a ten-page proposal and they would buy the book. It wasn't great money. We're talking about a six-thousand-dollar advance, so you had to write two or three of them per year.

So you're scrambling. The other problem for writers entering now is that publishing is in a crisis. Publishing is still trying to sell buggy whips in an era where we have a completely different prototype for how people receive their entertainment. Amazon, Smashwords, eBooks, and Barnes & Noble exist. And yes, there is a lot of junk out there. People can just throw up any old thing they've written without getting it edited, without getting a decent cover, and doing all of that stuff.

The traditional publishing market is really tough to get into now. It's really tough to make it. The George Martins and the Diana Gabaldons and the Stephen Kings are so unique. When I got into it, there was still what was called the midlist. There was a midlist of books where you would get paid $20,000 or $25,000 for a book. If you live in someplace like New Mexico, you could live for that year while you wrote the book. But that market is pretty much gone in publishing right now.

So my advice would be, unfortunately, don't quit your day job unless you have a spouse who can be the breadwinner. This is not a ticket to wealth. It's just not. You may get lucky. George got incredibly lucky. It can happen. But don't assume that it's going to happen. The old days of, "Yeah, I'll write a book. My publisher will give me $25,000 and I'll write another one," aren't there.

It all comes back to law. It's such a big topic. One of the things that killed writers is the *Thor Power Tool* decision.[4] It held that inventory had to be taxed as income. It killed the backlist. What used to support writers was their backlists. Fred Saberhagen had fifty or sixty books that he wrote. They included his *Berserker* trilogy and *Book of Swords*. In the old days, if a bookstore needed another Saberhagen book, they just called up and they'd send it from the warehouse. Well, suddenly, publishers couldn't keep the books. So the backlist died.

Now, with Amazon, the backlist is there. It doesn't cost anything. It floats in the cloud. So that's changed. But the *Thor Power Tool* decision really did a number on authors. Fred used to get these royalty checks every six months. He put five kids through college and two of them through medical school. But that was gone after that court decision. Then, all he could do was write frantically to keep up with the bills.

This is not an easy career. If you want money, then you go to Hollywood. There, they give you big wheelbarrow loads of money. On the other hand, they mess with your work. So it's a trade-off.

Going back to what you said, if a lawyer is reading this while working at their law job, they shouldn't quit that job. They should try to do it on the side. I'm assuming that they should just start writing and perhaps publish their work on the internet? Should they try to even go one step further and find an agent at that point? What would you recommend?

I'm so torn because I still have dear friends in traditional publishing. But I would say there's a middle ground. That is to go with indie publishing companies. Check them out and make sure you don't get a fly-by-night one. There are some out there that are no good. But you don't want to just try to do it yourself. For one thing, it takes a computer program to prepare your manuscript to go up on multiple platforms. Every one of them has its own algorithm. If you don't know how to program for each of them, it's going to be a disaster.

You want to get your manuscript copy-edited. If you don't know any great copy editors, a lot of these indie publishing companies (the one I work with is Prince of Cats Literary Productions) have the staff to do that.

---

4   Melinda is referring to *Thor Power Tool Company v. Commissioner*, 439 U.S. 522 (1979).

I pay the cover artist and then he pays the copy editor and the woman who prepares the manuscripts to be uploaded onto the platforms. He handles the marketing (which is good because I don't want to be a marketer). He sets up interviews for me and does various things. He does more for me than my traditional publishers ever did. Traditional publishers still tend to put all of their attention behind the Stephen Kings and George Martins and not give a boost to the new young writers.

So I think on balance, I would probably say I want to go with an independent publisher on the internet. Bookstores, apart from small boutique bookstores like science fiction specialty or children's book specialty, are dying. Waldenbooks is gone. Borders is gone. Barnes & Noble is in trouble. It's not easy.

Yeah. If I could go back to your earlier career, Vic was someone that was important to you. George R.R. Martin arrived later on. Can you discuss how you met them and perhaps the importance of mentors in becoming who you are now?

Mentors are huge. The writing community (particularly the science fiction writing community) pays it forward like crazy.

I met Vic in a bookstore. I was earning money working in a used bookstore to save up for law school. He came in, we fell to talking, and we just clicked. We were instantly friends. Then, he introduced me to role-playing games. A bunch of the other writers were playing these games. Then, George moved down to Santa Fe and the writing community reached out to him. This included people like Vic, Roger Zelazny, Walter Jon Williams, and all of these people. So he immediately was folded into the group and into our role-playing group. He not only played in games but became a game master himself.

It was the community. We had a weekly lunch where we'd get together. Then, we played games way more nights than we probably should have each week. There was one point when George was running Superworld for us. We were playing three and four nights a week until 2:00 or 3:00 in the morning because we were all writers and didn't have day jobs. Then, George and I turned that obsession from the game into a shared world anthology that, to this day, we still edit. He doesn't have time, but I write for a series called *Wild Cards*. That was how that happened.

Then, in the midst of all of this, George got swept off to Hollywood. He was offered a job on the new *Twilight Zone* and then on *Beauty and the Beast*. He called me one day and said, "Hey, Snod, I think you'd be really good at this screenwriting thing because you write really crisp dialogue and very powerful characters." Description has always been my problem. I hate writing description. Then he said, "If you write a spec script, I'll show it to my agent out here in Hollywood." So I wrote, "The Measure of a Man" for *Star Trek: The Next Generation.*

You embraced serendipity. Along with this, you developed really great relationships with members of your community. That led to so many different things.

Yes, it led to so many options. I didn't go out to make the network. The network happened. The other thing I first learned from my father was to always take the risk. Always take the risk. George said, "Will you write a script?" I went, "You've got it." Two weeks later, I had written a script. You don't let those opportunities languish. Grab hold of them immediately.

You acted quickly. Perhaps that was a little scary, too. You were a novelist and a short story writer and then you transitioned into screenwriting. Can you talk about that and what skills you needed to quickly pick up in order to succeed?

Well, I think I was born to be a screenwriter. If I balance my skills, I think I'm a better screenwriter than I am a novelist. But I would say it's a couple of things. You need a very strong sense of plot. I always plotted very strenuously. I think that was the legal training.

There's something called "pantsers," meaning that I write by the seat of my pants. George calls it being a gardener. He's a gardener. He's like, "I don't know what the seed is, but I will plant it and see if it's a kumquat or a stinkweed." And I'm going, "I want to know if it's a stinkweed before I start." He calls me an architect.

You do need to be more of an architect to go to Hollywood. You need to be really good at dialogue. The other thing you need is the ability to separate yourself once your work is done. It is truly collaborative and other people are going to mess with it. If you can't stand that, stick to novels.

You can have so many people coming in saying, "Change this. I don't like that." You've got the actors, the director, the studio, the network, and standards and practices. Then, there's the set designer going, "We can't build that. It's going to cost too much." So you're constantly adjusting. And you will be rewritten. Somebody is probably going to come in and rewrite your script. You let it go.

Right. If I can just ask you a specific question about writing in general. As law students and lawyers know, legal writing is very formulaic. You have CREAC (that's what I learned in law school). There is a specific way of creating legal arguments and crafting legal briefs. Fiction and screenwriting are considerably different than that. How did you navigate that transition from legal writing to fiction writing?

The truth is this formula is everywhere. Formula is not a dirty word. Every story has a shape. Kurt Vonnegut said that stories have shapes.

I read a lot, obviously. The thing you want to do is read people whose work you admire and see what they did. Also, join a writer's group. I think they're highly useful. It has to be a healthy group, however. It can't be toxic (some of these groups can be). But you want to be in a writer's group with people who are just a little bit better than you are so that they can challenge you. You also want to read each other's work and get critiques. By doing this, you get better.

If you go to conventions, there will be lots and lots of panels about the art of writing and how to craft a story. In Hollywood, there are books like *Save The Cat*. I would avoid Sid Fields. I think he was much too formulaic. But *Save The Cat* has some valuable lessons.

The thing I always tell young writers is first, you have to learn the rules before you can break the rules. So spend some time learning the rules and working with people. There are online workshops, too. A lot of people I know have had very good success with the Online Writers Workshop (OWW). That's a place to kind of dip your toe in and see how it feels. It also helps you see whether you can stand critique because that's a really important skill to learn. Editors are going to critique you, and if you're in Hollywood, one billion people are going to critique you. You have to learn those skills.

I had been an outliner, but when I went to Hollywood, we do this thing called "breaking a story." It is a very detailed breakdown of the story from the end to the beginning. We plot backward in Hollywood. I plot my books the same way. I plot everything backward now and you learn this skill. There are places where you can learn that. I just finished this convention and I said, "You can contact me through my website. You can get in touch with me on Facebook. A lot of people shared their knowledge with me. I'll pass it on to you as best I can." But again, don't be afraid of formula. Formula is not a dirty word.

How do you know when you're at that point where you can break the rules?

Some people say you need to have written one million words. I don't know if you need quite one million. I think you need to have written a lot. The other advice I give young writers is do not start with first-person. Everybody thinks that writing first-person is going to be easier. It is actually enormously difficult to do well. You should never tackle first-person until you've got some experience under your belt.

Why is it tougher?

If you are writing in close third-person (which is what most modern writers use), you have to sort of see the entire tapestry. If you're writing in first-person, you can only follow that individual. Unless you know how to craft within those parameters and limitations, it can get very difficult. It can get very self-referential and you have a much harder time telling the story.

Now, if you want to read the master of the first-person, you want to read Roger Zelazny. He was the finest first-person writer I've ever seen. I can write in it now, but I've been doing this for a long time. George gave me a nice compliment. He said that I write very, very well in first-person. But I certainly wouldn't have tackled it when I was first starting out. Having the ability to have other viewpoints and other characters gives you the chance to breathe and develop your skills a little more. So first-person is very difficult.

That makes sense. So whether you are writing your own novels or working in Hollywood with George, does your law degree or experience play any role? Does it provide you with any advantages?

Well, for advantages, I've got hired on *Reasonable Doubts* because I was the only lawyer on the staff. I use it constantly. Every time I give a lecture, I do my little PSA announcement of "Stay in school. Get your education." Nothing is wasted. The fact that I'm a dressage rider, that I've sung opera, that I have this legal training—I use all of these things constantly in my writing.

There was "The Measure of a Man" which is based on the *Dred Scott* decision. If I hadn't gone to law school, I might not have read and known about the *Dred Scott* decision. So I took *Dred Scott*, updated it, and turned it into a *Star Trek* episode. It applied when I worked on *Reasonable Doubts*. Even my first science fiction trilogy was about a federal court judge riding circuit. It applies even in my space opera series that I'm doing right now.

The one thing science fiction writers often overlook is law and economics (and politics to some degree). So I try to make a point of making sure that that's in there because law is foundational to everything. You can't have a functioning society without some form of a legal system. And then there is my urban fantasy *This Case Is Gonna Kill Me*, which is about a young woman lawyer working in a vampire law firm in Manhattan.[5] So I literalized the metaphor, right?

What's the title of the space opera series that you're working on?

The space opera is called the *Imperials* series. The first book is called *The High Ground*. Then, there is In *Evil Times*, which is book two. The third book (*The Hidden World*) is out and we're working on the fourth book. It's in the hands of the copy editor right now. Book five is done and waiting in the wings. Again, when I plotted it, I plotted all five books. I know exactly where it ends. I knew what the story was before I ever started.

I have to ask: from what you were just saying, you clearly write and release so many books. You quickly come up with ideas. Can you

---

5   *This Case is Gonna Kill Me* is part of Melinda's *White Fang Law* series. The second book in the series is called *Box Office Poison*.

take us inside your process, whether that's generating new ideas or actually sitting down and writing a specific book?

Ideas are the easiest part. Ideas are cheap. They are everywhere. Execution is everything.

For me, things usually start with a character. I will have a sudden vision of something and I'll wonder how that situation arose. With *Imperials*, I was sitting one day and was thinking about it. I thought, "We're always worried about the evil invading aliens coming to Earth." I had this sudden flash (literally an image) of this giant, eight-foot-tall ant-like creature with giant mandibles and claws and fangs just cowering in terror in front of a human holding a machine gun. I said to myself, "What if *we're* the evil invading aliens?" That was where it started.

I was also looking at how we are about "the other." We're terrified of "the other." I thought, "You know, if we actually did go out into the galaxy and we met up with alien creatures, the first thing we would do is kick the shit out of them." Honestly, we would. People are carrying on about caravans of evil brown people. Can you imagine if we meet the big mandible thing that's eight feet tall?

It's interesting with this series and this universe. Every writer has at least one trunk novel (usually more). Trunk novels are books that you start and try and they don't work. If you're smart, you just put them away. You put them in the trunk, forget about them, and work on something else. I wrote seventy thousand words of a trunk novel in this universe. It never worked. It wasn't right.

I put it aside. Then, a few years ago, I looked at it and thought, "God, I love that universe. I love that franchise. But my Chancellor of the Exchequer just didn't work out. He was the wrong character." So I went back and I thought, "What if I pick younger people? Who are they? What are they?" Then it all came together. Once I had my hero and heroine, everything just started to tumble into place.

I then did a plot break with my writer buddies Ty Franck and Daniel Abraham (who are the guys behind *The Expanse*). I had a plot break with them and Walter John Williams. I had the basic outlines of it. Then, we laid out the books and talked it through like a Hollywood writer's room.

So interesting. You could have an idea, put that to the side, see it in a new light, and then make it into something much better. But like you say, it's all about execution and getting feedback from others.

Also, getting help is important. It's helpful to reach out, talk it through, and ask, "Does this make any sense?" The *White Fang Law* books came because I looked at the urban fantasy landscape. It's always about a tough girl in the mean streets with a stiletto in her hand and stiletto high heels. I thought, "Yeah, but if there really were vampires in our world, wouldn't they be enormously wealthy and powerful? What does an urban fantasy look like if it's up among the highest levels of the elites and where the levers of power are?"

Nobody had written about that in an urban fantasy setting. I thought, "What would it be like if I was that young woman who suddenly went to work in a law firm where all the senior partners are vampires? And what if your stockbroker is probably a werewolf because they tend to be bond traders? The elves have gone into show business. They're all actors and rock and roll stars. What would that world look like? What does the law look like? How do ordinary humans make a buck in that society? Oh, you sell a sipping menu for your vampire clients who come to your restaurant. There are different types of blood."

I have to read this book.

It is first-person. Urban fantasy is always written in first-person. Then, you tweak it. You make it a little different. There are no women vampires and no women werewolves in my universe. There's a big secret about why that is. So you take the tropes of the thing you want to write about and you find a way to put a little twist on them to make it yours. What do I want to say about this?

Definitely. Let's take the readers back to when you were starting out your writing career (or even your career now). If you could do it over again, is there anything that you would avoid or anything that you would double down on? In other words, if the readers are reading this chapter and are inspired to become full-time writers, what should they do or not do?

Only write what you love. I felt like when I had to write just to make money so that I could pay the mortgage, it was never as rewarding. But sometimes you have to.

Write what you're passionate about. There's another point if you're going to Hollywood. In Hollywood, I could have continued to just work on TV shows as a staff writer (like I was on *Star Trek*, *Reasonable Doubts*, and *Profiler*). I could have continued to go from show to show. But I was offered the chance to create my own television shows (like Shonda Rhimes or J.J. Abrams). The rewards are much bigger on that path but the risk is also enormous. If you don't make it, you fall out of the memory of people that were on the staff track with you. If you get the brass ring, you make a fortune. If you miss, suddenly three or four years have gone by and everybody's forgotten who you are. And it's very hard to get back onto staff.

If I had to do it all over again, because I love writing on staff and being in a writer's room, I wish I had stuck with the staff track rather than trying to get my own show on the air. I wrote six pilots over the years, but only one of them got made and none of them were picked up. I did some good work, but it ultimately didn't pay off. It's very hard to get back in. I was older. Hollywood is getting better, but if you're a person of color or an older person, it was much harder to get work.

At that point, it's all about relationships, right?

Yeah. What you want is where you have a friend who's been hired to be the showrunner on some new show and he or she has worked with you before. When they put together their staff, they're like, "Oh yeah, I want Melinda again. I worked with her on this other thing."

Also, all the people I had worked with had started to fall out of the business. So then I didn't have the connections to get hired again. Unfortunately, it didn't get picked up, but I was the executive producer on *Wild Cards*.

Right. You recently wrote that script, correct?

Actually, no. I wrote a script to get the interest going, but then we set it up as potentially two television series at Hulu. I was an executive producer. We hired a showrunner. We had a writer's room and had eight writers.

We wrote a bunch of episodes for both shows. We did all of this fabulous work for ten solid months. It was fabulous.

Then, Hulu got bought by Disney and Disney did not need another superhero franchise. They had Marvel. They didn't need us, so we were dead. George and I are trying to get it set up again at another network. So I wrote a number of scripts, but none of them went anywhere.

Sure, it seems like bad luck. There's so much out of your hands that you just have to focus on what you can control. And whatever you can't control is up to fate, fortune, or something else.

Yeah, you just let it go. I've got a team, but then Covid-19 hit, so we haven't been able to figure out shooting. Hopefully, we're going to get it set up on one of the streamers.

As far as the business and marketing side, you were saying that selecting an independent publisher can be a good idea. Do you have any other best practices or tips in terms of selling or marketing new books?

I'm probably not the best person to ask. I'm terrible at it and I hate it. You need to be on social media. I hate to say it, but you need to be on Facebook and Twitter. If you're good at it, you probably need to be on Instagram (I suck at it). I'm a word person and not a picture person. But you need to have a social media presence. You need to be interesting without being too obnoxious if that makes sense.

My friend Connie Willis, who is the most decorated writer in science fiction, once said, "I make myself interesting and then people want to read my book because I'm interesting." What you don't want to be is the person who, every five minutes on your Twitter feed or Facebook page, is going, "Buy my book. Buy my book." A lot of people make that mistake.

When I have a book that's being released, I will announce it. Then, I stop. I probably should push it a little more than I do, but I find that nothing is more irritating than somebody screaming in your face. So I would ask, what makes you interesting? Be funny. Talk about your hobbies. Just be an approachable person and build up your following.

Don't forget about word of mouth. Word of mouth sells more books. The publisher of *Cold Mountain* did nothing, but independent bookstores and bookstore employees read that book, fell in love with it, and they started pushing it through word of mouth. So what you really want is to get people to start doing the work for you.

And never read reviews. Never, ever, ever read reviews. Bad ones just crush you and good ones just give you a swelled head. I don't read them. I just don't.

You are an equestrian rider. In your youth and even your legal career, you were singing and engaging in other creative hobbies. How important were hobbies as you worked to succeed as a lawyer and writer?

I think it's critical. If you're just focused on your work, first of all, it makes you boring and dull. Ultimately, I think it breaks your spirit. Writers have a horrible tendency to be awfully sedentary. The more physical things you do, the better your brain works.

I not only go to ride six days a week (when I could before Covid-19), but I joined a gym. Here at home where I have ten acres, I go hiking. I take a hike on days I don't ride. Sometimes I even ride and still take a hike. You work for a while and then get up and do something physical.

I don't sing anymore. Unfortunately, I had planned to find a voice teacher when I went to work on *Star Trek*, but the hours were so brutal. George and I were frequently meeting at nine o'clock at night to get dinner. He was just down the street on *Beauty and the Beast*. The hours are horrendous. They're like sixteen-hour days and I didn't have the energy. So the horses kind of ended up replacing that. But I think it's critical that you have something else you love outside of your work. Otherwise, you're kind of a dull person.

Right. And having these hobbies probably makes you a better worker or writer. So what are you the most excited about in the next year? Perhaps even the next five or ten years?

I want to continue doing my books. I want to try to get a TV show back up on the air that's all mine. I would crawl over broken glass to work on any *Star Wars* show. I also want to write a *Star Wars* novel. I know which one I want to write. There have been all of these shake-ups at their publishing, so my guy hasn't had a chance to really go in there. I'm like, "Let me write this story."

I'm fascinated with what makes people become okay with fascism and autocracy. I also want to know more about the Empire in *Star Wars*. All they ever show me are desert planets and Coruscant, which is one big city. There are also people selling food on the side of the road like it's the twelfth century. And I'm like, "Is there not a Minneapolis *Star Wars*? What does the average planet look like? Do they have Amazon? What does culture look like? What does the stock market look like?"

I want to write about those things. I keep throwing it out there in the hope that somebody at the *Star Wars* world would go, "Wait a minute. There's this very weird woman who wants to write about Minneapolis in *Star Wars*."

Well, I really hope you get the chance. It sounds super interesting.

It would be fun. And let me throw out one more thing as a cautionary tale to young writers. It isn't how many pages you write; it's how good they are. I set myself a goal of one thousand words a day, which is four pages. I work for about five and a half hours. That's about all the brainpower you have (unless you go away, do something else, and come back). Then you can write on a different project and maybe gear up again. But it's not about the quantity. It's about the quality.

CHAPTER 8

Richard Hsu

Legal Recruiter

If you are looking for some of the best career advice in just a few minutes, it's hard to do better than Steve Jobs' 2005 commencement address at Stanford University.[1] According to CNN, Job's speech is the most-watched commencement address of all time. With nearly forty million views on YouTube, Jobs' insights about life, careers, and finding what you love have inspired viewers to live life on their own terms.

There are the headline quotes that many of us know. "Your time is limited, so don't waste it living someone else's life," Jobs said. He added, "[H]ave the courage to follow your heart and intuition. They somehow already know what you truly want to become. Everything else is secondary." He concluded his commencement speech with four words that would follow Jobs until his death. Those words? "Stay hungry. Stay foolish."

Putting those iconic lines aside, one of the more interesting parts of the speech is toward the beginning, where Jobs describes his decision to drop out of Reed College. While he admits it was scary at the time, he also found it liberating. For instance, Jobs famously took a calligraphy class. He didn't have a master plan while he was learning about things like typefaces and proportionally spaced fonts, but he followed his curiosity. He had no idea that the lessons he learned from that calligraphy class would influence the typography used in the first Macintosh computer.

Therein lies one of the most important lessons from Jobs' speech. He said, "[Y]ou can't connect the dots looking forward; you can only connect them looking backward. So you have to trust that the dots will somehow connect in your future." Only by looking back can you see how random

---

1   You can find a full transcript of Jobs' speech at this link: https://news.stanford.edu/2005/06/14/jobs-061505/

events in the past were necessary for you to end up where you are today. In effect, what you are doing is writing your "career novel" without knowing the entire plot or theme. By reading the novel later, you can understand the meaning of certain "dots" that seemed random at the time.

Richard Hsu is a Managing Director at Major, Lindsey & Africa. Serving in the firm's Partner Practice Group, he works with individual attorneys, practice groups, and law firms. As part of his job, Richard helps lawyers think about the next steps in their careers. Whether that means working for a different law firm or leaving the practice of law entirely, Richard uses his knowledge and multi-decade experience in legal practice to help lawyers reach their career goals.

It's fair to say that Richard, while in law school, did not foresee a move from legal practice to the recruiting world. As he told me in our conversation, "Recruiting is just not a career that people think about." But in a LinkedIn post[2] describing his decision to leave Big Law for recruiting, he said that joining Major, Lindsey & Africa was "the perfect culmination of my background, knowledge, experience, interests, and relationships." Even though he may not have known it at the time, his experience as a young associate, a global practice head, and even a podcaster and blogger prepared him for doing his best work as a legal recruiter.

Richard's story provides so many lessons for us; however, one of the starkest is that it isn't too late to make a major career change. Richard decided to take a risk instead of resting on his laurels as a Big Law firm's global practice head. He chose to accept a challenge in a new field, even though there was a steep learning curve in doing so.

It's easy to think that you need to be early in your career to take on new work outside of the law. There are some advantages in doing so (for instance, you have more time to master your new craft in your new field and the "golden handcuffs" effect as a practicing lawyer isn't as strong). Nonetheless, there are plenty of advantages to making a substantial career move in your later career. As just one example, the network of relationships Richard had built in his multi-decade career as a practicing lawyer played a huge role in finding the opportunity at Major, Lindsey & Africa.

While the situation will depend on the new career you're pursuing, recognize that you may have a unique edge in making a change as a more

---

2   You can find that LinkedIn post here: https://www.linkedin.com/pulse/why-i-left-biglaw-partnership-become-legal-recruiter-richard-hsu/

seasoned attorney. Investing in your strengths and edges will likely put you in a great position to reach your new career goals.

* * *

Richard, I think that you have a really interesting career story. Many profiles in this book are of people who made the transition out of legal practice earlier in their careers. You made the switch later in your career. You also work in the recruiting world and encounter many lawyers that want to do something different, whether that's within the legal field or outside of it. I'm looking forward to hearing your insights on that. But to kick this off, can you talk about what first made you interested in law school? I was reading one of your blogs where you discussed how you didn't like the isolation of being a scientist or programmer. I suspect that was part of the catalyst for you going to law school.

I would probably say it was more of a catalyst for not getting a Ph.D. or other graduate degree in engineering. A lot of my colleagues became engineers and then they would go get a Ph.D. or other science graduate degree. Of course, back then, getting a graduate degree was kind of the natural thing you did.

My inspiration for law school was a little bit more of an interesting story. I didn't come from a family of lawyers. I really didn't know much about law school. If you told me in undergrad that I was going to go to law school, I would have been shocked. I would have said no to being a lawyer. But when I was working, someone I knew said, "Oh, you should think about going into intellectual property because that's an area where a lot of engineers go." At that moment, I probably barely even knew what a patent was. That's how little I knew about it. So that kind of inspired me to even look at the thing. Then, I took the LSAT.

There were two things about law school that actually made me do it. Number one was law school is the one professional school where there are zero prerequisites (unlike, say, medical school). With law school, you never need to take any kind of particular class. That was helpful because the last thing I wanted to do was go back to school to qualify. That's one of the reasons why I ruled out something like medical school.

That was one good thing. The other thing was that I figured, "Well, if I don't like it, I can always just go back to being an engineer." I didn't see a lot of downside. In fact, even when I started law school, I was thinking that there would only be a fifty percent chance that I would actually practice. I figured that if I really didn't like it, I would do something else. Who knows? Anyways, as it turned out, I did become a lawyer and went down that path. But when I started law school, I was not completely sold that I would actually become a lawyer *per se*.

Were you seriously thinking about this during college or did it start when you were working at Oracle?

It was more of when I was at Oracle. I was thinking about what I wanted to do, whether it was business school or something else. That's when somebody suggested this idea of intellectual property.

Right. You obviously ended up going. What made you actually pull the trigger and take a chance on law school?

One of the things that I wanted to make sure I had in law school was an experience in some other part of the country. I spent my whole life in California. I grew up in the Bay Area and went to school in Southern California. Getting into Columbia and having the chance to live in New York City also was kind of a catalyst. Not only could I go to law school and do something like I've never done before, but then I could also experience a new city on the East Coast. So that was actually a big part of it.

You said there was a fifty percent chance that you weren't going to practice law after law school. Because of that, what was the ultimate vision of how you would use your law degree?

Well, at the time, I really didn't have one. I wasn't sure how I would use it. I figured it wouldn't hurt, but I didn't have a vision of what I would do if I didn't become a lawyer. A lot of law students feel this immense pressure to get a job because if they don't get a job, what are they going to do with their law degree? I just didn't feel that pressure. It also made law school a more enjoyable experience because I just wasn't that pressured to get top grades or anything like that.

I really enjoyed it. It was a pretty fun experience. It was different from the kinds of things I had done before and I just wasn't that stressed out about getting a job.

Because you knew it would kind of work itself out. Columbia is a very prestigious school and you would eventually find some great opportunities. If I can ask you one thing related to the law school decision. You tend to hear many opinions on this, but what is your take on whether prospective law students should actually work in the legal field before they go to law school?

That's interesting. I don't have a strong feeling about that. I didn't do it, obviously. I'm on the fence about it.

On one hand, you can get a good sense of what being a lawyer is like. But in another sense, you really don't. Until you become a lawyer, the stuff that you're doing is pretty limited. You are working as a paralegal or you are doing some really mundane tasks. I'm not sure how good of a perspective it would provide on what it's actually like working as a lawyer.

So I'm probably mixed on that. I think it's fine, but I don't think it's essential.

And looking back, do you have any regrets about not having had that experience in the legal field before going to Columbia?

No, I don't think so. Not for me, anyway. I didn't think, "Oh, I wish I was a lawyer before I tried it."

Eventually, you do go to Columbia. You referenced the fact that location was an important factor. I'm sure the reputation of the school was attractive as well. Is there anything else that made Columbia shine over other options?

No. I had always wanted to live in and experience New York City. Columbia being in Manhattan made a big difference to me.

That makes sense. You entered law school with a background in the hard sciences. You went to Caltech and worked at Oracle before going to Columbia. Looking back, do you think having that sort of

background in the hard sciences gave you any type of advantage or disadvantage in your law school courses? Or perhaps was it neutral?

It gives some advantages and disadvantages. The analytical thinking and all of that was the easy part for me. It was easy for me from an LSAT perspective. Breaking down legal issues and putting those puzzles together is similar to what you do as an engineer and as a scientist.

As far as what wasn't as helpful, I'm not as strong of a writer as others. That was somewhat of a weakness. Then, I wouldn't say legal skills take advantage of the scientist's skills. If they did more, I probably would have done better. I think I was a good law student, but I was definitely not at the top of the class. I was not on law review.

So I think it's a good background to have, but I honestly wouldn't say it was great. I'll just put it that way. That was my experience.

I came from a political science background. I've noticed that there are some pre-law students who choose these types of liberal arts majors (like political science or history) because they think they can get higher grades and get into a better law school. Correct me if I'm wrong, but I believe you would say that you shouldn't game the law school system like that. You should actually be interested in the major before you choose it.

Yeah, that's probably true. But also, I think a hard sciences background helped me get into a good law school because they probably want diversity and people with different backgrounds. I think it was helpful in getting in.

You were saying a few moments ago how law school for you wasn't as stressful or competitive because you weren't as concerned about getting the big firm job after graduation. If there's a law student or potential law student out there that wants to get the most out of their law school experience, what would you say?

I think my biggest tip for law students is to really try to take advantage of summers. Try to get different experiences and get the widest breadth of practice you can. Try different law firms or different practices.

I went into IP law (which was fine). But part of it was I thought I had to because of my engineering background. Of course, it turns out that wasn't true. But as a result, I never got a chance to experience corporate or other transactional types of practices that I might have enjoyed more.

So I would say the summers are the best time to try different practices or different kinds of law firms. I actually think that's more important. Law school is law school—regardless of whether you go to number one or number fifty. It's pretty much the same curriculum.

What did you do during your first and second summers?

I clerked at the exact same firms that I ended up working at. Lyon & Lyon was an IP firm. Again, I was just so pigeonholed and focused on becoming an IP lawyer. I had this notion that that was what I would do or could do or whatever. So that's what I did. But I sort of regret that. I would have maybe tried out other practice areas.

Right. So you did end up practicing after graduating from law school, even though you gave yourself a fifty percent chance of doing so. What caused you to ultimately embrace that path? Were you just looking at your general career options? Or was it something else?

I think I based that decision on the work. I wanted to see what the work experience was like and see if it was something that I would enjoy. I would say that it crossed the threshold. It was high enough that I said, "Okay, let's just go for this."

I mean, it wasn't like I love being a lawyer or anything like that. I liked it well enough. I probably liked it more than most lawyers like being a lawyer, but I wasn't going to die for it. It was good enough to say, "Okay, let's give this a try. Let's go forward."

And like you were saying, getting that experience during the summer is super valuable. Law students should think hard about that. I feel like the pipeline from law student to recruiter is very rare. I'm assuming you need a significant amount of work experience. You need a lot of connections within the legal industry. But let's say that there's some reader out there who is in law school and thinks that recruiting or headhunting is something that interests him or her.

They want to go directly into recruiting from law school. Is there any way to do that? If so, what can that reader do to better his or her chances?

Well, first of all, it's very rare. Recruiting is just not a career that people think about. It really isn't. People stumble into it accidentally. It's generally not a career that people want to do. So I think that's pretty unlikely.

You absolutely could go into it right out of law school. There's absolutely a path. But so much of recruiting is a network and experience. If you don't have any of that, you're really handicapped. I just think that's a really, really hard business to go into without those two important things. And networking is not something that you can just really learn. That's the other thing. It takes years—even decades—to develop. There's no substitute for that.

Right. Time is fighting against you on that front.

Yeah. Exactly.

So Lyon & Lyon was your first law firm. How did you select that firm over others? Was it the firm's IP practice that interested you, your summer experience there, or something else?

It was a little bit random. The main reason I went to Lyon & Lyon was that there were a few Caltech undergrads that worked at the firm. I knew them (or knew of them) from college. I kind of figured that way, I would have some familiar brethren. People with similar backgrounds were there. That was a big factor.

How did you initially hear of this firm?

This was before Google. Back then, you did research in Martindale-Hubbell and you would see the IP firms. I knew Lyon & Lyon was in Los Angeles, which is where I went to college. So I thought, "Okay, this is something that I should pursue." I think I just wrote to them. I don't think they recruited at Columbia. That's my recollection.

That's how I got my big firm job, too. I think writing a letter like that and directly reaching out to firms is an underrated strategy. It's natural to rely on the firms visiting your campus as your "investable universe," when, in fact, there are plenty of other outstanding firms out there that may not be visiting your school. From Lyon & Lyon, you went to work for a venture-backed company called Cyrano Sciences. You wanted to work with Robert H. Grubbs, who was a Nobel Laureate with Caltech roots. That's really interesting because getting a general counsel position is rare for any new lawyer. It's difficult. I think a lot of new lawyers want to do it, but it's hard to find those positions. Can you explain how you found this position at Cyrano Sciences?

Yeah, it is interesting. This opportunity stumbled onto my lap because it was a Caltech company that was spun out by three Caltech founders. They found me through a recruiter, but one of the founders was actually my professor at Caltech. Considering my background and everything, they thought it would be such a perfect fit. I thought so, too. I was like, "Well, I'm uniquely qualified to join a company that came out of Caltech." So I thought it would be fantastic. I thought the company would be super successful. I thought, "Well, I will do this and then retire." But like a lot of things in life, that's not what happened.

I learned a couple of things. First of all, the company was not successful. But the thing that I learned (which really surprised me) was that between being in-house and being in private practice, I enjoyed being in private practice a lot more. So I came back out to private practice (which I know is rare). But that's what I learned.

Can you talk about that more? What you specifically liked about private practice compared to being a GC?

What I really liked about private practice that I missed in-house was something that nobody told me. Everyone said, "Oh, you don't have to do billable hours and all of that." But actually, I was like, "Whatever. That's not a big deal to me."

There were two things that I really missed about being in private practice. First was the variety. When you're in private practice, you get to work with a ton of different companies in a ton of different industries.

You get to work with different-sized companies. You get to work with general counsels and founders. By working at a company, I missed the variety of both industry and the client. At a company, there is just one (main) business.

Then, the other thing was just the autonomy. When you're working at a company, you have a boss. No matter how great the boss may be, he or she is the boss. You're still accountable to them and doing what they tell you to do. Whereas in private practice, you get to decide what projects or clients you want to work on. I missed the autonomy and the variety. That is one of the reasons I went back to private practice.

Interesting. So if there are readers that read that and still want to become GCs at startups, is there anything that they can do to increase their odds? I'm specifically talking about readers just graduating from law school or readers who are in the earlier years of their legal careers.

Well, I think talking to recruiters is a good idea. I also think it's important to ask themselves that question about why they want to leave the law firm. That's not something that a lot of people consider.

I give this advice a lot. A lot of lawyers think they want to go in-house. Then, I start asking these questions like, "Are you really fit for in-house, or are you really fit for a law firm?"

I think the people that do well with an in-house position really love the technology and/or business and the company. That's obviously very important. The other thing about being in-house is that you have to really enjoy (or not mind) living with your decision. Because when you're in-house and you have a problem, you're the one that has to solve it. You're the one that lives with it.

At a law firm, you give this advice. You say, "You can do A or B." The company then decides. That's another thing that I think a lot of people don't realize when they move in-house. They have to be prepared to really want that or enjoy that. I think that's important.

So for those law students or lawyers, it's about looking inward. They should see what their priorities are and, if they are interested, find a company that suits them well. This means being at least interested in the product or service and those sorts of things.

Exactly.

You ended up going back to private practice. You've also had plenty of leadership positions at several large commercial law firms. When you're looking back at those experiences and making those incremental decisions to work at different law firms, what factors were important in your mind? There may be some readers that hear your story and think, "Oh, I'm thinking that I actually want to stay in private practice. However, I may want to go to another firm, but I don't know what I should be looking for when making a lateral move." Do you have any insights on that?

I give this advice every day now. I think it is about finding a firm where your practice can really explode. One of the things I like to say is "Teach a person how to light a fire and they'll be warm for a day. Set a person on fire and they are warm for life."

So it's very important to find a place where your practice can really, really grow. Otherwise, you're not going to be happy. That's the other thing. What's a fantastic fit for person A could be terrible for person B. It's really important to be able to evaluate that.

Now, that doesn't necessarily mean moving. It could be that you already have these growth opportunities at your firm. You may be in the best possible situation. One of the things I like to pride myself on as a recruiter is to often tell people, "Look, I think you're really in a good place right now. Even though it's against my economic interests to say it, I do. "

I think it's important to have conversations and understand what other firms offer. But it may very well be that someone is already at the right place.

How do you get a sense of that before making the transition? You can read all of the Glassdoor reviews that you want. You can maybe even speak with associates or partners. But until you actually get there, I can imagine it's difficult to determine the firm's culture, whether there are real mentorship opportunities, and similar attributes. Do you have any tips or hacks that readers can leverage before they make the switch?

It is a good point. You can do all of the diligence you want, but until you get to a new place, it's really hard to tell. I think the best thing is if you know people that work there. That's really the best way because they'll kind of give you the inside scoop. They'll tell you the warts. Every place has warts. Probably the best way to do it is to find someone you personally know or through another personal connection who can honestly tell you about the firm. You'll want to hear what it's like being at the firm, what the firm's culture is like, and what the practices are like. But you're right that reading a review about a firm isn't always going to be helpful.

Yeah, it's tough. Sometimes you just have to take a leap of faith.

Yeah. Part of it is that, too.

You have worked with many partners and associates during your legal career. What do you think makes a good partner or associate? Along with this, what mistakes do associates or partners make when they begin their new roles?

I think the most important thing that people must realize about being a successful partner or associate (or really, a lawyer) is to embrace the service mentality. That's really the thing. At the end of the day, a lawyer is a service provider to clients. A lot of people don't understand what a service provider mentality is.

A very successful lawyer that I interviewed said that he learned this from when he was a waiter before law school. Because when you're a waiter, you have to manage up and manage down. You have to be a service provider. That's very important to understand. I think the most successful lawyers are ones that really understand the service provider mentality.

I would agree. Also, it sounds like managing expectations is a huge factor. It's part of being a service provider.

Absolutely.

You spoke with *Above the Law* several years ago. In that interview, you mentioned the importance of mentorship. I'd agree that it is crucial when evaluating any job or career opportunity. Many Big

Law firms offer specific mentorship programs, which can be useful. What do you think about mentorship programs or finding a mentor in a general sense?

Well, mentorship is super important. I'm a big fan of that. My perspective is that there are two really important things on how to identify a mentor. Someone who is a really good mentor is somebody who takes a vested interest in the success of your career. It's hard to find.

I've been lucky to have a couple of mentors in my life. They were Craig Johnson of Venture Law Group and Jim Gilliland, who was the chairman of Townsend. Both, unfortunately, passed away. It's very sad. But both of them took a serious vested interest in my career. Those are the mentors that you want.

The second point is, "Well, how do I identify who is going to do that?" Here's my answer to that. The best mentors are the ones who themselves had a great mentor. The only way to become a great mentor is to have been the recipient of a mentor. Not only do you understand how to be a mentor, but you understand the benefits of having received great mentorship. Then, you are able to give back.

For example, both my great mentors talked about the great mentors that *they* had in their careers. They explained how they benefited from those mentors. You know that they are much more likely to be great mentors. A person who has never had a great mentor is probably not going to be a great mentor. That's my experience.

I give this advice to law students and associates. Those are the two criteria and they are important.

Those are great points. You practiced for several decades, right?

Yeah, it was two and a half decades.

Then, you made this transition to Major, Lindsey & Africa. You have written two great LinkedIn posts describing your thinking behind that.[3] One of the many interesting things you said was that your decision was the perfect culmination of your background, knowl-

---

3   You can find both posts on Richard's LinkedIn page (https://www.linkedin.com/in/richardhsu/).

edge, experience, interest, and relationships. There were five key elements. Can you describe how you discovered their importance and how they helped you navigate this big career move?

Well, it was actually through somebody that I knew very well. A close friend helped me make that discovery. What happened was that through some random connections, I had a conversation with somebody at Major, Lindsey & Africa about becoming a recruiter. I remember walking into that conversation thinking, "Am I really going to go from being a law firm partner to a recruiter?" I thought there was like a five percent chance of that being the case.

I went to the meeting and spent three hours talking to this person at MLA about the job. I remember describing this experience to somebody who knows me personally. I said, "I had this meeting. It wasn't a non-starter, but I don't see myself leaving a law firm partnership to become a recruiter." This person who knew me really well said, "Oh my gosh, you would be perfect for that job."

It's interesting because people who knew me really well were the ones who basically said, "Well, that's perfect. You love building relationships. You have this blog (at the time I had a blog). You have the interview podcast thing going.[4] You love meeting people. This is so you." A lot of times, you yourself don't even realize that. You don't really know, but when somebody else tells you, it's different.

I mean, there were still other things that finally helped me make the leap. But those conversations with people who knew me well made the initial step from something like a virtual impossibility to something that was much more realistic.

Yeah. That's so interesting. You can just imagine if you didn't bring up this opportunity to your friend. Things may have been very different.

Totally.

---

4 Richard started a blog called HsuTube and a podcast called Hsu Untied. Richard started Hsu Untied to interview individuals in the legal community. But as the show grew, Richard started to interview fascinating individuals outside of the law. Some of those individuals included Tony Robbins, Angela Duckworth, Steve Wozniak, and even Big Bird.

After you spoke with this friend, how confident were you in making the change? While the conversation with this friend helped you get to that point, it was solely up to you to make that change.

So my current partner at MLA is Keith Wetmore. He was the former chairman of Morrison & Foerster and somebody that I've known for many, many years. He's been sort of an informal mentor to me. I've talked with him in the past about leadership because he had been Chair of his firm.

I was seeking his career advice about a few different things—including this potential career possibility. He basically said, "Well, it's funny that you should mention that. That's actually something that I've been thinking about doing after I retire from Morrison & Foerster. He had been their Chairman and he had been there for thirty-five years. He's about ten years older than I am. Basically, we sort of talked each other into doing it. We were like, "Why don't we go do this together?" And that was we did.

Would I have done it alone? It's hard to say what I would have done. But definitely having someone like Keith (who I really enjoy and respect) made the decision easier. It has been a great partnership. We have worked together now for three years. It has been fantastic.

Were there any financial or non-financial roadblocks that perhaps gave you pause before making the transition?

I think for me, two things allowed me to make the transition. One was that my kids were much further along with their college degrees. So a lot of my big expenses had gone down. Also, I just have never had a very lavish lifestyle. I still live in the same exact house that I had as a third-year associate. That really gave me more flexibility.

But the other thing that was interesting is that I remember how I made my final decision. The reason why I ended up making the change is that I asked myself, "If in ten years I didn't do it, would I regret it?" It was the first job where I felt that I might regret not taking the opportunity. That's actually the ultimate reason why I pursued it.

Like I was saying at the beginning of our conversation, you are one of the few people in this book that had a later transition. Others made the switch out of the legal field when they were junior associates or younger attorneys. First, do you think there are any advantages or

disadvantages of making the transition later? Second, are there any best practices that older attorneys should consider?

That's a good question. Of course, everybody is different as to when it would be the right time to transition. But I think it's also good to do it at a point where you feel like you got everything out of being a lawyer that you wanted.

I certainly felt that way. I didn't feel like I really had another rung to reach. I had already been a partner at a major firm. I had already been in law firm management. I had been a practice group leader. I had been the managing partner for an entire firm. I had done the merger of two firms. So I didn't feel like there was anything I needed to still accomplish as a lawyer or wanted to still do as a lawyer. Then, it felt like making the transition made sense.

You've been at MLA for how many years now?

Almost four years.

What do you think is the most rewarding part of working there? Along with this, are there certain rewards that you didn't get or couldn't find in legal practice?

Well, helping people find new jobs is really fulfilling. By the very nature of being a recruiter, you do tend to talk to unhappy lawyers. They are the ones that want to talk to you. So I probably hear more than my fair share of unhappy lawyers or lawyers who are struggling in their practices. Helping them find a better place to help them unlock their careers is very rewarding. It sounds kind of cliché, but it's actually true. I would say that's probably the most fulfilling thing. It's probably something I didn't really expect. I always thought it would be a very fun job because of the nature of what we're doing, but I didn't realize how fulfilling it would be.

Were there any growing pains within the first few months or years after making the switch?

For sure. It's a steep learning curve. You have to really be used to and okay with rejection. There are a lot of "nos" to this job. You have to understand that. I think that's a very big factor. It's also a business that is hard to break into. There are two things you discover. One is that no matter how big you think your network is, when you go into something like this, you realize it's much smaller than you initially realized. The world is much bigger. What you realize is the people that you don't know are a much bigger number than the people you do know. It's kind of daunting to realize that.

The second thing is when you're much further along in the profession, many lawyers already know or work with a recruiter. It's kind of like a mortgage broker. When you talk to somebody who has owned three houses, they probably know a mortgage broker. It's very unlikely that they don't know any brokers. So you're also having to basically steal a relationship that they've already had with someone else, which is also hard. For many reasons, those are challenging things.

Do you think you had any particular edges coming from your legal background?

I'm not sure that I had an advantage coming in with a legal background. But what served me well (and I didn't realize it at the time) was that I had already been at a number of firms. I probably knew more lawyers than someone who had been at one firm.

Secondly, I was always kind of a natural networker. I always took the time to get to know other lawyers (even at other firms). A lot of lawyers network with clients and may think there is little value in networking with other lawyers. I never felt that way. I've always enjoyed talking with other lawyers. That kind of led me to my podcast. I think that served me well.

Speaking of networking, there are some lawyers that just hate the idea of networking. As a natural networker, do you have any tips or advice for those lawyers?

The reason I'm a great networker is not so much that I'm a great networker per se. The thing is I'm really fascinated with people. I'm more interested in hearing their stories and their personas. That's why I launched the podcast. Because I have such a natural interest in people, networking is not hard for me. I can just imagine that if you're not that interested in people, it can become very painful or tedious.

So I think trying to tell somebody who's not naturally interested in people to "Go be a networker" is really hard. It's like telling somebody who doesn't like to jog to go run ten miles a day. But for me, I've never even really thought about it as networking. I've thought about it as following my interests. I never felt like it was a job or tedious because I just really enjoyed doing it.

It really sounds like those lawyers should at least try to follow their curiosities or interests. By doing so, the "networking" will happen from there.

Yeah. Exactly.

Let's say there's a lawyer reading this book who wants to make the switch into recruiting or headhunting. Is there anything that they should do or avoid when making that transition?

Having now met a lot more recruiters, I think a lot of people have a sense of whether they would like it or not. If you've been a lawyer for a while, you've probably had elements of recruitment. Trying to find clients is, to some extent, like recruiting. You can kind of isolate elements of being in law practice. If you like doing those things, then you probably will like recruiting. If you didn't, then you're probably not going to like recruiting.

The best example is if you did any recruiting as a lawyer. I certainly did it as a lawyer and I really enjoyed it. My partner Keith Wetmore recruited hundreds of lawyers during his career at Morrison & Foerster and he loved it. He knew that he would probably like it. I had a pretty good sense, too.

There are other elements (for example, whether you enjoy getting new business). If that's something you really enjoy, you'll probably like recruiting because recruiting is about getting new business and new connections. This is kind of a negative, but it also works better if you didn't love being a lawyer. That was me. I enjoyed it and had a successful career. I think I was pretty good at it. But I never really loved practicing law.

I think that's kind of important. I think people who really love the practice of law are not going to turn to recruiting since recruiting is not like being a lawyer. There's no question about it. The things you get to do as a recruiter are talk about being a lawyer and talk with lawyers all the time. You are not a lawyer. So if the aspect of being a lawyer is something you really love, then it's probably not a good idea.

I'm sure you would recommend that part of that judgment is speaking with friends. Like you did when speaking with your friend, an outside source can help you identify what you are good at or what you are naturally inclined to do. Are there any prerequisites to taking on a recruiting role? For instance, things like law firm leadership positions? When can, say, a mid-level associate start considering the switch?

Once you start to be a mid-level associate, you can certainly start to pursue it. A lot of people have successfully done it and have built an entire career as a legal recruiter. I think there is a trade-off. The longer you wait, the bigger your network is. However, that also delays your start in terms of being a recruiter.

Is there an optimal point? Probably. I don't know what that is. But definitely, at the very beginning, you want to get some legal experience, some practice being a lawyer, and build up your network.

That makes sense. At MLA, you help attorneys make transitions. I'm sure you have noticed patterns—both in your clients' thoughts and the decisions that they make. I'm also assuming this includes both good decisions and bad decisions. Do you have any tips or advice on lawyers making any type of transition? Perhaps things they should think about or things they should do?

Well, whenever I meet with a new lawyer who says that they're unhappy about their firm or career, I try to go through a lot of the questions that are similar to the ones you're asking me. For example, how they became a lawyer. We go back to square one and what they enjoy (and they don't enjoy) about being a lawyer. That's particularly helpful if they want to go in-house. A lot of times people think they want to go in-house, but they may not be well-suited for it.

I think those are some questions that you need to ask if you want to take a leap. You have to look at the kinds of things that you enjoy or do not enjoy about being a lawyer. Then, see if you could actually replicate those elsewhere.

A lot of times, people who become lawyers go to law school for a very specific reason. That's probably why it's more well-suited for them than they think. For example, lawyers are notoriously known to be risk-averse. You hear this all the time. I think that is largely true. They go to law school, by and large, because they are risk-averse. They are looking for a very specific career. When they become a lawyer, they think they want to go into business and they don't realize how much riskier business is than being a lawyer. They probably went to law school to begin with because they didn't like taking those sorts of risks.

Yes, it's an interesting transition. If you leave legal practice to become an entrepreneur, for instance, you are taking on risk every day. Ideally, it's calculated and managed risk, but there is much more risk than working at a firm. So in your later career, you created a podcast interview series called Hsu Untied. You created a blog called HsuTube. What caused you to start both of these things and what rewards did you get from starting them?

Well, I started the podcast because my childhood dream was to be like Charlie Rose or Terry Gross. I always thought that would be a great job because I could interview people every single day. One of the beauties of the internet and technology is that anybody can do that. You don't have to get hired to do that job.

So when I started the podcast, I literally just did it by interviewing friends and lawyers that talked about interesting topics. When I started, I remember thinking that if I could interview five or ten people, I would be excited. And then the thing just organically took off.

It really was a labor of love. Because it was my own show and I didn't do any advertising, I only interviewed people that I wanted. I was under no pressure with reaching a certain number or having to reach a certain sized audience. In fact, my criteria for picking people and doing the interviews were those who I thought I would enjoy interviewing. If the only person listening to the interview was the interviewee and their mother, it was totally fine with me. It didn't bother me. I deliberately don't track any statistics because I don't want that to be the driver of the interviews. So if there is somebody that I wanted to interview, that's all that matters.

And you have had some well-known guests on your show, so congratulations.

Oh, thanks.

Like you say, you did it mostly for intrinsic personal reasons. But I also think creating a podcast, blog, or YouTube channel can be a career accelerant. Would you recommend a similar thing for lawyers? Let's say that a lawyer has a certain niche or specialty practice. Should they create content like a podcast, YouTube channel, or something else?

I always encourage people to do them—as long as they are doing them for the right reason. The reason is that they intrinsically enjoy doing it. Because otherwise, it is just a chore.

If you are doing it for the right reason, though, you should absolutely pursue it. It really allows you to meet other people and gives you an opportunity to talk about interesting things. Interviews in the podcast format are so easy to do. It costs zero dollars and the technology is all there. It doesn't cost anything to do any of this stuff. It allows you to really talk to people and get more perspective in some expertise that you want to learn. There's nothing better than doing a podcast and learning from others.

Definitely. It's also about staying consistent and finding interesting guests. It just builds on itself like that.

For me, it was great because I learned a lot about rejection. It was a natural fit with recruiting. People say no and that's just the way it is.

And it's a great way to pitch yourself.

Exactly. Pitching yourself and hearing people say no. That was a good precursor to being a recruiter. I just didn't know it at the time.

Do you have any general advice for law students or lawyers that may not be exactly satisfied with their careers, but feel afraid of making a transition? They may feel anxious and inertia may be keeping them

stuck in a job they don't necessarily like. Is there anything you would say to guide them on the next step of their career journey?

A lot of it depends on how unhappy they are. A lot of times, their unhappiness is not as bad or a lot worse than they think. They don't realize what else is out there.

But I think there is something important to do. As you are working in your legal job, really take note of what you enjoy and don't enjoy about it. To find something that makes you happy is to find a job that has more of those elements than not. But if you don't really know what it is you enjoy about being a lawyer, then it's hard to find another career.

For example, some people really enjoy business development. Some people really enjoy talking to clients. Some people really enjoy the drafting part. I would say really take stock in your current career on what it is you enjoy and don't enjoy. It may turn out that being a lawyer is the best way to have those elements. That's what I've told a lot of people. It may be that there is another job that has more of the elements you enjoy. But that's the part that you need to figure out.

So you need to set aside some time where you can sit down and write down what you enjoy and don't enjoy. From there, you'll have a better idea of what you need to do.

Yep.

CHAPTER 9

Diahann Billings-Burford

Nonprofit CEO

Life is full of difficult decisions, but our backgrounds and experiences influence the way that we handle those decisions. In some instances, we rely on emotion and gut feelings. In others, we create pro-con lists or conduct cost-benefit analyses. And then there are some decisions that are galvanized from the advice and wisdom of a mentor or close friend.

In an uncertain world with countless variables, we try to make the best decisions with the information that we have. As we weigh that data and anticipate the future, we can drastically improve our decision-making skills by combining mental models and personal experiences.

Mental models, as you may already know, are frameworks that help us understand the world.[1] Charlie Munger, the vice-chairman of Berkshire Hathaway, famously espoused how a "latticework of models" can help us become better thinkers and decision-makers. Mental models help us get out of our own heads and adopt different perspectives. You can think of them as individual tools in an ever-expanding toolkit. When you encounter a difficult problem or decision, you can pull out one (or several) mental models to help you chart the best possible course forward.

Jeff Bezos, the founder of Amazon, famously defined a mental model that I particularly like. He calls it the "regret minimization framework." As he described in an interview, Bezos thought about leaving his safe and secure job at D.E. Shaw to start Amazon. It was certainly a risk for him. While internet usage was growing at around 2,300 percent per year, leaving a well-respected hedge fund to start an internet company was much rarer compared to today. As he contemplated his decision, Bezos transported himself into the future. He pictured himself as a much older

---

1   If you'd like to view a list of one hundred mental models, check out Shane Parrish's post on the *Farnam Street* blog. You can find it here: https://fs.blog/mental-models/.

man looking back at his life. He knew he wanted to minimize—or eliminate—any regrets from his life. From the perspective of his eighty-year-old self, he looked at the decision to leave D.E. Shaw and asked himself, "Will I regret not doing this?" Everyone knows how Bezos answered this question.

The regret minimization framework can be a fantastic mental model when making difficult decisions. It helps us reach the core of what we *truly* want to do. It may be a more emotionally based mental model than others, but its power comes from understanding that emotions *are* a factor when making career-altering decisions.

Diahann Billings-Burford is the CEO of Ross Initiative in Sports for Equality (RISE), a nonprofit that "empowers the sports community to eliminate racial discrimination, champion social justice, and improve race relations." At RISE, Diahann and her colleagues use sports as a way to educate, empower, and engage on important social issues. Before working at RISE, Diahann had extensive experience in service-based or nonprofit roles, including at organizations like Time Warner, NYC Service, City Year New York, Achievement First, and Prep for Prep.

Prior to all of that, however, Diahann was an associate at Simpson Thacher & Bartlett. A practicing litigator for around two years, she decided to leave Big Law and work full-time in the nonprofit space. In part, the move was caused by the unexpected death of her mother, but she arguably relied on the regret minimization framework to make the final decision and start a new chapter in her life. She asked herself the following question: "If I only had fifty-eight years of life on this planet, would I have accomplished what I wanted to have accomplished?" She wanted that answer to be "yes."

Like Diahann, we can use mental models—like the regret minimization framework—to make major decisions in our personal and professional lives. Looking at these decisions from different perspectives can make the right choice seem completely obvious. It just emerges, and with that new clarity, you can go forth and live the life you truly want to live.

* * *

Diahann, I'd like to start by asking you how you started thinking about law school. Was it something that sounded interesting when you were younger? Or did that interest grow when you were older?

For me, it was definitely as a child. Sometimes when I look back now, I'm not sure I would define my family as poor. But at best, we were lower middle class.

I was great at school. I remember being young and in church where I gave speeches and used big words. So law school was kind of a social expectation, right? Like, "Oh, she is going to be a doctor or a lawyer." It was clear early on that I was scared of blood, so I wasn't going to be a doctor.

I think some of my attraction to the law came from that. It came from this socioeconomic expectation mixed with my academic abilities.

So it was mostly your speaking and academic abilities that led you to more of an academic route as opposed to, say, something more entrepreneurial?

Absolutely. It's interesting because my dad was an entrepreneur. My abilities led me the school way and the law way. Then, I will say that as I got older (by older, I mean by high school and college), it became clearer that I was always aware of the legal underpinnings of the things I cared about.

How so?

I went through a program called Prep For Prep. This meant that I was identified fairly young and put into independent schools. Between friends from my neighborhood and my family, it became very obvious how different my educational experience was. I began to see the impact of that. I started realizing how much educational equity was rooted in the law. In fact, one of the reasons I practiced at Simpson Thacher & Bartlett was because of its pro bono work. One of the partners there (Joe Wayland) was the counsel for the Campaign for Fiscal Equity. So even though the law started as this kind of societal expectation or community expectation, once I started even figuring out what I cared about, I was aware of the legal implications in that space.

Unfortunately, a lot of my family was impacted by drug addiction and the criminal justice system. I joke that I was sitting in a Civil Procedure course at Columbia Law School and had this moment of, "Oh, there's a procedure that isn't for criminal law." Because quite honestly, up until law school, most of my interaction with the law was criminal. Even though I understood that the law was connected to justice and social issues, my interaction was on the criminal side. So there definitely was this external expectation. But there came a time where I just realized that the law was attached to so much of what I cared about.

Like you were saying, it was always in the background. I believed you studied psychology in college, yet law school was still on your mind.

Yes.

Looking at your biography, you took a significant break from college to law school.

Yes, I took five years.

What changed that prompted you to actually go to law school?

Quite honestly, I got some energy back. I'm not sure it's related, but I always tell the story. I got to Yale and my mom was dropping me off freshman year. I said, "Mommy, I heard about this thing called a gap year. I'm tired." Having gone through Prep for Prep at ten years old and done the independent school thing, I was tired by the time I got to undergrad.

Let me tell you something: my mother looked at me and said, "Diahann, I'm going to be back up here in May 1994 and I need to hear your name." So there was no gap year. That wasn't happening. But I was tired of school when I graduated from Yale. I loved Yale, but I was exhausted. So my break was mostly about, "I cannot read another book, write another paper, or take another test. I just need a minute."

I also felt like I still had some deciding to do. One of the reasons I'm so excited about your book is that I do think something like this would have been helpful. I knew I was really committed to education. I did not know what I wanted the next step in my career to be, but I knew school would cost money and my mom had been footing the bill for quite a long time. Working wouldn't. Working would allow me to give as opposed to pulling. So I took a break because of that.

Besides law school, what other options were you considering at that time?

I thought about law school and different types of grad school. It's interesting. I majored in psychology because I did think about getting a degree in organizational psychology. I love that type of work and I feel like I get to engage with that when leading organizations. But I was considering different types of work. It was like, "Am I going to go to Prep for Prep or another community-based organization? Am I going to teach in a school?" At Yale, I did everything to be certified to be a secondary school teacher. So it was going to be teaching or going to a community organization and working in the ed space.

From my experience in law school (and I'm sure from yours as well), you've seen law students that have gone directly from college to law school. You clearly took a more significant gap.[2] If a prospective law student is thinking about law school right after college, would you recommend some sort of gap?

Absolutely. I don't like to be pessimistic because I think you can get to anywhere from anywhere. But I think I would always suggest that people take time if they can. In retrospect, I didn't make the decision because I was so wise. It is easier to transition out of the law if you have done something before. It just is. It doesn't mean you have to have done something before. It doesn't mean there's not another way. But it's easier.

I also think it means that you approach law school differently. I felt like I loved law school. One of the reasons I picked Columbia is that there was a significant percentage of older students there. When I walked on campus, I didn't feel old—even though I was out for five years. I had plenty of classmates older than me. Some had kids. It was diverse in that way and I appreciated it.

_____

2   Diahann graduated from Yale in 1994 and started at Columbia Law School in 1999.

That's really interesting. It's easy for prospective law students to focus on the prestige of a targeted law school. They want to get into the highest-ranked school. Columbia is obviously a great law school, but prospective applicants that are overwhelmingly focusing on prestige should consider these other factors.

Absolutely. I hear that other schools have that as well. But I really liked that at Columbia.

Can you talk about your time there? What did you enjoy? And to go one step further, for law students that are reading this book, what advice would you give them to not only succeed in law school, but to have a less stressful time?

So I loved law school. I liked school. It was good for me because, again, I had been off for five years. By then, I'm no longer tired. I'm ready to go back to school. It fed that desire I had.

I would say one of the most difficult things I did (and I think most law schools acknowledge this) is legal writing. But I think legal writing has been invaluable throughout my career. I think the mindset and the way that some law schools teach you to think is transferable to every setting. So I jokingly say, "I think I IRAC everything."[3] Even when we're talking about what's going on in the organization, I'm like, "What's the issue? What rule do I apply? How do I apply it? What's the conclusion?" It's not always that clean but it's a way of thinking that I've transferred, whether I'm in government or the private sector.

I enjoy the issues. I enjoy being emotionally attached to things. I think I'm mission-driven, but I also need to be very thoughtful and look at different perspectives before I take a stance. To me, that is the best part of law school. It's being analytical and saying, "Okay, here's where I stand, and here's why I stand here."

So I enjoyed law school. It also gave me a diversity of subjects. Like, Civil Procedure was great for me.

---

3   IRAC stands for "issue, rule, application, and conclusion." It is a way of organizing your thoughts and structuring a legal argument in a memo or brief. In law school, you may learn a derivation of IRAC, which includes CREAC or CRAC. While the details slightly vary, the overall objective is similar.

It wasn't my favorite.

Yeah, I can imagine that. I got to study human rights law with Louis Henkin.[4] One day, Professor Henkin was saying something and one of the students said, "Well, we don't really know what the special commission at the UN intended on this particular issue." Professor Henkin could say, "Yes, we do." The law student said, "How do we know?" He's like, "Because I was the chair." So it was great to study human rights. It is interesting to see what's in the news now. I didn't think as much of it then, but I chose to study a bit of Native law.

I think people sometimes see law school as vocational. While it is, there is an opportunity to almost have this liberal arts approach to law school.

Right. The 2Ls and 3Ls reading this book may not know which courses to take. So you're saying that they should follow their passions or interests to some extent. Don't exclusively focus on the vocational side of it.

Yes, you should follow your passion. But I did both. I think most law schools allow you to do both. I took negotiations. I think it has been great for me. Schools don't require it, but they really should. All students should have to do clinics and clinical work.

I was in another clinic focusing on prisoners' rights. Again, I was always interested in social justice. So there, I was able to marry an interest in family law. What we were seeing in New York State was this confluence of Rockefeller Law[5] and family law changes. You had parents' parental rights being terminated only because they've been sentenced to so many years in jail. So it was about going into the prisons and teaching incarcerated folks about those laws, what they could do, and what their options were.

---

4   As described by Columbia Law School, Louis Henkin is a pioneer in the study of human rights law. Among other things, Professor Henkin helped many foreign governments incorporate human rights principles and laws in their constitutions.

5   Spearheaded by New York Governor Nelson Rockefeller, Rockefeller Laws were stricter sentencing guidelines for individuals convicted of drug crimes, including the possession and sale of small amounts of drugs.

It was great. I enjoyed it. I would recommend that for students. Get some practical skills. Get out there. It's your chance to get out there, be scared, and be nervous. But also, it's cool, right? Develop your mind. Don't forget that.

Right. As far as clinics, I joined one as well. You really get the best of both worlds. You're able to obtain that practical experience. Even though you may feel like you're nervous and don't know what you're doing, you have world-class people behind you.

Right. You have a professor that has done this seventeen thousand times.

Yes, you're not going to get into that much trouble.

And they are going to catch it before you do it exactly wrong before a judge.

You try your best and you go from there. So during your 2L and 3L years, I believe you're thinking of a position at a commercial law firm. You ended up at Simpson Thacher & Bartlett. Can you talk about why you chose that route, considering your interest in public service?

Yep. I think this will speak to a lot of people. I'm very driven but sometimes, life can just take the starch out of your wings.

When I was going through law school, the easiest route (if you had decent grades) was to go to corporate law. I remember one day, you go into the hotel and all the firms have their different suites. You go in, you interview, and people call you back. That was the easiest route.

The truth of the matter is that up until 2L year, I was still wavering. Did I want to go into public interest or did I want to go into the private sector? After my 1L year, I did an internship at the U.S. Attorney's Office in the Southern District of New York. I liked it but realized that I wasn't meant to be a prosecutor.

Oh, really?

Oh my gosh, yeah. The most troubling moment was when I helped on a really important case. I got to actually interact with Mary Jo White[6] and listen to Janet Reno[7] on conference calls. It was amazing. There was a man who was considered responsible for basically building the Crips in the Bronx. He was using a lot of young people to commit murder. Janet Reno had taken a pretty hard line. She was pro-death penalty if it involved children. Mary Jo White did not like that. Mary Jo consistently thought it wasn't the way to go. It was interesting just to be an intern and to be there.

But even with him: when it came time for the sentencing, I remember (I think it was Judge Shira Scheindlin) reading his sentence. The sentence in the federal courts is given in months. So you had that moment of people calculating how many years his sentence was. I thought he got exactly what he deserved. And even with him, I was like, "I cannot do this. My job cannot be to incarcerate people every day." It's not to say it shouldn't happen. There are people like him who need to be incarcerated. It was great to see the interaction. Janet Reno was on the conference call and was like, "Listen. I'm telling you right now. If this man does not agree to this deal, we're seeking the death penalty. I'm finished talking about it." She and Mary Jo White had an excellent relationship (at least from what I could see). But she was done.

It was also great to see Mary Jo White and the Assistant U.S. Attorney (who was actually the lead on the case) sit down with him and say, "Listen, this is it. This is our final offer or we go to trial. And we are here to tell you that our boss is clear: you are going to die. So what do you want to do?" I was like, "Okay, I don't know if I want to do this."

That's great you discovered it that summer.

Sorry about the long-winded answer. That was after 1L year. 2L year, I was still contemplating public interest or private law. My mom suddenly passed at the beginning of my third year of law school. I was also pregnant with my daughter. It was everything I could do to get up, get to class,

---

6   Mary Jo White has held a variety of major positions in the U.S. government, including the U.S. Attorney for the Southern District of New York and the chair of the SEC.

7   Reno was most famously U.S. Attorney General under President Bill Clinton.

and get the grades that I wanted to get. It was all I could do, along with preparing for the bar exam. It was a lot.

But to get the right public interest job coming out of Columbia, I would have had to do a lot more compared to getting a firm that I felt great about. I felt great with Simpson. I was like, "I don't have any more mental energy or emotional energy to spend on this thing. I'm going to go with the firm I feel is right."

And at that time, were you thinking that you would stay there for a long time? Perhaps become a partner?

I don't know if I thought I would become a partner. Again, I really liked Simpson because the partners were doing great things. There were two to three women partners that I thought were amazing. They were so honest with me. Remember that I'm interviewing with one child. When I was interviewing for my second year, I didn't know that I was expecting my second one. But I found the partners there were so great. I'm not sure I went in thinking I would be a partner, but I certainly thought, "I like the partners here."

I went in thinking, "This is where I'm going to work." I remember talking to a guy who went in with a three-year plan. He knew he was leaving. He was paying down bills and he even had a spreadsheet. I didn't go in like that. But when the fog of grief really began to lift for me, I remember looking around thinking, "There are people that are really happy to be here. Now that I'm awake, I don't belong here." But again, I didn't have the energy to spend on it to even have that realization before.

That's not the only instance I have heard of someone having a very specific date where they would be leaving their firm.

Yeah, there are some people that go in like that. I didn't have that. I just thought I was going to work.

Were you a litigator?

Yes.

Were there any especially interesting trials or cases that you worked on?

You know, it was so interesting. It was this case that had actually finished. I felt like I kept getting plum assignments and I loved it. I got to work at Simpson and the firm had one of the first African-American partners. His name was Conrad Harper.[8] Conrad was technically retiring, but State Farm had lost a fairly big case at the U.S. Supreme Court. The way we understood it is State Farm stayed with Simpson to make sure that everything that they needed to do to respond to the decision was in order. They really wanted Conrad to lead in that and I got to work with him on that case. Other than that, no. One of the drawbacks of big firm life—especially on the litigation side—is that there is a lot of uninteresting work.

Did you ever appear in court?

I did not. But I didn't stay long enough.

It's easy for prospective law students (or even current law students) to have this vision of becoming a litigator at a big firm. The vision is about making court appearances and completing depositions. The reality is that this often occurs later in their careers.

Yeah, it's like three or four years. I did it all through the pro bono side. The other thing I would say is Simpson had (and I'm sure there still is) a great pro bono practice. I actually was able to continue some of the family law-type work I had begun at Columbia.

I was going to ask you a little bit later, but perhaps it's appropriate now. Let's say an attorney is reading this book and they work at a big firm. They may not necessarily want to leave right now, but they may want more impactful work. What insights or advice would you offer?

---

8   Along with being a former partner at Simpson, Conrad Harper was a former president of the New York City Bar Association.

Well, especially at big firms, I don't think we see ourselves as good court-room lawyers. But I actually think most people at big firms are incredibly intelligent. They know the law.

There are literally thousands of families impacted by the inability to get good counsel. And I mean *impacted*. People could lose years of their lives in jail because they don't have a decent lawyer. They couldn't afford a decent lawyer. So for attorneys at firms: even if you don't feel super great about your courtroom abilities, your ability to understand the process, get answers that you don't know how to get, and your ability to be tenacious could literally make the difference in someone's life or a whole family's lives.

On the family law side, all of my clients were women. Some of them had been formerly incarcerated. Many had not, but they may have been victims of domestic violence. They were trying to get out of visitation agreements and any number of things. I feel like most people coming out of law school can figure out how to get through a problem.

Exactly. We learn how to learn.

Right. Help them figure out how to get through the problem. You don't need to know it going in. You just need to apply the fact that you can figure it out.

I'm just thinking back to my firm. From my recollection, there were many pro bono projects that dealt with both domestic and inter-national issues. For instance, I was working on a project that was helping Iraqi legislators work through some issues of international law. It was a great experience. Do you think people should try to focus more on what's happening in their communities or the U.S. as a whole?

No, I think it goes to passion. It's the same as the way I felt about my courses in law school. I think it's about passion and skill-building. So again, even if you're not exactly sure what you want to do, where can you build the relevant skills? If you are going to have a job that requires you to engage in public speaking (like mine), do your pro bono work in a place that is going to force you to get in front of a judge. Do work in a place that will force you to speak. Build some skills. But also do what you're passionate about.

I think it's a mix of both. There are some people coming out of law school who are really interested in are international issues. Then, your route would have been the smarter way to go.

A substantial part of this book is about moving from legal practice into non-legal roles, so I'd like to speak about that for a bit. You alluded to it earlier that part of the reason you took this position at Simpson was because of things occurring in your personal life. Once the grief wasn't as intense as it was, you kind of came to the realization that you may want to move on. Can you speak about that more? Specifically, how did you look at that decision before choosing to leave your firm?

It was more like an epiphany. It really was cloud lifting and saying to myself, "Diahann, what are you doing?" But again, I went in thinking this is what I was going to do. My mom really did not live that long. I said to myself, "If I only have fifty-eight years, is this what I would have wanted to have done?" I need to get up and go to work saying "yes" to that question every day. I couldn't say that in the position I was sitting in. I needed to change because of that. So I started having informational meetings.

What do you mean by that?

I began to think, "Okay, well, what things would I feel great about every day? If it ended tomorrow, am I doing what I'm supposed to be doing?" I started meeting with people that I knew (and some that I didn't know) in organizations where I felt like I could say, "I'm doing what I'm supposed to do."

At the time, I don't think that I was looking for any particular roles. I thought it would take me longer to leave than it did. What I didn't expect was that I would go back to Prep for Prep. I only went back to Prep for Prep because my mentor (the founder) was leaving. So they asked me to come back. They said, "From a continuity standpoint, we want you to do this. Here's the position we can put in front of you that will help you grow past what you have already done." Quite honestly, without reorganization, the position didn't exist. Before that meeting, I didn't see anything in Prep for Prep that was right for me to go back to. So it took me a little less time because of that. But in all honesty, I didn't stay there that long.

At the firm?

No, at Prep for Prep. That initial move to Prep for Prep wasn't that long. I was only there for about a year and a half. I think that if I had taken a year to really figure it out, I would have ended up in the charter school space (where I ended up right after Prep for Prep).

But as far as concrete steps, talking to people is important. Make your interests known. I think there's always going to be that type like me where I was kind of concerned about wanting to leave. There's a guilt in wanting to leave. It's important to get over that and just be explicit when you're talking to people. "I am looking to leave and I am trying to figure it out."

How did you get over that? Did someone help you get over that?

Yeah. Definitely speaking to senior associates helped. I love what one of them said. They said, "Diahann, do you want to be in a pie-eating contest?" I was like, "No." They were like, "Okay, then you should leave because they only want two or three people to win the pie-eating contest every year." So speaking to senior associates helped me on that front.

How long was it from the moment you thought, "Okay, I need to leave," to actually leaving the firm?

About six months. Again, it was faster than I thought. I thought it would be one year.

At that time, you're reaching out to different people and trying to see what opportunities are out there. Towards the last month or last few weeks, did you feel any last-minute hesitation or risk aversion to take the leap?

Nope. I am risk-averse, but I tend to worry on the front end. Once I make a decision, I'm like, "We're there. Let's go."

So you didn't try to hedge or think, "Oh, maybe I can try this for a bit and then come back?" It was over at that stage.

No. That's my personality. I am risk-averse, though. But I am also a decision-maker. I'm done. I'm there. Let's go.

For readers that may be interested in nonprofit or philanthropic work, there seems to be a big transition from Big Law. It's true not only in the work that they are doing but in the compensation that they are receiving. How did you think about or navigate that?

I was just talking to my kids about this. I think it took me about eight years to get back to what I made when I left Simpson. Everybody needs to be ready for that. It's not the longest road ever, but it is a long road.

I think coming out, unless there are extenuating circumstances, people have got to be ready for a changing financial situation. Unless they are like my friend who had the spreadsheet. He set it up so his life really did not feel that different. He was just throwing money at debt while he was at the firm for two and a half years. He was in a good spot, so when he left six months later, his lifestyle was pretty much the same. Quite honestly, he never really lived like a corporate attorney because he was paying off debt.

So I think you just have to prepare—whichever way works for you—in figuring out how you're going to take that hit.

Let's say there are readers who aren't like this lawyer with the spreadsheet. If those readers are thinking of leaving within six months, are there some financial steps they should take to prepare? If so, what are they?

For me, I grew up with the idea of, "Hopefully, you make enough to pay all the bills." It wasn't necessarily about planning. So for the first time, I really began to plan. The six months were fast because my plan was to have one year before I left the firm. But Prep for Prep came through. The other thing I'm going to say is I think the world (especially in the nonprofit space) is more open now to negotiating and giving higher pay when possible (considering certain circumstances). Prep was able to do that for me and it helped me with not needing the full six months more.

But plan. Look at your expenses and figure out which ones you can drive down. It's stunning. When we're working at places like corporate law firms, there are expenses we have just because we could be buying certain brands and doing certain things that are more expensive than necessary. But there are also real expenses coming from the fact that we have a job where you basically could work twenty-four hours per day.

So some of my expenses were coming down because I just needed less childcare. They were coming down because I could clean a little more. I didn't need a person to come in every week. It really is planning and figuring out, "What can I take away from the expense side to even this out?"

And there are probably other things. We traveled differently. We intentionally went on a really nice trip and said, "We might not go on a trip like this for another three or four years." You just plan and budget. Budgeting is probably not that big of a deal to some, but if you're not in the habit of doing it, it can be a big step.

So with that transition, I'd like to ask you about mindset. People making these types of career changes may have this idea of what they want to do in their careers and in their lives. But they may have people around them that are naysayers. They may say things like, "Oh, that's kind of stupid. That'll never happen." Have you ever experienced that?

Oh my goodness. Are you kidding me? I don't say this to make my family feel bad at all. I think my family is great. But I think the first words out of almost every family member's mouth were "Let me get this straight. You make six figures—just for going to work every day. And you want to walk away? Oh no." They were like, "You've arrived. What are you doing?"

It was also, "You've already given back. What are you doing?" So there was a lot of pushback. That part, I will say, was probably the hardest for me. I'm risk-averse, but I also like nice things. I was like, "I'm making a choice. This is going to hurt."

Right. You still ended up leaving, though, so how did you do so amidst some of these objections?

Inner moral confidence was important. I don't think anything was pushing me more than this: I needed to be doing what I should be doing with the skills God gave me. Nothing was pushing me more than that. Even the external forces pushing me to stay were not nearly as great as the thought of, "If this ended today, what are you doing?" That was pushing me more than anything.

I asked myself a similar question. There are also different frameworks that you can apply when making the decision. But really, it comes down to the thought that if something happened today, is this what you want your legacy to be? So considering all of this, you did go back to Prep for Prep. You were saying the role was kind of created for you. Can you talk more about that?

Well, the role was created and then they realized I would be the perfect person. They never thought I would come back for it. It was fortuitous for me and the organization. Prep had reorganized prior to that. The organization had been organized based on the age of the students. So you had a person in charge of activities for the kids from the seventh and eighth grade, and then the high schoolers, and then college.

When Gary Simons left, the new CEO arranged things according to function instead of age. So I was able to come in and lead something we call "leadership development opportunity." Literally, every leadership development opportunity that we give Prep students from seventh grade until they graduate high school fell under that docket. So it included some college counseling (which I had done), but also our leadership development curriculum, our summer and school year job banks, and camps for our young kids. All of those leadership development opportunities fell under this one group. I got to come back and head that.

That's really cool. When you transitioned there, I'm sure you were very excited.

Yes, I was ready to go.

I know we talked about this earlier, but what about your legal background or training did you rely on? I think you said critical thinking skills were important.

Absolutely.

Is there anything else that lawyers making this transition should try to leverage?

So again, I can't underplay the critical thinking skills, right? The other thing I think is a blessing and a curse for lawyers in government (and especially not-for-profits) is we get this smell test. Like you're in this space where everyone's like, "That would be a great idea." And then there's the lawyer that is like, "Or it wouldn't because..."

When I got to NYC Service, everybody was big on climate. We had to reduce our carbon footprint and the mayor put out this mandate. We were asking ourselves how we could get volunteers involved. One of the big initiatives we came up with was called CoolRoofs and we were going to coat rooftops white to reduce the buildings' energy consumption. It is highly effective, but it was the lawyer in me that said, "I'm sorry. Wait. What? We're putting volunteers on roofs? I think we have an insurance problem. I don't think that's covered under anybody's insurance policy."

It was kind of great because when I sat down with corporate counsel, they were like, "So this plan is not going to work." I was like, "No, it is. We need insurance. I found a not-for-profit to do this and X, Y, and Z." They were like, "Oh, okay." So in a way, I think it hinders us because we always have that smell test and it can cause us to be naysayers. But I also think good lawyers are taught to figure things out. So I think we use the smell test and then figure it out. It's not "no," it's just "how."

Yes. I think the stereotype for lawyers is that they always tell their clients "no" or what they can't do. Like you were saying, if the readers of this book could embrace the "how," that could be a major advantage when transitioning into something else. So you were at Prep for Prep and then went to two other nonprofits (Achievement First and City Year New York). Then, you went to NYC Service, Time Warner, and now RISE. So you have all of these different experiences. I suppose for lawyers that are trying to do something similar to what you did, what should they know about transitioning from the nonprofit world to perhaps the government and corporate worlds and then back to the nonprofit world? Is there anything that they should know or keep in mind?

I think mission is important. I think my resumé looks crazy, but I know that it has always been about mission. Even as I'm at Prep, Achievement First, and then City Year, for me, it goes back to when I was young and talking about educational equality. That was my passion. That was the thing. If I woke up every morning and am making for a more equitable educational experience, then I could say, "Yes, I'm doing what I'm supposed to be doing."

All of them afforded me that feeling on larger and larger scales. I went back to Prep for Prep because I love Prep. I also think my educational opportunity came directly from there. With the charter schools, it was about how we can bring great schools to places where kids don't have great schools that are free. Then, they can't test into schools, right? Charter schools are about putting your name in a hat for the school that is sitting in your neighborhood and you have a good academic environment in your neighborhood now. Then, with City Year, it was an even larger focus on the quality of the educational experience. It just allowed me to impact even more traditional schools and ask, "How we can make those schools better" so those kids are getting a great education as well.

I would say that if possible, any transition—especially when you're coming out of the corporate space—really needs to be passion-driven. I think I've always been able to look for and pick opportunities based on my passions.

Or, like you said, the mission.

Yep. Right. So their mission matches your passion. That's what should lead you—no matter what you're doing at that organization. The other thing I would say is I think more attorneys need to be involved in the not-for-profit space—even when they are in the corporate space. I think every attorney needs to be on a board. I really mean that. Whether it's a board of a small not-for-profit or a large not-for-profit, every attorney should be on a board. It should be like a requirement for us. The rest of the world has to do jury service because nobody ever picks us to be on their jury. We should have to help this way.

So if attorneys find an organization, they should maybe send a cold email or get an introduction and try to get involved?

Absolutely. You would be stunned at how many not-for-profits are like, "Do you want to be a board member?" Again, when you're in the corporate space, there are so many not-for-profits that, if you are a board member and you give $5,000, they'll think that's a big deal. If you're in the corporate space, $5,000 is not a lot of money. So I would say board service is key.

Just going back to something you said. Your mission was defined over the decades—even before college. I feel like a lot of attorneys go to law school because they don't really know what they want to do. So when they want to make this transition, they're trying out different things. Sometimes it works out and other times it doesn't. But say an attorney is reading this book. They don't really know what they want to do, yet they want to get out. I know you don't have personal experience with that, but what would you say to that person?

Here is what I would say. If you want to get out, get out. It sounds simple. But the reality is if you want to get out and that is your focus, then do it. Like you and I were talking about, that's the first hurdle. Once you cross that hurdle and you're like, "I am going to do this," the rest of it actually seems relatively easy.

The other thing I would say is the same thing that I say to young people now. Quite honestly, because so many people go from college right to law school, you're actually in the same place as the kid coming out of college. If you went to college, then law school, and then a law firm, you are, from an experience standpoint when having thought about these things, in the same position as a 22-year-old that just came out of undergrad. The thing I say to them is, "Just do something. If it's wrong, it's fine. Do you know how many jobs you're going to have before you get to stop working (unless you're independently wealthy)?"

When I was at Time Warner, I thought it was interesting. They had a group come in because now, apparently, we live so long that 401(k)s are not even going to cover retirement. They were built for people who were going to finish working and die about fifteen years later (or twenty at the most). That is actually not what's happening anymore. So we're going to have to work. We're going to have so many careers. Don't spend that much energy worrying about if it's right in the long term. If it feels right right now, just do it and do it well.

Right. You don't know what opportunities will open up later. Eventually, you took on the CEO position at RISE. Can you talk about how you got here and the work that you are doing here?

I will say this was another fortuitous opportunity. I think the groundwork was there. Whoever was selected to lead this organization had to have a lot of different skill sets in place. I had been in corporate philanthropy. I loved it. Time Warner was bought by AT&T, so it was a great time to raise my hand and say, "Hey, I would love a package." I felt like I wanted to get a little bit more back into the direct kind of work and this is an interesting space for me. It's not so much about sports. I have always been involved in sports (plus I have two kids that are athletic). I spend so many hours of so many days in sports. It's amazing. I've always played sports, too. We came from a sports family.

So from that perspective, RISE was a match for me—specifically understanding sports and understanding the impact that sports could have. I will say with the election of Donald Trump, I really have been thinking back to that same thing. What do I need to wake up and say I'm doing? What do I need to do to say, "Yes, I am in the right place and doing what I am meant to do?" I remember posting on Facebook that whatever we think we have or don't have, as a country, we have a race problem. We just have to grapple with it.

It was always part of the educational opportunity work. It was really explicit in my work at Time Warner. I was funding diverse artists. At Sundance, I was funding diverse fellows in all of their programs. So I was always looking at race and racial diversity. But it just became clear. I just needed to be doing more in that space because I feel like this is where our country is hurting the most. I actually was planning on leaving Time Warner. I was considering teaching or taking money from my package and taking a minute. This job came up. A friend who works for the Miami Dolphins asked me to look at it. I first said, "No, I have something lined up," but then the same position came back again. A couple of people asked me to look at it, so I felt, "Okay, God is saying look at this position." Sure enough, when I really looked at it, it was amazing.

That's great. And again, it fulfills the mission that you've been working on for decades now. I have two questions for lawyers making the transition into philanthropy or the nonprofit world. First, what

advantages or disadvantages do they have? Second, how should they pitch themselves if they're making the transition?

So I actually think it is an easier jump into philanthropy—even though it's not the jump I made right away. With philanthropy, it literally doesn't matter who the philanthropist is. It is fully a legal entity. Everything about foundations, individual givers, private foundations, public charities—they are legal entities and most of what they are doing in moving funding is connected to some regulation. I actually think that it is an easier job and I think lawyers should see that, know it, and try to be involved.

It's interesting: working on not-for-profits can make you appealing to the people that fund them. So I think that's an easier job. I think they appreciate lawyers in the space quite a bit. In the not-for-profit space, I usually think there are tons of different types of positions that lawyers can fill well. I think it is about learning how and being willing to pitch yourself. Help people understand that the skills you have are transferable and how they are transferable.

What particular skills would you recommend for those attorneys?

Well, I think analytical thinking is important. A lot of attorneys, especially if they are coming out fairly junior, have project management skills. Even junior and mid-level attorneys have these skills. Mostly, what they have been doing is managing projects and managing them incredibly well. So I think of project management skills. Again, one of the things that I some-times see in the not-for-profit space is that lawyers' attention to detail is invaluable. I can be your person who comes in and has great attention to detail.

The other thing I think we as lawyers miss is human resources. I think most lawyers looking at any space, but particularly the not-for-profit space, are predisposed to fill in HR roles. Again, HR is mostly law.

Is there anything unexpected that you didn't see in the not-for-prof-it world before your transition that lawyers should recognize before they make their own move?

You touched on something before—risk-aversion. Most lawyers I know are more risk-averse than the average population. I will say at every organization, I have moments where I'm looking at my organization like, "Are they serious right now?" It becomes a mismatch. So I've had to grow in my comfort with risk. Be ready for that. Maybe be ready for facts and rules not to rule the day. It is a mental transition to make. We like the specialization of function. That does not really exist. I have come in and been like, "Who does what? Oh, absolutely not. This group does this, this group does that, and this group does this." We tend to appreciate specialization of function more. Now, I'm in a position where I'm able to put those things in place. You have to be comfortable coming in and being in a place where it feels a little chaotic since everybody is doing a little bit of everything.

Almost like a startup mentality.

Yeah.

So as far as practical steps of leaving from law to the not-for-profit world, serving on a board is one thing. Networking is obviously beneficial. Is there anything else that could help?

Budget is huge. Serve on a board if you can. You can do coursework, too. It's sometimes hard when you're in corporate spaces, but I would say now, the courses you can take online are amazing. There are tons of courses in not-for-profit management or any other field that you think you're interested in. In the not-for-profit space, there has increasingly been this appreciation for substantive expertise. Building up that substantive expertise is helpful.

CHAPTER 10

Jay Bilas

College Basketball Analyst and Sports Personality

Our career arcs are influenced by plenty of variables. Sure, things like sheer talent, hard work, and drive are extremely relevant. However, I would argue that there are other subtle yet impactful variables that can dramatically impact the course of our careers. For law school graduates and legal professionals, I believe one of those variables is maintaining hobbies and interests outside traditional legal practice.

We aren't robots. All of us have interests and passions unrelated to the law. At the same time, it can be surprisingly difficult to pursue those interests as a law student or practicing attorney. All too often, the demands and challenges of the legal profession become an increasingly larger force in our lives, thereby crowding out some of our other passions and interests.

During law school, the overwhelming focus is on doing well on exams and finding a job. All-nighters (or near-all-nighters) aren't out of the question. As practicing attorneys, our work can be all-consuming. Obviously, we want to provide the best possible work for our clients. But at the end of the day, demands of the *now* may come at the expense of following our other interests.

This is unfortunate. Maintaining those outside hobbies and interests provides plenty of benefits, whether or not you plan on building a long-term career in legal practice. For starters, they can make you a better lawyer. Clearly, you want to make sure those pursuits don't interfere with your day-to-day duties and responsibilities, but by pursuing passions outside of the law, you bring balance and energy into your life. You can then bring that energy into your day-to-day legal work. Consequently, you become a better attorney and will better serve your clients and colleagues.

Another benefit to actively pursuing your hobbies and interests is that you may unlock compelling career opportunities. Certainly, there is no guarantee that this will happen. However, I believe that by staying well-rounded and maintaining your passions outside of legal practice, you may come across an opportunity so intriguing that it would be difficult not to entertain it.

Whenever we think of college basketball, it's hard not to picture Jay Bilas. From providing color commentary on the biggest games in college basketball to breaking down the latest March Madness bracket, Jay lives and breathes the sport. While Jay is well-known for his work in the college basketball world, many don't realize that he used to be a practicing lawyer. He still holds an of counsel position at Moore & Van Allen, which is a large law firm based in the Southeast. In his almost thirty years with this firm, Jay has specialized in commercial litigation and served all kinds of clients, including a costume manufacturer sued by the partnership who owned Barney from *Barney & Friends*.

Along with building a stellar legal career, Jay has reached the highest levels of college basketball broadcasting. It's safe to say that basketball has been an extremely important part of Jay's life. Playing for legendary Duke basketball coach Mike Krzyzewski,[1] Jay was a four-year starter at Duke and later drafted by the Dallas Mavericks. After playing professional basketball in Europe, Jay returned to Duke. He became an assistant coach under Coach K while simultaneously attending Duke Law School.

Even when Jay arrived at Moore & Van Allen, his passion for basketball didn't fade. While at the firm, he obtained an offer to be a radio broadcaster for college basketball games. ESPN then offered him some games. He kept getting more broadcasting opportunities, and through hard work and dedication, he has become one of ESPN's most well-known college basketball commentators and analysts.

As Jay describes in the interview, his initial opportunity to broadcast college basketball games didn't just fall into his lap. It was the result of years of experience in the basketball and media worlds. Not only was he a player at both the collegiate and professional levels, but he worked with Coach K *while in law school*. In college, he was a runner and production assistant for ABC Sports. Ultimately, broadcasting wasn't completely

---

1 Coach Mike Krzyzewski, also known as Coach K, is one of the most legendary coaches in college basketball history. The accolades are too long to list. In his forty-one years at Duke, Coach K has more than one thousand one hundred wins, five national championships, twelve Final Four appearances, and twelve National Coach of the Year honors. As the head coach of the U.S. Men's Basketball National Team, Coach K has also received six gold medals.

off the radar. Though he moved in a different direction and became a practicing lawyer, he was still extremely passionate about the sport. His long-standing experience and interest in college basketball was an asset as he started his new career in broadcasting.

Jay understood that his legal career came first. He told me that if he thought his broadcast work would negatively impact his practice, he would have stopped broadcasting. That said, he did great legal work and received a compelling offer from ESPN. Since then, he has become *the* voice of college basketball in America.

Even if you aren't interested in college basketball, you can learn a lot from Jay's story. Although law school and legal practice can be stressful and all-consuming, don't ignore your other interests. Take the time to indulge them. Anything can happen after that.

* * *

Jay, thanks so much for taking the time to speak about your career journey. I'd like to start by speaking about your initial decision to go to law school. I always find it interesting to ask this question because you often find plenty of reasons. Some prospective law students are inspired to take the leap since some family members are lawyers. Others may want to be lawyers because of what they see in pop culture. There is also another group that is interested in the potential financial rewards from legal practice. There are many other reasons. What prompted you to at least start considering law school?

I was encouraged to do it by my parents. Both my mother and father thought that an undergraduate degree wasn't enough for the world that I would be living in. Neither of my parents had the opportunity to go to college. So that was a big step for me. They felt that a graduate degree would be really important.

My dad was the one that really felt that a law degree would be the right thing to do. He always felt that it was a good education and you didn't have to be a lawyer if you didn't want to be. The degree would still serve you well. He used to say that if you ever ran into a problem in whatever career choice you made, you could always hang a shingle out and make a good living. That's the way he looked at it.

But he really sort of sold me on the idea that just because you go to law school doesn't mean you have to be a lawyer. If I felt like I had to be a lawyer after going to law school, I don't think I would have wanted to go.

Interesting. When did these discussions happen? When did you first start thinking about law school?

You know how it is with parents. Seeds were planted earlier on. But it really became a discussion point when I graduated from college.

I played professional basketball and played overseas. I was drafted by the Dallas Mavericks and then wound up playing in Italy and Spain. My dad felt like I should take the LSAT, apply to law school, and then get in. If I could defer my acceptance, then I could keep playing if I wanted to. He felt like if I didn't take the exam early and get admitted to a law school, I probably wouldn't be motivated to do it later. That if I were in my early thirties or something, I would just move on. I wouldn't be interested in going back to school.

He was right. I wasn't all that interested in doing it when I did it. But things worked out timing-wise where it made itself available.

When you're thinking about going to law school, did you have an ultimate goal in mind? I know you said the flexible nature of a law degree was attractive, but did you see yourself in any particular job or position?

No, I did not view law school as something I wanted to do. That was something I was encouraged to do. When all of the pieces fell into place, it seemed like the best option.

What happened was that I was offered a coaching job at Duke. I was offered the job where I played and by the coach I played for (Mike Krzyzewski). I was admitted to Duke Law School around the same time. When that became available, it made some sense to me. The pieces fell into place so I decided to quit playing. I had not anticipated stopping that early. I was going to play ten, twelve years professionally if my body held up. Then, I would move on from there. But when the coaching thing came up and I could do law school at the same time (which was a little bit unusual), I thought it was a good thing to do.

But I never went into law school with the goal of becoming a lawyer. It just sort of happened.

Did you apply anywhere else besides Duke Law School?

I did not apply anywhere else. I was going to, but it was so far off into the future. When this opportunity came up with the Duke basketball team, I applied to Duke Law School.

I find that so interesting. For one thing, many law students may feel overwhelmed or inundated during their 1L (or even 2L) years. But at the same time you're going through law school, you're working with Coach K. You must have excellent time management skills. Can you talk about how you managed both law school and coaching?

Well, I was older. I had been out in the world a little bit. So law school wasn't the be-all and end-all for me. I wasn't worried about it. I wanted to do well, but I wasn't going to let my grades define me.

Basketball was a top priority and I just prioritized each day. I had certain things I had to do each day for basketball and certain things I had to do for law school. I dealt with them and just prioritized them. I didn't have a whole lot of time for anything else, but I managed it.

Look, law school is different for everybody. It's different at every school. But in my experience, law school was really difficult the first semester because I didn't know what I needed to know. It was fear-based. It had nothing to do with the difficulty of it. After the first semester, you're like, "Okay, I can handle that. That wasn't that bad." It's just like anything else, but law school brings this aura with it that probably isn't true (at least in my experience).

This was back in the early 1990s. Scott Turow had written this book called *One L* and it was basically like reading *Jaws* before you went to the beach.[2] It wasn't anything like the law school experience I had. One

---

2   *One L* is one of the most-read books about the law school experience. While somewhat dated, a 2007 story in *The Wall Street Journal* reported that around thirty thousand copies of the book are sold every year.

prominent professor that I knew before arriving at Duke Law School encouraged me to read that book. That might have been the dumbest book recommendation I ever received. Law school was nothing like that book.

I suppose in the beginning, there is always the fear of the unknown. You may need to study more than you expect. Sometimes, you may just not know what you're doing. But if I can just go back for one second: you're studying and taking the LSAT while you're playing professional basketball, right?

Yes.

How did you handle that?

That was easy. The test wasn't easy, but the preparation for it was. I was playing in Spain at the time. I took the LSAT at an Air Force base called Torrejón. I had to take some time away from the team to fly there, take the test, and fly back. But it really wasn't that big of a deal.

The truth was, at the time, I didn't know I was going to be in law school the next year. I don't want to say I didn't care how I did, but I wasn't worried about it. I wanted to do well and I prepared myself to do well. But when taking the test, I wasn't tapping my fingers on the desk and feeling all anxiety-ridden. As far as I knew at that time, I wasn't going to be in law school for a period of years. So it seemed like it was so far ahead. It really wasn't of much consequence to me—other than the time I'd invested.

But when I was playing overseas, I had a lot of time on my hands. You played and you practiced. You prepared that way, but the rest of the day, I had plenty of time to study.

It was sort of like preparing for the bar exam. After I graduated from law school, I had a lot of time on my hands. So preparing for the bar exam really wasn't that difficult. You treated it like a job. I had a certain amount of time each day that I devoted to studying for the LSAT. I just did it and it wasn't that big of a deal.

That makes sense. You said you weren't anticipating going to law school for some time. So it really all came down to that coaching gig

opening up and you thinking that it would be the perfect time to also study at Duke Law School.

Yes. I wasn't sure how long it would be until I went to law school. I thought I was going to continue to play. That was a goal of mine and something I enjoyed doing. I was young, in shape, and loved to play. But I had an opportunity come to me and I wasn't sure it was going to come back. That opportunity was the coaching gig at Duke. Combined with going to law school at the same time, it was a great opportunity.

I just decided to go ahead and take it. I applied to law school. I don't know how the admission process worked, but it didn't seem like deferment was an option on the table. So when admission was offered to me, the coaching job was offered to me, and then Coach K said, "Why don't you do both," it seemed like a good opportunity. But if I struggled with one, I honestly don't know which one I would have quit.

I was going to ask you about that. Everything worked out, but if you were at a crossroads, you would have had to make a tough decision.

Yeah, I don't know how tough it would have been. I didn't have to make it. But the powers that be at the law school were not excited about me coaching while I was in law school. They fought it.

Did they?

Yeah, they did. It became a sticking point before I arrived. Would I be able to do it? My argument was, "Look, you guys aren't policing what everybody else is doing. I don't see why you should be policing what I'm doing. If it becomes a problem, we'll deal with the problem. But you're not out there patrolling the bars at night and wondering what other students are doing. Why are you worried about what I'm doing? And you know exactly where I'm going to be. I'm going to be across the street or I'm going to be here. It's not going to be hard to find me."

Coach K sounded supportive. Did he provide any advice on time management or how you could juggle your coaching responsibilities and your law school responsibilities?

No, there was never any discussion about that. That was up to me. I had played for him already. He knew me. He didn't need to provide me with advice on time management. I knew how to handle that.

Right. So at that time, you're traveling with the Duke basketball team. You're going on road games and are coaching during March Madness.

Yes.

Were there any moments where you felt overwhelmed with how much you had to do?

Just the first semester. That was it. It had nothing to do with the time demands. It had more to do with just law school. I would have felt the same way whether I was a basketball graduate assistant or not. Law school is nerve-wracking in the first semester. It was just a different feeling. I'd never really gone through anything where your entire semester was based on your final exams. There was nothing in between.

Basically, that's the way it was. Except in my small section, you got very little feedback along the way. You didn't know whether you were doing the right thing. You kind of found out at the end. Usually, if you're in a race, you don't find out at the finish line if you won. You know where you stand among your peers. I didn't know where I stood so I assumed that I was in the back of the pack.

Was that extra motivation for you? Did you work harder and stay up later?

No. I always want to do well. There's never a time I want to fail. I always wonder about these commencement speeches where they're encouraging people to go out and fail. That's not advice I would give. Don't be afraid to fail. Like, I wasn't afraid to fail. I wanted to do well and I did not want any part of failing. I wasn't extra motivated by that. I did what was required in both coaching and law school.

So you were out of school for several years playing professional basketball. Was it difficult to get back into the academic mindset— especially during that first semester of law school?

No. School isn't that hard. They tell you what to do, you do it, and you take the test. It's really not that big of a deal. Some things are harder than others. But you're not splitting the atom every day. It's not that hard. You just apply yourself.

There were many smart people that went to law school with me. They were nothing other than helpful. We had study groups, and if you needed a hand, someone was there to help. People got it on different levels. I went to school with some genius-level minds. I know I didn't process the material the same way that they did. They thought on a different plane. I knew I wasn't the smartest person in any room I was in, and I knew that I wasn't the dumbest. So I figured I could handle it.

It sounds like you have a generally positive view of your law school experience.

I liked it fine. If I had the choice between spending a year in the Italian Riviera or going to law school, I think I would choose the Italian Riviera. But I didn't look at it as some sentence either. It was somewhere in the middle of that.

I loved the people I went to school with. I loved a number of my professors. I stay in contact with some. The whole experience was very good, but I understand why people don't like it. It's not easy. But I didn't have my identity wrapped up in how I did. I was not worried about that. There were a lot of people who were. Their status as a student was very important to how they viewed themselves.

Being out of school was helpful because I knew that when you're walking down the street, people don't care what your grades are. I also knew that when you became a lawyer, you walked into court and no judge gives a damn about what your grades are. They want to know whether you have a case and whether your argument is a winner. That's the end of the story.

Exactly. As graduation approached, what were you assuming your next steps would be? Did you have a discussion with Coach K about

sticking around? Or were you thinking of perhaps going into private practice?

I always assumed that I would stay in basketball. I was not particularly concerned about being a lawyer after law school. But I took all the appropriate steps while I was in school. I always took a little bit of time each summer to clerk for a law firm. It was available to me and I had a little bit of time where I could do it during the summer. So I did it.

I would take care of my duties at Duke. I worked camp every summer, but I always took one month and worked as a summer associate. I did that for two years in Los Angeles with a law firm called Lillick & McHose. Then, that became Pillsbury, Madison & Sutro. They merged when I was in law school.

Then, I believe you graduated from Duke in 1992. You began working at Moore & Van Allen. Is that right?

Yes. During my third year of being an assistant at Duke, I became engaged to my fiancé Wendy. We had dated all through college. So when we were deciding what to do in our family life, coaching didn't seem like the right thing for our family. With coaching, we would have to move every once in a while. It's not always the most stable thing for a family and that's not the way that we wanted to do it.

I needed to find a job. My wife did not particularly care for the idea of living in Los Angeles. That's where my job offer was. Pillsbury had offered me a full-time position. I thought, "Okay, well, maybe I'll take that." My wife didn't want to go. So we decided that we wanted to live in Charlotte, North Carolina. I didn't know anybody here. However, I was able to get connected with some people at Moore & Van Allen. I interviewed there and a couple of other places but I went with Moore & Van Allen.

But I did all of that stuff. I figured I went to law school so I should take the bar exam. I tried my hand at being a lawyer. I can't imagine that anybody in my class at Moore & Van Allen would have thought that I would be a guy that would stay at the law firm for almost thirty years. I'm still there. I almost can't believe it.

Just going back to when you first heard about the opportunity with Moore & Van Allen. Are you basically just pounding the pavement

and trying to meet as many attorneys as possible? Is that what led you to the firm?

Aside from basketball people, I didn't know anybody in Charlotte. So I asked a friend of mine if he knew anyone in the legal community in Charlotte that could give me a lay of the land. This friend directed me to a guy named John Fennebresque who was the managing partner of Moore & Van Allen. So I went to Charlotte and I met with John and he gave me some advice. At the end of our meeting, he said, "So you're in the market for a job here in Charlotte?" I said, "Well, yeah. That's why I'm here." I remember exactly what he said. He said, "Well, we want in."

That's how it happened. I interviewed with Moore & Van Allen starting right after that (maybe even that day). In a very short time period, I decided that's where I wanted to be. I sort of formally interviewed with another firm in town and chose Moore & Van Allen.

Say some law students are weighing offers at two or three different firms. What sort of factors would you recommend that they weigh or analyze?

I wouldn't presume to give advice to somebody else on what they would choose in their career. When I was interviewing, I met a guy named Ben Hawfield (who later became the managing partner of the firm). He has been a mentor to me and is one of the smartest human beings I've ever been around. I left my meetings with him saying, "I want to work where he works. If he works here, this is where I want to be."

That was basically it for me. The way law firms do it is you meet with somebody for half an hour. Then, they walk you to another office. You have five or six meetings in one day. How are you going to tell? I can't tell anything from that. I couldn't tell anything about the firm. I could just tell from the people.

After I met Ben and got to know him, I was convinced that Moore & Van Allen was the right firm. That's also basically how I made my decision on going to Duke. It was through Coach K. After I met him and got to know him, I was like, "I want to play for this guy." It had very little to do with Duke and more to do with him.

So for both Ben Hawfield and Coach K, it wasn't only their sheer intelligence, but their leadership qualities that were attractive to you?

It was the whole thing. You meet somebody, you spend time around them, and get to know them a little bit. From there, you just know. It's like what the Supreme Court said on obscenity. I can't define it, but I know it when I see it.

At Moore & Van Allen, you became a commercial litigator. What made you prefer litigation over the transactional side?

Well, I didn't start with litigation. I started in bankruptcy because I wanted to get into court right away. I didn't want to wait, and with litigation, it seemed like there was somewhat of a wait to get in the courtroom. I wanted courtroom experience right away, so I went the bankruptcy route. I had done some of that during my summer with Pillsbury. They called it creditors' rights.

I enjoyed it. That's where Ben Hawfield was practicing, so I worked for Ben, David Eades, and guys like that. I just sort of learned how to do it. Then, I gravitated toward litigation. I had spent a fair amount of time in court and liked it. I wanted to go the litigation route, so I switched it up after a couple of years. Since then, I have spent the rest of my practice years in litigation.

I can't remember the exact date, but I signed a full-time contract with ESPN. I was doing ESPN work on the side and I decided that's what I should do. So I went full-time with ESPN and gave notice to Moore & Van Allen that I was going to have to quit. When the firm found out that I wasn't leaving town, they offered me an of counsel position. I don't practice full-time anymore and have not for some period of years now.

I'd like to ask about that in just one second. But is there a specific matter or trial earlier in your career that you are especially proud of?

I was proud of all of it. But we had a bunch of cases that were memorable for many different reasons. The one that everybody knows about (because it has become inescapable) is the Barney case.[3] I represented a costume manufacturer against the partnership that owns Barney the purple dinosaur. It started out as a very simple trademark and copyright infringement matter. I thought that the partnership that owned Barney was just trying to protect its marks. It turned into this vendetta-like lawsuit. Because of their demands, we had no ability to settle the case. So we had to take it to trial in federal court.

We appeared before Judge Graham Mullen in the U.S. District Court for the Western District of North Carolina. We had a lengthy trial and it was sort of absurd in that, when I was in law school, I didn't think I'd be in federal court arguing over what looks like Barney the purple dinosaur. But I did and we wound up arguing the case in the Fourth Circuit Court of Appeals. It wasn't really a First Amendment case or something like that. But it was pretty memorable.

When you were preparing for legal argument, did you approach it like you would in the moments before an important basketball game? In other words, did you rely on skills or experiences from the basketball world to help you prepare?

I'm not sure I did. Basketball and law are very different things. Law requires a little more thoughtful approach. It's not that it differs in your preparation. In both endeavors, preparation is vital. I didn't really have an opponent in law. Nobody was going to stand up and make it difficult for me to make my argument. You got your turn. You may look at it as having an opponent, but you really don't. There's nobody physically trying to stop you from doing what you're intending to do.

So I don't look at it as being similar at all. You could argue that some of the characteristics that make a person successful—perseverance, preparation, and all of that stuff—cross over. But I never went to work saying, "Okay, here's what I learned in basketball and it's going to make me a better lawyer." It was already ingrained in me.

---

3   In *Lyons Partnership v. Morris Costumes, Inc.*, 243 F.3d 789 (4th Cir. 2001), Jay and his colleagues were defending Morris Costumes, a company that rented out costumes. Lyons Partnership, the owner of Barney, argued that one costume in Morris Costumes' collection too closely resembled Barney the purple dinosaur.

In fact, a lot of the lawyers that I worked with were a heck of a lot smarter and tougher than a lot of the basketball people I dealt with. I think a lot of people in sports are looking for motivation and inspiration from outside of sports. They can certainly find that in the law profession if they are willing to look there. Folks in other industries always look toward sports because it resonates with people. But other than the obvious, I didn't see that I used basketball for my law practice.

I think something that is especially interesting about your career is how you were able to stay at your firm while being able to pursue other opportunities. You alluded to this a few minutes ago on how you were working with ESPN. Correct me if I'm wrong, but you were doing great work at your firm and building your reputation, yet you wanted to pursue this other career in broadcasting. You said you were thinking of leaving to pursue it full-time and your firm strongly wanted you to remain. Is that how it played out?

No, that's not what happened. When I started my job with Moore & Van Allen in late 1992, I got an offer to start doing broadcast work. I talked to my superiors about it at the law firm and said, "Hey, if I can do a couple of games per week and it doesn't take me away from my law practice, I would like to be able to do it." They were fine with it.

My law practice came first. My clients came first. But I always looked at broadcasting as something that would be enjoyable to do. I wanted to do it and I wasn't going to say no because I thought it would negatively impact my law practice. If it did, I would quit. I'd stop the broadcast stuff. But if it didn't, it was something I wanted to do and I was going to do it. If my law firm had said no, I would have said no to the opportunity. But they didn't. They said yes.

So for six or seven years, I did broadcast work. I started in radio and then ESPN started giving me games. I started working in the studio as well. My opportunities kept increasing, but I never let them affect my job. My job came first. After some time, however, I gave notice. I accepted another job. My law firm had a going-away party for me. Somebody had asked me, "When do you move up to New York or Connecticut?" I said, "I'm not moving. I'm staying here in Charlotte. My work requires travel, but I can live where I want."

A few days later, the managing partner came into my office and asked me to stay. I told the firm I would stay to handle a few cases that were headed toward trial or arbitration. A couple of them settled and one of them actually wound up going to arbitration. But we handled those and then I moved into an of counsel position. I've been in that position ever since.

Just to backtrack a bit. How did that first opportunity in radio come about? Were you actively searching for it or did it kind of fall into your lap?

Well, I don't look at anything as falling into your lap. When somebody offers you something, they're actively seeking you. I was sought out by a radio company called the Capital Sports Network. The guy's name was George Habel. He came to Charlotte, took me to lunch, and offered me a slate of games to do on radio. So I took it.

I had always thought about broadcasting. When I was younger, people asked, "Hey, what do you want to do when you're done playing basketball?" It seemed like that was a fashionable thing to say. But I'd worked in the industry when I was in college. During the summertime, I worked for ABC Sports as a production assistant and a runner. It was something I expressed interest in and I thought I could do, but I'd moved in another direction.

When I got this offer, I thought it would be fun. I had already said no (at least for that time period) to coaching. I thought it would be something that would give me an opportunity to see a lot of my friends and stay around the game a little bit. I felt like I would really enjoy it. So I said yes.

I certainly didn't do it for the money (because there wasn't very much of it). But after doing that for a couple of years, ESPN reached out and started offering me games. I started doing games for ESPN and that's when things took off a little bit. I got more and more work to the point where I couldn't do both jobs and do them the way I wanted to. So I chose to pursue the broadcast avenue when ESPN offered me a full-time position.

I'm trying to imagine what your schedule would be like. I'm assuming you get into the office early. Do you leave at around 5:00 or 6:00 and then go to your games?

It depended on the day. If it was a road game, I had to go on the road and fly. The first couple of years, I was broadcasting Duke basketball games. So if it was a home game, I could drive there. Door to door, it was a two-hour drive. I would go to the game, the buzzer went off, and then I would go home. Oftentimes, I went back into the office. Sometimes I went home. It just depended.

Back then, it was a little more difficult because you didn't have current technology. Basically, nobody knows whether you're at your desk or whether you're on the road. They knew back then. So I spent a lot of time in the office and burned a lot of late nights. But that's what the job required so I did the job.

Sure. When you're gaining more responsibility at ESPN, were you thinking something like, "If I don't pursue this, I'm really going to regret it?" How did you approach that decision to leave when you were getting more gigs with ESPN?

I received an offer and the offer was too good to turn down. So it wasn't anything I necessarily pursued. I received an offer, negotiated it out, and realized that it was the best course of action at that time. And I decided to take it. I felt like if it didn't work out, I could always turn around and go back into my law practice. We could move. There were all kinds of things we could do.

I didn't look at it as some sort of decision that was the be-all and end-all of my life. I thought it would work out. If it worked out, great. If it didn't, that's great too. I would do something else. It was just a great opportunity and I took it.

I know it's hard to give general advice. But if someone wants to move beyond the law and do something else, should they work on that idea or passion at night (almost like a side hustle)? If not, what would you do?

I've always taken a first things first approach. I was not pursuing broadcasting. I was a lawyer. I'd made my mind up to be a lawyer and I had responsibilities as such. I not only had responsibilities to my clients and to my law firm, but I also had them to my family. I know it's just a word, but I didn't look at anything as a side hustle. That sounds a little odd to me. I was doing something that made sense and that was within my area of expertise. It was also something that my law firm approved of and knew of from day one.

I didn't look at it like somehow I was pursuing something on the side and trying to end run around my current job. If I didn't want to be a lawyer at that time, I wouldn't have been one. I would have pursued broadcasting. I had made money playing professional basketball. I didn't have to practice law. I could have done whatever I wanted and had enough money to get going. So I did what I wanted to do. But after six or seven years of it, when I got the offer, I knew what I was leaving and I knew what I was going toward. But I didn't look at it like I was going to pursue something from the beginning just to get myself out or practicing law. That's not what happened.

Right. So ultimately, you were very upfront with management and the managing partner about what you wanted to do. I'm sure that you would recommend that readers follow that same approach.

I can't imagine if you're going to do something else that there's any other way than to let your firm know. I think you have an ethical obligation to do that. It's not just what I think. I can't imagine you could do that without informing and seeking the blessing or permission of your law firm. If you hang your own shingle out, you can do whatever you want.

What I was doing was a public matter. I don't think I could have done that without informing everyone. I would not have gone forward without having the express prior consent of my law firm. I can't imagine not having done that. I don't know if it's my advice. That seems like ethics 101.

Now, in your role at ESPN, do you find your law degree and legal background helpful? If so, to what extent is it helpful?

I think my law degree is helpful in everything that I do. It's not helpful in this area or that area. There's not a day that goes by that I don't feel my law degree and the education I received when I was working as a lawyer. It's a fabulous education. I met unbelievable people and I've continued to benefit from it every day since then.

Oftentimes, people that don't work in the industry may know as much about it as anybody. My dad was as right as anybody I've ever come across in the legal profession with how he viewed the value of a law degree. He was right and I'm glad I listened to him.

So it really doesn't come down to one or two particular skills, right? It's essentially the whole package and the whole experience.

Yeah. Different people take different things from law school. You have some that are interested in specific areas of the law and could not stand up and give an argument in front of a judge to save their lives. You have other people that can do that in their sleep. People have different talents and use their law degrees and education in different ways. I can't imagine it's one thing to any group of people. It's different for everybody. For me, I learned a ton in law school, but I learned way more in the practice of law.

I'd like to ask you a question about transitioning into the sports arena. Some attorneys may want to do that, whether that's working in a front office, doing something in the broadcast media space, or even becoming an agent. Do you have any tips or advice on what those attorneys should think about if they are planning to totally break off from traditional legal practice and build a career in sports?

Well, I don't know. I don't think I transitioned into sports. I was in sports. I never left it. I've been in basketball my whole life. I was out of basketball for a period of months—not a period of years. I took the side job in broadcasting within a period of months after I started at Moore & Van Allen. So it wasn't a difficult transition for me. At least, I didn't view it that way. I didn't view myself as transitioning. I was in a business I'd always been a part of and that was basketball. I didn't look at it so much as the business of broadcasting at first (later on, it became that).

But I don't know. If I'm a lawyer, I'm not looking to get over the wall. I made a commitment to be a lawyer and something pulled me out of it. If I wanted to do something else, I would have just done it.

I realize that some people may have certain obligations and may want to make a certain amount of money and all that stuff. I get that. But if I want to work in a front office, I'm not going to work at a law firm first. I'm going to go after what I want to do. I think it's kind of inefficient to do it through a law firm. You can certainly do that, but you'd better be prepared to be a lawyer for the duration. Otherwise, you have a chance to be awfully disappointed. Unless you're working with a pro team, representing a pro team, or have a job where you are actually in that area, I think it's an awfully inefficient treadmill. It's like being on a treadmill to reach the finish line. It's a difficult thing to do.

Right. Just to clarify what I was asking, let's say there was an attorney that has worked at a law firm for several years. They were initially really interested in the law but have recently become more dissatisfied with it. Maybe they're even having a midlife crisis and thinking, "Sports is something I've always been interested in. I have a passion for it, and I want to leave my job to enter the sports world." In other words, this attorney may have been extremely interested in legal practice at the beginning of their career, but they somehow lost interest. In that situation, is there a way to best navigate that transition?

I can't speak to that. I have no experience in midlife crises or wanting to do something else because I'm dissatisfied with what I'm doing. If I was dissatisfied, I like to think I would quit and move into what I wanted to do.

At least to this point in my life, I've never done anything that I didn't want to do. I count myself as extraordinarily lucky and I'm very grateful for that. I don't think it has anything to do with some sort of makeup that I have. I've been very fortunate that I've been able to pursue what I want to pursue.

I didn't think I wanted to be a lawyer. But when I made the commitment to do it, I jumped in with both feet. I didn't look back. I did not turn away from law; instead, something pulled me away from it and I actually never really left. I'm one hundred percent devoted to my job at ESPN and now I do law on the side. When I started, I was a full-time one hundred percent devoted lawyer that did broadcast work on the side. That script has been flipped based upon an offer I received. But I didn't turn my back on anything or become dissatisfied with anything. So I don't know that I could speak to that.

Looking back, it sounds like you wouldn't do anything differently with your career. Is that right?

I don't know that I could say I wouldn't do anything differently. But I don't have any regrets as to the decisions I've made. I made the right decisions for me and my family at the time I was required to make decisions. So I don't regret one second of it.

I'm assuming you're going to stick with work at ESPN and at Moore & Van Allen for the foreseeable future.

I don't know what I'm going to do. I've had numerous offers in between to do other things in basketball, but I've chosen to remain in the position I'm in. I hope I'm of value to the firm. I do certain things for the firm, but I don't practice like I did when I was practicing full-time. I'm one hundred percent a broadcaster now. When there's something to do in broadcasting, that's my number one priority.

Makes sense. One final question here. In your broadcasting job, you get to speak with many different basketball coaches. What's the most useful life or career advice that you've heard from Coach K or other basketball coaches?

I'm kind of out of the career advice business. I don't really get much of that anymore. At my age, I'm just looking for retirement homes.

Or what about general life advice?

Coach K has been a profound influence on my life in a variety of areas—not just in basketball. The thing I took most from him (among so many things) is probably the value of preparation. I think whatever success I've been able to achieve in my life has been due less to talent and more to being prepared for the opportunities that are out there.

So I prepared myself for life after basketball. It came a little sooner than I expected, but I was prepared for it. As best I could, I took care of the "have-tos" in my life so that I could experience some of the "want-tos." I'm very fortunate that I basically get to do what I want to do.

But I took care of the "have to" part. I took care of the school part. I paid attention to the steps I needed to take on the education front. When there were opportunities to work in broadcasting during the summers when I was in college, I took them. When I had the opportunity in law school to work for a law firm—even though it was only for a month—I did it.

I never said no to an opportunity. I made sure that I was prepared for the steps that may be ahead. If I chose not to take those steps, that's one thing. But I was going to be prepared for them. I think I took that more from Coach K than anything. Prepare yourself for what's important. We always did that as a basketball team, and certainly, I tried to do that in my personal life and professional life.

Chapter 11

Ayelette Robinson

Actress and Entrepreneur

No matter our career paths, I would argue that we all need to develop technical skills and marketing skills. Both skills are important, yet it's all too easy to spend an excessive amount of time on improving the former.

For starters, it's critical to develop our craft in our chosen line of work. The term "legal practice" includes the word *practice* for a reason. We may learn foundational skills like legal writing and research in law school, but we can spend the rest of our legal careers mastering those skills. Not only that, but the law is constantly evolving. A single legal decision can send ripple effects throughout your practice area, causing you and your colleagues to think of new ways to best represent your clients.

I would go one step further and include "softer skills" in this bucket. This includes things like finding clients, setting client expectations, managing paralegals, and building strong relationships with judges and court staff. While these skills aren't necessarily taught in law school, they are extremely valuable in our day-to-day lives as practicing attorneys.

Ultimately, we want to master these technical skills so we can provide the best possible legal representation. Having said this, our focus on mastering technical skills may come at the expense of other critical skills, which can help us reach our career goals. These are things like building our personal brands, marketing ourselves within our industry, and meeting mentors and other influential figures in our chosen lines of work.

Doing great work is a necessary—although not sufficient—condition of reaching our highest goals. Along with great work, we need to advocate for ourselves and aggressively pursue those objectives. There's no guarantee of success, but we substantially increase our odds by strengthening our technical and marketing skills.

To some, working on these marketing skills may seem awkward. It may feel too self-promotional or pushy. However, we all have a personal brand. Whether we realize it or not, we are implicitly broadcasting those brands every day. By taking control of our brands, *we* craft our public image—no matter what we want that image to be.

Ayelette Robinson knows how important it is to build technical and marketing skills in any given career. She is a former practicing attorney and knowledge management professional who left the legal world to pursue a career as an actress. Through an unexpected layoff and an "acting for non-actors" class she found on Groupon, Ayelette made the leap to acting and hasn't looked back.

Since then, Ayelette has been an actress, voiceover artist, and producer. Her talent as an actress and creator is evident on the screen. As just one example, Ayelette created, produced, and acted in a web series called The Couch. The Couch was a widely celebrated series. It won the Oniros Film Awards Best Screenplay and Best Web-Series, and Ayelette was selected to appear on the Emmy Awards nomination ballot for Outstanding Actress in a Short Form Comedy or Drama Series. Since then, Ayelette has gone beyond the actual craft of acting to help other actors and actresses pursue their dreams. She founded ActorsGuru, which helps actors track their relationships, events, and auditions. In acting, the "craft side" and "business side" are equally important. Actors must not only perfect their technical skills, but they must also market themselves. Tools like Actors-Guru can help actors and actresses better handle the business sides of their careers, but tools can only go so far.

Whether you remain in legal practice or want to leave the legal field to do something else, be your best advocate. While your craft is important, spend time shaping your personal brand, meeting others outside your company, and representing yourself in your chosen line of work. It is an investment, but that investment will likely pay off.

* * *

In your interview with *Authority* magazine, you said that you grew up in this extremely academic community. You also said that you didn't have many career role models at the time. Before you went to law school (and even when you were in law school), did you ever think that you would eventually build this career in film, television, and theater?

No. I grew up as an Orthodox Jew (Modern Orthodox) and went to a private Hebrew day school. There were literally two extracurricular activities: basketball and drama club. Most of my friends were on the basketball team. I personally was always a dancer, but never a sports athlete, so I became a team manager so I could spend time with my friends. I always had a seed in my mind that acting was interesting so I was also always part of the drama club. But we didn't have any training. There was no teacher. It was just all of us students finding a script, memorizing the words, and finding costumes and props.

Although it had always been in my mind that acting seemed interesting and cool and fascinating, I never actually knew what the technique involved. I assumed it was memorizing lines and pretending to say them in a certain way. So the seed was there, but I never had any contact with anything in the creative world. It always seemed like there were only two ways your career could go—you were either related to someone famous or you were waiting tables at 2:00 a.m. It really seemed either-or. And since I didn't want to be a stereotypical starving artist, it never seemed like a realistic career.

After college, I still didn't know what I wanted to do. I had studied Japanese in college, so I started working at a Japanese bookstore. I eventually got to a point where I felt that I wanted to have *some* career. I wanted to be able to say that I am an expert in something—even though I didn't know what that was.

My sister was a lawyer, so we started talking about that. She said, "I think you would do really well." After some thought and wondering if I wanted to be a student again, I decided to apply and made the decision to go to law school. The seed of wanting to be an actor was still there, but I had no information about what that actually meant as a career, so I never pursued it.

I even feel like that's the case within the legal industry, too. As I've spoken with other individuals for this book, many of them in their earlier days had some inkling of what a lawyer was. But it's hard to really know unless you're working in the industry. Considering that, however, you have to start somewhere, right? There has to be some spark of inspiration that leads you down that path. For you and the legal field, it was your sister. I'm sure she spoke about her experi-

ences. But how could you relate to them? At the time, what did you think that you would be getting out of a legal education?

Well, you said the word "education." I've never enjoyed being a student. The fact that I had to go back to school was a real turnoff for me. I've always felt, "If I'm going to be working, I want to get paid for it, I don't want to pay you for it." Obviously, education is important. But I thought, "I've been through college. I'd rather work and contribute to the world, rather than pay you to read books."

However, in talking to my sister and coming from this Jewish background that is very analytical, there is this mental analysis from Judaic studies that bridges well with legal analysis. I don't remember more details, but it seemed like my skill set would fit well.

At that point, you went to the University of Michigan Law School. I went to Michigan for college. It was a terrific experience. Why did Michigan stand out?

There were a few things. First, when I was applying, my mindset was, "I know I have to go back to school, but I don't want to be a student." I really didn't want the stereotypical competitive experience. I wanted a school that was going to be more supportive than competitive, and Michigan stood out for having a collaborative culture.

Being work-focused, I also really wanted an opportunity to do a clinic. That was important to me. And, while it might sound superficial, I never studied abroad during undergrad so I wanted an opportunity to study in a foreign country. Michigan is one of the few schools that has an amazing study abroad program for law school.

The final big piece for me was that I had family in Michigan, including my mother. I grew up near Boston, but my mom was living in Ann Arbor at the time. So there was a strong family reason to be there.

Ultimately, it was a combination of the vibe (which was fantastic), the clinical opportunities, the opportunity to study abroad, and family.

Did you end up studying abroad?

I did. I studied at University College London and it was wonderful.

Well, as a Michigan alum, I can attest to what you are saying about the atmosphere. Ann Arbor is a great place to live. The people are very nice. There are plenty of reasons to go there.

Absolutely. I have to say that I had the best law school experience. I'm so glad that I went to Michigan. It was perfect for me and I had a wonderful experience there.

Can you provide some more details about your experience? Perhaps how law students can maximize their law school experiences?

Yes. So again, I think the vibe of the community is important. I think it lived up to what I expected (which was that the students really were collaborative). There really was not a competitive environment at all. Certainly, that's how I felt with my class. That was huge.

Although I did have a very challenging first week. Before your first day of class, the reading assignments were over one hundred pages per class. It wasn't necessarily over one hundred pages for every class after that, but in that first week, it was around one hundred pages for each of your four core classes (Civil Procedure, Property, Criminal Law, and Torts).

They put up the assignments about four days before the first class. I'm a slow reader and I was up at 1:00 a.m. trying to get through all these assignments and started bawling. I didn't think I would be able to finish. I was wondering whether I made this horrible mistake. It was really bad. But then you get into the swing of things. Obviously, it turned out fine.

So for those readers that are potentially in that situation, it is mostly about developing grit and just grinding out the work, right?

Yeah. I think there's a very quick ramp-up period in the sense that it might be different from whatever you've been doing before. If you're coming straight out of undergrad, it's also probably a little bit different because maybe you've been in that reading mode beforehand.

But the core of class is discussion. While you certainly have to do your reading, if you have good professors and a good class where everyone is engaged with each other, it really becomes motivating to do the reading. You want to enter into these stimulating discussions. I think as soon as you get into the culture of it, it becomes easier.

You also don't want to get called out either. The Socratic Method forces you to do your reading because you don't want to be embarrassed if you're called on. So whether it was your 1L or 2L year, I'm sure you were thinking about what you wanted to do after graduation. I believe you went more onto the corporate law track in the beginning. Can you discuss your thought process behind that? Perhaps how you got your job and why you picked your firm?

Sure. I wanted to pick a profession that would suit me, but I definitely didn't have a specific direction. I certainly wasn't thinking, "I need to practice this type of law because that's where my heart is." My decision to become a lawyer was a purely professional one. I didn't have a personal connection to practice a particular area of law.

I definitely knew that I wanted financial stability. My point of view was that the reason I chose the career was to have professional stability. So private practice for me was kind of an easy decision. However, because I did not know what type of law I wanted to practice, when I was summering, I wanted a firm that would let me rotate among different areas so I could see what each practice area was like. My two criteria for accepting a summer associate position were, first, allow me to rotate across different areas so I can see what it's actually like day-to-day. Second, growing up on the East Coast, California always had this exotic reputation. I wanted to spend half my summer in San Francisco.

Now, I had been living in New York prior to law school and I always assumed that I was going to practice in New York. Especially since law firms only hire you if you have a connection to the city where they're hiring, I was applying to New York law firms. But I wanted firms that had San Francisco offices and would let me split my summer with that office.

Were you able to split your summer?

Yes, I did. Then, I received separate offers from the two offices. I could go back to whichever one I wanted. I decided to go to San Francisco. I ended up loving it there.

Just to back up for a bit: when you were at Michigan, were you spending time on your creative pursuits? Or did you put that to the side and solely focus on your coursework?

So again, acting to me was like ether. I never actually knew what it was. It seemed like this ethereal, wonderful place that was like paradise. But it didn't have a grounding in any reality whatsoever. It never even dawned on me to pursue a situation where I'd actually be acting. It just never even entered my brain. It was so far from reality.

But I had grown up dancing. I had started ballroom dancing in college, and I took the opportunity to be a part of the ballroom team in Michigan. I didn't pursue it 1L year because I was focusing on school. But starting my 2L year, I joined the Michigan ballroom team. And then for my third year, I spent my fall semester studying abroad at University College London and was lucky enough to be a part of UCL's ballroom team.

That's great. I'm sure it was also a great way to manage stress. So you ultimately get this offer from O'Melveny & Myers' San Francisco office. Looking at your career in corporate law, what did you find the most rewarding or challenging?

I liked the analysis, problem solving, and creativity. People think of the law as being stodgy or boring. But I found it creative, resourceful, thoughtful, and analytical. It was very engaging and active. You're also never bored. I have always been a person who thrives when I have more going on, so to me, being busy and having lots of projects at the same time was very positive.

And I ended up choosing corporate work over litigation because I felt like the core of litigation is being antagonistic with the other side, while the core of corporate work is getting both sides to agree to something. I wanted to be in that more positive kind of framework, where you are trying to get to a place where both sides are happy.

When you say corporate work, what specifically were you doing?

For my first year, I was focused on lender-side financing work and also some M&A. In my second year, I moved to the Silicon Valley office, so I began doing venture capital and public securities work.

In that sort of situation, I think every Big Law associate has this interesting eye-opening experience. Law school teaches you a very theoretical foundation of the law. It can be great in and of itself. But

when you get to your firm, there is the surprise of not really know-ing how to practice law. How did you learn what you didn't know? Along with this, how did you handle the stress in those early days?

I don't know that I have a great memory to provide much detail. I will say that it probably wasn't as much of a transition for me because I had been working before law school. For me, the bigger transition was going back to school. And when I went back to work, I thought, "This feels so nice. I'm back home again."

In fact, I had been a paralegal for a year before law school. That was at a small litigation boutique in New York. While litigation and corporate work is different, I still had some sense of the day-to-day. Between that and just yearning to be in the thick of actual work versus theory, it was more like water in the desert than a struggle.

As far as your paralegal experience, do you think that prospective lawyers or law students should get that type of experience before starting law school?

I wouldn't say that it's required. It really depends on what information you need in order to make the decision. What actually prompted me to make the decision was talking to my sister and thinking, "Oh, why don't I at least start work and see if it feels like a fit for me." Being a paralegal let me get a little more information.

I also had this perspective that, "If I'm going to be working long hours in a complex and high-activity environment, I'd rather get paid more." So I thought, "I might as well just go to law school and be a lawyer." There are people who seem to just know that they want to be lawyers. If so, I certainly don't think they would need to be a paralegal first. But I think it does make sense if you feel like you need more information.

There may be a good number of readers that are considering a Big Law path. This is especially true at the so-called "Top Fourteen" schools. The financial rewards are compelling, but along with that, it is an easy path to follow. Recruiters come to you. You attend on-campus interviews for two or three days. You can talk to many firms in a short period. It is very easy. So what should those readers

think about if they are going down this path and considering a Big Law career?

I think you need to be aware of the world that you are joining. Make a conscious decision that it's a world you actively want to be in, or at least don't mind being in.

Big Law is a very high activity and potentially high-stress environment. A lot is expected of you—both in terms of quantity and quality. If you thrive on that or are okay dealing with that to get some other benefit that you want, then great. Go for it.

But I think it's really about being aware of that environment. For some people, I certainly have seen it take a big toll. I think it's really about being aware of that situation and deciding that it's okay (or even great because you thrive in it). Make that conscious choice to go into that environment in exchange for the benefits that you're getting.

Yes, I think that's really important. You shouldn't let inertia take over with a decision like that. You must make a conscious, active decision to go down this path. So let's discuss your transition from corporate legal work to acting. Can you take us back to that time? Can you give the readers a sense of what you were thinking and what those early days looked like?

I transitioned out of legal practice because I knew I didn't want to be a partner. I really enjoyed the practice of law but I didn't enjoy being a salesperson. When you're a partner, fifty or eighty percent of what you do is selling—that's the business development side of it. And that was not something I ever enjoyed or wanted to do. Funnily enough, this comes back to you later when you're an entrepreneur. You kind of have to do it.

Anyway, when I first started researching other opportunities, I thought, "I'm still very happy to practice another two, three, four years until I find the right thing." I was not in a rush to leave. But I happened to come across this wonderful opportunity. It was in the professional development department at Morrison & Foerster, and they were hiring attorneys into that role. The role was about helping attorneys grow their careers, so they wanted people who knew what it meant to be an attorney at a firm. I fell in love with the people there and found the work really interesting. Relatively quickly, it felt like a very natural fit.

So I went into that role. At that point, knowledge management (KM) was under the professional development umbrella. I had never heard the term "knowledge management" before, so I had no idea what it was. But a project opportunity came up, and I thought, "Sure. Tell me what it is." From that moment, I was completely hooked on the knowledge management world. It was an amazing fit for me because it's this marriage of analysis, understanding how people work, and envisioning what they need to make their jobs easier. Also, it's understanding the processes and technology that need to be developed to support those changes.

I ended up focusing mostly on tech more than process, and I've always found technology really fun. I'm not a coder but I'm very comfortable with technology and tech language. Part of this knowledge management role is being that liaison between a practitioner (like an attorney, paralegal, or someone on the business side) and the tech professionals.

I loved that liaison role, and I learned that I have a deep interest and knack for usability, UI design, and stuff like that. It became this really natural fit. So that's when I ended up staying in knowledge management and developed that career. I was doing some speaking and writing. I fully expected that to be my career.

Once I transitioned into KM, I had a little more time on my hands. In the time that I was practicing law, I had not been dancing. I just didn't have the time. But now, I was able to go back to it. My dance coach, who had taken acting classes early in her career, said, "To enhance your dancing, you might want to consider taking an acting class." She just kind of threw that out as a recommendation. And it brought acting to the front of my mind again.

A few weeks later, there was a Groupon for an acting for non-actors class in San Francisco. I knew nothing about acting studios or coaches or even what to research, but I lucked out because it just happened to be at a really wonderful studio. And as soon as I took that class, I knew, "This is what I was meant to do with my life." It wasn't even a question.

Can you talk about that a bit more? Like what did you find there that you weren't getting in your knowledge management role (or even your role as a practicing attorney)?

If you don't really know what acting is, imagine that a painter uses paint and color as their palette. For actors, their palette is their emotions. Your job as an actor is to be whatever emotion is necessary for the conversation you're having.

Growing up, I had a very chaotic family environment. A lot of emotional evolution happened through my youth and into college. As I processed all of it, I had discovered that I loved feeling all of my emotions. That was something that was really wonderful. It made me feel human.

I had done that personal work, so for me, learning that acting was all about living in your emotions was the most wonderful discovery. I immediately knew, "If I can spend my life living in my emotions, that's amazing. Count me in." I just had no idea what it was before.

So this all came to you during this acting class?

Right. While it was a basic class, I got the foundation of, "I get to call on my emotions—joy, anger, sadness, or ecstasy—whenever I want?" To be able to call on any of them at any time filled me so much. It was also the fact that there was this whole career that I could build off of. It was like a switch went off in my mind. I knew it was my calling.

That's really interesting. Nonetheless, even when you had this realization, you still needed to take the next step and pursue acting more seriously. I'm sure it's a scary thing—especially because you were in a good position. You were enjoying your knowledge management role. How did you go one step further and actually commit to a new career in acting?

The studio happened to be founded by a woman who had studied directly with Sanford Meisner, and he had developed a two-year training curriculum. After the initial six-week class, I discovered that the two-year curriculum was going to be starting the next month. I thought, "Should I do it? Do I have the time?" I was really torn. But I knew in my gut that I was going to do it. So I did it and I kept doing it as I was working. The classes were only once per week, but we always had homework in between.

The first few months were going by. The classes were progressing. I was thinking, "Okay, I know that this is what I'm meant to do. But how am I going to make this happen? How can I get a job that's flexible and that allows me to go on auditions? How am I going to make this work?"

And lo and behold, about six months into the Meisner course, I got laid off from the new firm I had recently joined. I was thrilled. I now had the time and some financial resources (severance) to figure out what I wanted to do. I knew that I wanted to switch. It was the gift that I had been dreaming of. I had really been stressing about leaving a job before I had something else. So this was the answer to my prayers.

Right, it was almost like divine intervention.

It was just perfect. When I was transitioning from legal to knowledge management and suddenly had more time on my hands, I had taken a Pilates certification course. I had always loved Pilates and thought, "I want to dive in and learn more about this." I never planned to teach it but wanted to understand it more deeply, and it dovetailed well with my body knowledge from dancing. Well, now was the perfect time to put the education to use. I became a certified personal trainer (this was still in Northern California) and now had the flexibility to start going out on auditions and being on projects. That was really, really wonderful.

Well, you've certainly had successes in your acting career. One of your most prominent projects was called The Couch. Not only were you selected for the Emmy Awards nomination ballot for Outstanding Actress in a Short Form Comedy or Drama Series, but you were also the creator and producer for that same series. Looking at your success with The Couch, are there any key insights or takeaways that you have from that experience?

I think it was an example of two things: the business side of acting and the fact that you have a lot more control than you may think.

Control over your career?

Yes. There are absolutely aspects that are out of your control. But there are certain aspects where you do have control. Part of that is learning the industry, building relationships, and marketing yourself. Part of marketing yourself is creating your own projects. Especially now where you can put your stuff out into the world, there's a major assumption that you will be creating your own projects. And because of my work background, it was an organic transition for me to become a producer. Note that in addition, a lot of actors are also writers. I'm not personally a writer, but many actors do that as well.

The key is that there are opportunities for you to have more control and take more control. You don't want to come in with the mentality that you are waiting for an agent, casting director, or someone else to discover you. You have control over a lot of what happens in your career.

So at least from the marketing and business sense, that's what led you to create The Couch? It was the fact that you had this idea, you wanted to bring it out into the world, and there are tools and people to help you do that.

Exactly.

And I'm assuming you would do more of those projects in the future?

Absolutely. There have been two different features along the way, but a lot goes into making a project happen and they can take a long time. For a while now, I have had a feature script. I've also been looking at optioning this book series. There's so much that goes on behind the scenes before you get to a point where it's in front of people. But I'm absolutely still wearing that producer hat.

One of the big successes for me with The Couch was that the Emmys have a short form series. This was a project that I completely envisioned, brought the team together to do, and submitted to the Emmys. For this short form category, they get hundreds of submissions and only put thirty on the ballot. I was among thirty on that ballot for outstanding actress, and that was something I had key control over.

I think the real takeaway is to know you do have control over your career. Do you have control over all of it? No. But if you want to progress, you can take a significant amount of control. It's there for the taking.

So I'm just trying to think of the lawyer who is reading this book and is maybe interested in making a career change that is similar to yours. Maybe they are still at their job and are giving this acting idea some serious thought. How can those readers prepare themselves or better their odds of successfully making that career transition?

For any creative pursuit (maybe you want to be a sculptor, singer, or actor), you'll need to have flexibility. You do need to find some role—whatever that is—that allows you to attend events, auditions, industry meetings, and such on an irregular schedule. And now that we're dealing with Covid-19, I think everyone's more flexible with working from home which is helpful.

This is a bit of a digression but goes to whether it is potentially hard to make the transition. While I'm not full-time acting yet, for me, the transition is such an easy decision. When people ask me about whether it was hard to make that career change, I think, "Should I spend one hundred percent of my time doing something that isn't leading me anywhere that I want to go? Or should I spend forty percent of my time doing something that is supporting the other sixty percent that I know is exactly where I want to be in five to ten years?" To me, it's such an easy comparison. I think, "How can you even ask that question?"

When you put it that way, definitely.

So do you need to find that forty percent to support the sixty percent? Yes, you do. But for me, it's a no-brainer. I just think, "Okay, part of this track is finding that forty percent thing." That still seems one thousand times better than spending one hundred percent of my time doing something that's not what I want to do.

The key part of that is flexibility, right?

At least as an actor. Again, other roles may have different needs. As an actor, because you specifically have auditions and gigs that you need to attend, that flexibility is important. Although auditioning now is much more self-tape, which is helpful. You might have twenty-four or forty-eight hours to record a tape, so you can do it in the evening, for example. Certainly, when things are in-person, you have to go to your audition in the middle of the day, but more and more projects are using only self-tapes or are at least open to self-tapes.

Just to be clear: self-tape is just recording yourself instead of attending an in-person audition?

Exactly. Putting Covid-19 aside, most auditions were typically in-person. You show up and, depending on the role you're auditioning for, any combination of the casting team could be running the audition. It could be one person (like a casting assistant who will run the camera and show the tape to everybody else later) or a few casting people, the director, and producers. You could literally have anywhere from one to twelve people in the room.

But with Covid-19, most auditions have become self-tape or at least done remotely over video software. In addition to addressing health safety concerns, there are a few other benefits to self-tapes. The casting team can see more actors because, for each audition, they're only spending three to five minutes watching a tape instead of fifteen to twenty minutes in a room talking and taking multiple takes. And with self-tapes, the production saves money because they don't need to pay for a physical space.

I should highlight that my career focus has been film and that's where these self-tapes come in. Theater is a little bit different. With film, in all cases, they are going to record the audition. As they are going through everybody's auditions after the fact, they want to be able to re-watch the tapes of the top choices to compare them. Also, the final product, the film, is going to be on camera, so they want to see you on camera.

Theater is a little different. The audition will typically be in the theater where the show is. Although I have seen them recorded because, again, it makes their job a little bit easier when they're going back and trying to compare different people. However, the recording is less directly relevant because the final deliverable is the live performance on stage.

So in film, they do always record it, but the auditions themselves were in-person. But now that's changed. It does put more responsibility on the actors though. Self-tapes mean that you as an actor have to have a basic filming setup. It doesn't have to be complicated, but there are a few basics you need. In addition, you have to find your own reader, a person to read the other characters' lines. And now, that's more challenging because you need to have someone do it virtually (or maybe even over audio), and you have to imagine the person you're talking to and look at a spot on the wall as though it's that person.

Now, there are many self-tape studios. For example, you can go and pay fifteen dollars for fifteen minutes. But most people can do it from home because phone quality filming is just fine.

Yes, it sounds like it has become much more convenient.

Exactly. So going back to the flexibility question, since there is now a higher percentage of self-tapes, you may not need quite as much schedule flexibility for your auditions. But at some point in your career, you're going to have in-person auditions.

The other thing is unless they are really independent projects that tape more on the weekends, most projects are taping Monday through Friday. When you do book something, you will need to have that flexibility to actually go and do it.

So if I can take another step back really quickly. In those early days, you took your acting course and I'm assuming that your skills were quickly improving. But how do you get those first couple of auditions? Does it come down to cold calling or just taking anything that you can?

Different cities have different resources. Cities like Los Angeles and New York (and other mid-sized cities like Boston, Atlanta, and San Francisco) have casting websites. You put up your headshots, reels, clips, resumé, and special skills you have such as foreign languages, accents, activities such as sports, martial arts, or dancing, or experience like medical knowledge or other specialized techniques. What happens is when someone has a project, they put the project up on the casting site. They have what are called breakdowns, which describe the high-level summary of the project, shooting dates, and other details. This is so you can confirm whether you're actually able to do it. Then, for each character that they're casting, there's a mini summary of that character. For any character that you think you're a match for, you click on that character to submit your profile. Then, the casting team goes through all the submissions and decides who they want to call in for an audition. That's the process for all independent projects.

For network projects, it's a similar process but there's an extra layer. The main casting site in Los Angeles is called Breakdown Express. While anyone with an independent project can post to the actor-facing side of this platform called Actors Access (where actors can submit themselves), network projects post only to the Breakdown Express side. Only agents and managers have access to these projects, so you're not able to submit to them without agent or manager representation.

But then on top of that, to your point about cold calling, there is a whole other aspect which is the business side of acting. Just clicking submit is not enough. You need to pitch yourself, put your work out there, and build relationships. But from a logistical point of view, that's how submitting to projects works.

So to answer your first question about how I got my first few auditions, I created a profile and started submitting for just a couple of background roles. I had never even been on set before. I was like, "What does that even mean?" For a background role, they don't have you audition. They are just picking people who look different and diverse. But you get to be on set. So I highly recommend doing that to start because you get to hear the terminology, see how the day flows, and how shooting even works. You want to be experienced with that so that the first time you're on set with a speaking role, you're not asking questions that everybody else knows and expects you to know. You want to know how everything works so that you can focus on doing your job as an actor.

Also, a benefit to starting your acting career in a smaller city like San Francisco is that it's a much smaller acting market and is ninety-nine percent non-union. This is great when you are first starting because you're not in the union yet, so you get a lot of opportunity with such a high volume of non-union projects.

That all makes sense. I'm just thinking about the lawyer that is just starting out their acting career. It seems like the basic toolkit involves a headshot. Would they need an agent? In other words, what would they need to start on day one?

To start out, you need a craft. You need to actually know what you are doing. I would not get headshots until you have been in an acting class for at least six months. I know it can be hard to imagine when you're outside of the industry. But it would be like saying, "Oh, you want to practice at a law firm? Just show up in a suit. Go to a law firm's reception lobby in a suit and say, 'I want to practice law here.'" They would give you a funny look and say, "What are you talking about? You need to go to law school and you need to know what you're doing." So I would say be in a class for at least six months to get started so you understand the core.

At that point, the actual package includes headshots. You should also include a reel or acting clips. I think it's nice to have both options. Some casting directors like to have a reel where one file includes short snippets of acting in different types of roles. But casting directors are very, very busy, and for some, their approach is, "Just send me the clip that relates to the role that I am casting. I don't need to see clips on seven other types of roles that I'm not looking for right now." So it's nice to have both versions.

You do not need to have an agent or manager to start. In fact, one of the common sayings is that agents get ten percent of the money because they only do ten percent of the work. In your career, you are expected to do ninety percent of the work. As you evolve and get to the point where you will be auditioning for a network, then absolutely. Getting an agent or manager on your team is going to be part of that growth. But when you are first starting, you absolutely do not need that. You are going to want to do non-union projects, and you absolutely do not need an agent or manager to get on those non-union projects and get started.

Correct me if I'm wrong, but I'm assuming starting actors have a better chance of getting on independent projects compared to network ones.

Getting on a network is almost like becoming a partner at a law firm. No one's going to hire you to be a partner at a law firm until you've been practicing. You have to be really good at what you do. It's like talking to someone who has been in law school for six months versus someone that has been practicing for six years. They can see the difference right away. There's no comparison.

So first, you need to be really good at what you do. The other thing is logistical. That is the fact that network projects are basically all union (whereas independent projects can be union or non-union). When you're first starting, I think you want to jump right in and get that on-set experience. Get on those non-union projects. See what it's like.

But eventually, to start expanding your career, you are going to want to join the union. There are a few ways to join the union, and in each case, you must meet some requirements. When I was starting, you could join the union by producing a web series with a union actor. By having that SAG-AFTRA (union) actor on the project, it would be considered a union project. Then, a non-union actor on the same project can fill out the appropriate forms saying, "I was on this union project. Now, I get to join the union." Note that they've modified the rules now.

Joining the SAG-AFTRA union is definitely something you want to look at down the road. But when you are first starting, you don't even want to join the union because there are so many more non-union projects and it's much easier to book those. You want to just get the experience of being on set and it's easier to do that when you're non-union. Get the experience first and then join the union when you're ready.

So if I want to become an actor right now, I wouldn't know any of this stuff. I'm assuming it is helpful to find a mentor, right? It seems like it would almost be a requirement.

I was really lucky. The Bay Area Acting Studio where I started helped students understand that there is a craft side to the career and a business side to the career. If you have this legal background, you kind of get it. To be a partner, you can't just be in the books or on paper drafting documents. You have to be building a clientele. You have to be building relationships with partners. You may have to write, speak, and publish. There's a whole business side to convince the partnership why you are valuable as a new partner at the firm. It's not just being able to draft a document.

It really is the same thing with acting. Again, I was really lucky that the first studio had both technique and business courses. Since I had worked before and had other careers before, I immediately understood why that made sense. I started studying up on that right away.

To your point, there are many classes and ways to learn about the business side of acting. But absolutely from day one, I would recommend attending a studio where you get coaching on both the technique side and the business side.

Speaking of that business side, do you use any of your legal background or training in your career? Do you think it gives you a certain advantage over others (or perhaps a disadvantage)? I'd ask this both on the acting side and what you are currently doing as an entrepreneur.

I would say that as an actor, just having had other life experiences (as opposed to starting a career straight out of high school or college) can be helpful. One of my acting teachers used to always say something great. New people joined the studio and would say, "Oh, I have never really trained as an actor before." He would always say, "Have you been a human being for the last few decades?" They say, "Well, yeah." And then he would say, "Well, then you trained as an actor because what you're doing as an actor is being a human being in whatever situation you're given to be in." So having had a lot of life experience and different careers, I have more insight into different angles of being a human being.

Then, from a business point of view, I do feel grateful that when it comes to things like contracts and transactions, I feel comfortable with them. But I also know what I don't know. I've never been an entertainment lawyer, so I do not rely on my own skills in terms of knowing the ins and outs of entertainment contract terms. I don't know enough about entertainment law to know what the standard is, for example, or if something key was left out, or if this specific contractual term is actually good or bad within the industry. I have an entertainment lawyer that I rely on. But I'm completely comfortable at least reading the contract and being able to say, "I understand what this is saying. I just have no idea what's normal." The fact that it doesn't intimidate me and that I feel comfortable with it feels unusual as an actor. I think a lot of actors think of legalese and think, "They're trying to cheat me out of something," as opposed to saying, "Okay, we're two parties. We need to come up with terms that are comfortable for both of us. How do we get there?"

Right. The focus is on creating mutual value.

Exactly.

As far as the financial aspect of quitting a legal job or knowledge management job to become an actor, it seems like there is always this stereotype. It's really about the starving actor or actress. The consensus seems to be that it is such a financial struggle to try to reach many acting dreams. How can readers overcome those financial struggles, whether or not they have law school debt?

This may not be a very satisfying answer, but the key is don't be a starving artist. I say that because there are some people who have this vision. It's like this grand thing to say, "I'm starving for my art." I think there actually are some people that have that idea. It's not the mindset I come from at all, but I have seen that.

Really, the first thing is to say, "Okay. I know that this career can take a while. It's being an entrepreneur, just like if you were starting a startup. You can't quit the day that you're just starting to develop your software. You still have to have your job and then also be working on that." The way to think of it, really and truly, is that you're being an entrepreneur.

You know that you're building something that is going to be your future. But until you get to that point, you need to have something else that's going to complement it. So part of the task is to find the thing that's going to complement it. That's it. Can that take a few months? Of course. But reach out to other creatives and find out what they do.

For me, starting off as a fitness trainer was perfect. You still have that in-person obligation and certainly, you don't want to be canceling on clients at a moment's notice. But when you're starting, you're not going to have tons of auditions all the time. You have at least some flexibility to be scheduling sessions around when you want to be doing them. So anything that's like a consultant-type role (where you have control over your schedule) is a great place to start. Eventually, you would want to be in a position where you don't ever have any face time requirements. That lets you be much more flexible. But usually, the easiest thing to transition to is some sort of consultant-type role. Even though you have the face time requirement, you have control over when that happens.

So really canvas your own skills, see what you're good at, and see what you could sell.

That's right.

I'd like to ask you about ActorsGuru and the marketing side of acting. Can you further discuss how lawyers transitioning into acting can make a name for themselves (especially in the early days)? And how does ActorsGuru help them with this important task?

So now we've talked about how there's the craft side and the business side. ActorsGuru's job is to make the business side easy for you. Actors-Guru came about because of my knowledge management background and wanting a source of passive income (in the sense that I can do it on my own schedule, though there's still a lot of work involved). It's a way for you to keep track of your projects and industry events, the relationships you're building, your auditions and patterns in those auditions, your training, and then make plans based on all this aggregated and linked information you have. There's a lot of business stuff in terms of building your craft, your industry relationships, and your marketing package (headshots, reel, and resumé). ActorsGuru helps you manage all of that in one place so that this part doesn't become stressful for you.

For example, you might notice that casting directors call you in regularly for medical roles. Knowing that pattern can help you pitch to casting directors by creating your own medical acting reel with clips in different roles (for example, doctor, nurse, or EMT) and in different show styles (for example, *Chicago Med* versus *Grey's Anatomy*), and display that you're comfortable with technical medical lingo.

When it comes to marketing, you're going to go through lots of different headshots. One casting director is going to say this headshot is so you and it's perfect. Another casting director is going to say, "If I saw this headshot, I'd pass right over you." So you want to remember what each person's preferences are for when you interact with them next. And, by the way, that subjective analysis is going to happen with everything—your performance, your headshot, your reel, everything—so not taking feedback personally is a big part of the career.

Right. I'm not in the industry, but if I was in that position, I would feel like it certainly fits a need that I would have. While marketing and the business sides are huge parts of it, I would probably want to spend more of my time focusing on my technical craft. Is there anything that I didn't ask that you would have liked to know as a lawyer or knowledge management professional transitioning into acting? Alternatively, do you just have general advice for lawyers that are unsatisfied with their careers and want to do something else?

The biggest personal advice I would give is that you are the only one living your life. No one else is living it. You need to do what you are driven to do and not let other people's opinions affect you. Everyone around you is going to have an opinion. Hopefully, many of them are supportive. Almost certainly, there will be some that are not, and those people can live their own lives however they want to live them. But you're the only one who is living your life and has to live with the consequences of that life.

So make whatever decision is right for you. If transitioning into acting isn't right for you, then don't do it. But don't make your decision based on someone else's opinion.

You need to make that decision for yourself—even if it is uncomfortable. I'm paraphrasing, but like you said, you could be one hundred percent in the direction that perhaps gives you more money. However, it could be in the complete opposite direction of where you want to go. So you want to be heading in the right overall direction. Do you know of any helpful resources (besides ActorsGuru) or classes that lawyers or law students can look at to facilitate their transition into acting?

In terms of acting teachers, I absolutely have my favorites. But really the biggest thing (and I've already touched on this) is to recognize that it is a skill. It is a craft. You need to invest in becoming good at that craft. You wouldn't expect a doctor to perform surgery on their first day of medical school. You wouldn't expect a glassblower to create something incredibly intricate and detailed on their first day of glassblowing.

So because it's a craft, expect to invest in the craft. As far as specific resources, my experience is in San Francisco and Los Angeles. Obviously, readers will be in different cities. I have my personal favorite classes. But because acting is about you as a person becoming something else, you need a teacher who brings out the best in you personally. Many teachers will know the same information, but you need a teacher who helps you be the best you can be.

This is in contrast to many other professions. For example, you can go to law school and learn how to read a contract. You may not love the teacher, but they're going to teach you what the terms are. But as an actor, you must have someone that's speaking the language of your humanity (both in terms of actual terminology and support for you). I would say the key is to audit classes in at least three or four different studios before deciding where you want to study.

Yes, I was going to ask how you would get that information before-hand. But like you say, it's about testing the waters, auditing different courses, and sticking with the one that speaks to you.

Yeah. That shows you what's common across all teachers. Acting is like five principles and everyone just teaches them in a different way. So when you audit a few classes, you see what's common. And then that highlights the differences among the teachers so that you can find someone that helps bring out the best in you. That's going to help you grow the most.

That makes sense. It takes some patience. You need to keep putting yourself out there and trying different things. Hopefully, you'll eventually find that one person that helps you perfect your craft.

Absolutely. And as you evolve, you develop different tools in your toolset. For example, joining an improv company isn't my dream, but I do have a goal of taking at least take one improv class per year to maintain that muscle. And there are other helpful and powerful skills as well. For example, Linklater voice technique is amazing. I would say as you evolve, be open to expanding your toolset by studying other complementary techniques.

We've alluded to this in the conversation, but you are also an entrepreneur. You started your own business and that requires its own set of skills. How did you quickly pick up those skills and how did you take on the many challenges that come with becoming an entrepreneur?

You know, it's funny. Acting was an obvious decision. It was that light switch that I talked about. I didn't care what challenges there were. I was just going to do it. But when it came to ActorsGuru, I grew up being sure that I never wanted to own my own business. I always felt, "I don't want that pressure. I don't want that stress. I just want to do my job and get paid." And lo and behold, here I am.

I launched in January 2019. That first year, honestly, was pretty crushing in a lot of ways. I was doing so many things. As you know, it is just so, so hard to really gain traction in the first couple of years. I was pursuing every possible marketing angle, partnership, or affiliation that I could think of to grow the business. I knew what it was like to be an actor, so I knew points throughout the journey that I could insert myself.

There is so much uphill work. "Actor-preneur" is another word that people use. In any creative career, you're basically an entrepreneur. You have to put in an enormous amount of work and then eventually the returns come in. As much as it wasn't surprising to me as an actor, it was surprising to me as an entrepreneur. I had a hard time with it. The key is just being prepared for it. Understand the ratio of how much work you're initially going to have to put in. But as long as you're prepared for it and expect it, then it won't bring you down as much. Ninety-nine percent perspiration, right?

Yes, it's also about managing your expectations.

Right. The surprise was how much work was involved—especially because I felt like I knew the career. I was like, "I know how to do this. I know how to market to actors because I'm an actor." I think I initially underestimated the marketing work involved. That was my personal challenge.

The other thing is to be mindful of who you ask to join your team, whether that's temporarily hiring someone for a project or a more permanent partnership. Because this is your baby and something that you care about so much, you don't want to have some voice in there that's going to make that world start to feel negative. You need to have voices and collaborators that are all working to build your product or service up.

CHAPTER 12

Sander Daniels

Entrepreneur

It is safe to say that working for or founding startups has become an extremely appealing career option. Startups are inherently exciting. They represent the opportunity to leverage new ideas and technologies to create immense value in the world. Not only that, but the financial rewards can be life-changing.

For attorneys, the most obvious path into the startup world is to go from their current practicing gig to an in-house counsel position at a startup. There is nothing inherently wrong with this. In fact, by following this path, you can make a huge difference in a young company's life *and* take on challenging legal work. That said, it isn't the only way to get involved with startups. Some law school grads and practicing attorneys choose to take an operational role in young companies. Others may take the leap and create their own startups.

Whether you want to start a brick-and-mortar business or have a killer app idea, there are plenty of resources to help you get that business off the ground. This is especially true if you have any interest in a tech startup. In the past, non-technical founders may have found it nearly impossible to transform their nascent ideas into working websites or apps. Now, there is an extensive ecosystem that makes it substantially easier to transform nearly any type of startup idea into a minimum viable product.[1]

That's not all. The stigma against entrepreneurship in the United States isn't as strong as it used to be. In the past, if your startup failed,

---

1   Specifically, so-called "no code" tools let non-technical founders launch all sorts of software applications without writing a single line of code. Putting aside the debate of whether startup founders should learn how to code, these no-code tools let technical and non-technical founders quickly create and iterate on all types of digital products. For instance, Bubble.io is a website that lets anyone prototype and build a new app in just a few hours.

it may have been extremely difficult to bounce back from that failure. It would have been tougher to find a new job or fundraise for a new venture. Today, a failed startup isn't a career-ender. In fact, that failure can be the first stepping-stone in a ludicrously successful entrepreneurial career.[2]

Just because it is easier to start a business, however, doesn't mean that it is easier to grow and scale that business. No matter what product or service you are selling, it is critical to find product-market fit. It can take a long time. It may not even happen at all. That said, the barriers to entry are low enough that you can enter the arena *right now*, whether you are a law student or a practicing lawyer.

Sander Daniels is a cofounder of Thumbtack. As you may already know, Thumbtack is a digital platform connecting local professionals with individuals who need to get things done. On the Thumbtack platform, users can find everything from movers and electricians to roofers and personal trainers. Founded in 2008, the company has experienced both highs and lows, including layoffs during the height of Covid-19. Nonetheless, the company continues to evolve. In June of 2021, the company raised $275 million on more than a $3 billion valuation. With Thumbtack allocating more resources to becoming a "home management platform," Sander and his colleagues continue to provide significant value to their users.

Sander traces his Thumbtack origins to his time at Yale Law School. At the time, Sander was looking for ways to balance the gauntlet of law school with hobbies and interests outside the law. He and two of his friends chatted and realized they were all interested in starting something together. It wasn't necessarily a "tech startup" *per se*. Sander and his friends considered things like political advocacy groups and nonprofits. But after thinking of several different startup ideas, Sander and his soon-to-be cofounders settled on the idea that became Thumbtack. Sander, however, didn't just jump ship and go all-in on the Thumbtack idea. Instead, he went to Sullivan & Cromwell and practiced for around two years. Once he amassed enough savings and hit his pre-planned exit date, Sander made the leap and joined Thumbtack full-time. He has remained there ever since.

---

2   There are countless examples of startup founders that failed at their first ventures. Some of the few that come to mind include Travis Kalanick (eventual founder of Uber), Kathryn Minshew (eventual founder of The Muse), and Nick Woodman (eventual founder of GoPro).

Sander's story shows that law students and lawyers can thrive as entrepreneurs. While the road to entrepreneurial success is never easy, law students and lawyers can rely on their intelligence, drive, and work ethic to better their odds of success. While these qualities aren't sufficient to create a successful startup, they will certainly help in getting started on the right foot.

* * *

You've had quite an interesting career, from Yale Law School to Sullivan and Cromwell to Thumbtack. But to start at the beginning, when did this idea of law school or becoming a lawyer first enter your mind?

While I was in college. My dad went to law school and got his law degree, but he never practiced. It wasn't until I was in college[3] that I seriously considered going to law school. In college, I double-majored in environmental engineering and international studies. I studied a lot of history, politics, and public policy.

I always had a passion for politics. I grew up in the Washington, D.C. area. I had interned on Capitol Hill during college. Since I loved philosophy, public policy, and politics and thought I would have a career in Washington D.C., law school made a lot of sense.

What did success look like to you at that point? Did you think of running for office one day or working more behind-the-scenes in the political world?

I thought I would maybe like to run for office one day. I also thought that being chief of staff in a political campaign or for a senator or a governor could be awesome. That's what I had my eye on.

And I'm assuming you would use your law degree to perhaps work in the legal field for a little bit. From there, you would transition into a political role?

---

3   Sander attended college at Yale University. He graduated in 2005.

Sure.

Besides law school, were you seriously considering other options at that time?

There were other paths I was considering. I was considering a Master's in Public Policy at the Johns Hopkins School for Advanced International Studies. I was also considering a JD/MBA. I did have this potential interest in getting an MBA in the back of my mind. But in all of those cases, they were going to be dual degrees with a JD. A JD was always a central part of it.

When I speak with prospective law students, a good number think that law school will open doors to some other career. Other prospective law students may go to law school because they really don't know what else to do. What do you think of those justifications? First, did you believe them? And second, do you think they're valid?

I'll never forget when I showed up at law school in the first week and met my classmates and learned that ninety percent of them actually wanted to be lawyers for the rest of their lives. I applied to law school and attended not at all because I wanted to be a lawyer but, first, because I was intellectually interested in the law, and second, because I wanted to build a life in public policy. So that was really surprising to me.

I really wish somebody had educated me beforehand—exactly why people go to law school, what you study in law school, and the fact that it's reading cases and case law for three years straight. I was very uneducated about it when I applied and was accepted.

One thing that I think is unfortunate about law school is that it naturally funnels you into very specific career paths. It's kind of built to do so—mostly by the recruiting processes that happened on campuses. So what I have in mind are clerkships and law firms. At least at Yale, there was this incredible social pressure to apply to clerkships in your second year of law school. There was this incredible social pressure to apply to be on law journal during your first year. There was this incredible social pressure to get a law firm job during your third year. Those were almost inescapable.

I knew that doing a clerkship was the last thing in the world I wanted to do. It was way too academic and way too professorial. I had always been very interested in a practical career (something where I was able to build something). Even though I knew that a clerkship was not the right fit for me, it was still so hard and anxiety-inducing to be surrounded by people who were going after a clerkship. It was difficult to try to stand aside from the tide of clerkship applications and do my own thing.

I can't say that going to law school was a bad decision for me—even though I didn't end up really using it that much. But it was so hard to go in an independent direction. I got very lucky in many ways that I was able to go in a different direction—something that was truly right for me. I think there are so many people that get caught up in the tide of clerkships, law review, and law firm applications. They just go down those routes as the default path, which ends up turning into their career in their life. It's just not the right path for them and they end up medium satisfied or dissatisfied. It's just a recipe for disaster.

Circling back, there are quite obviously many reasons why you could have chosen Yale Law School. But what was the one reason for you that stood out?

Its reputation as a place where you can learn a theoretical application of the law rather than the more practical application of the law. I knew I didn't want to be a lawyer. So I thought, "Okay, this is a place where I can get even more exposure to the history and philosophy of public policy and the political aspects of the law."

And why did you decide to attend when you did?

Because I wanted to knock it out as early as I could. Normally, if there's something I know I want to do, then I just want to get it done.

Right. Looking back, would you recommend that same perspective or same choice to other prospective law students?

Yes, if it's something you know you really want to do. I would just say get it done as quickly as possible. I guess the real question is this: how much time should you give yourself after college to discover if it's really something you want to do? If I had to rewind the clock, it almost certainly would have been the right life decision to wait two or three years after college before deciding to go to law school. This is because it turned out there was this other opportunity that came into my life that was totally separate from having gone to law school (this whole Thumbtack thing). I would have taken advantage of it even earlier than I did.

Yeah.

The opportunity cost of having gone to law school with only one year in between college and law school turned out to be huge. I think that I was a particularly unusual case. But I do think that's probably the case for many people.

Right. And we're going to get into Thumbtack in a bit. But before that, could you just talk about your law school experience in general? What elements did you enjoy or not enjoy? For prospective law students reading this book, is law school as good or bad as people say it is?

The thing I loved most about law school was the people that I met there. I made great friends. I keep in touch with many of them. I just had breakfast with one of my classmates an hour ago. I went on a family vacation to visit another law school classmate over the Fourth of July.

But otherwise, I didn't really like it very much. It was, first, way too political for me. Turns out that even though I thought I was going to spend a career in politics, I love building things more than politics. I love the practical applications of things. I have discovered over the years that my personal strengths are in building new things and operating things and less so in debating abstract ideas and political ideas. So I had three years where I was debating abstract and political ideas—which are things that are weaknesses of mine—and not able to build or operate anything, which is a strength of mine.

So I found myself very frustrated in classes and very frustrated by the never-ending political dialogue and debate in classes. I was also frustrated because I felt like I was really thrown into the deep end in an unfair way. In law school, I didn't really understand the case method of teaching until maybe halfway through law school. I wasn't able to really build a strong foundation in constitutional law, which was frustrating because so many of the classes—at least at YLS—kind of assumed you had a foundational knowledge of the basic cases (which I didn't have). So the pedagogical method didn't really work for me either.

I think your experience may be all too familiar for some people. If you're really frustrated with law school, it can be tempting to think of dropping out or leaving to try something new. Now at the time, it was early days for Thumbtack. I suppose this question is a little different for you. But did you think of dropping out at that time? And if so, what stopped you from dropping out?

I never thought of dropping out. What I did was, over the latter half of my second year and third year, architect my classes so it was much more black letter law (which I was much better at) and less theoretical and philosophical law. I also started engaging in outside interests that kept my attention. I was able to be a teaching assistant in an undergraduate history class for a professor that I knew pretty well. It was fun. I was able to pursue other passions over the course of time. By the end, I became more comfortable with being independent and pursuing what I cared about, rather than following the herd.

So if someone is not interested as much in the theoretical or abstract aspects of law school, they should try tailoring their courses to more practical areas of law. What else can people do to make the most of law school?

Another thing I would say is to find some way to get off the hamster wheel—whatever that means for you. So the toughest thing about law school and the legal field generally is that in many ways, it's a zero-sum, cutthroat competition of IQ against IQ. If there is any way that you can step aside from that super competitive competition, you'll be way happier.

So once I decided I would not pursue a clerkship, that was a huge burden lifted off my shoulders. Once I decided no law review, that was also a huge burden off my shoulders. Once I got a job I was happy with, that was a huge burden off my shoulders. It turns out that once you're out of the legal field, the difference between Sullivan & Cromwell and Baker

McKenzie and Wachtell Lipton and on and on is meaningless. Nobody knows.

Right.

But you get so deeply wrapped in that. It's super healthy if you can find a way to mentally step aside and separate yourself from that and not worry as much about the competition.

Do you have any tips on how people can do that? Because, like you said a few moments ago, the pull towards these things can be so strong, even if you inherently don't have an interest in them.

I think probably the best way to do it is to have an outside interest or activity that you aggressively pursue. So some of my friends knew they were born to be trial lawyers. They just went into mock trial and coached undergrads interested in mock trial. They found very specific jobs in prosecutorial offices around the country or in their home districts. And that's awesome if that's your passion because you're going after a very local, specific passion rather than the most competitive, toughest clerkships and jobs in Washington D.C. or New York or whatever. So those people were generally very happy.

I found the same thing by being a teaching assistant with a professor in undergrad. Another thing that kept me happy during my third year at least was that I lived in Washington, D.C. while attending school in Connecticut.

Oh really?

My wife was at Georgetown Law. I commuted up on the train on Monday mornings and came back down on Wednesday or Thursday nights. I took a pretty quiet course load that year and decided to read as many of the great books as I could. So I put together a list of books that were written from, you know, 2000 BC to one hundred years ago and got to the Enlightenment and the American founding. I never got beyond that. I still have to do that. But I did that in my last year and made it a personal pet project. That was fun.

That's cool. It seems rare for someone to commute that far for classes every week. Did you get used to it? Was it that difficult?

No, it was fine. I just studied and read the great books on the Acela or Amtrak.

Obviously, you took a different path compared to other law students. I'm specifically talking about working on a startup while you were in law school. It seems more commonplace now. I'm assuming it was more of a rarity back when you were at YLS. I read[4] that in 2008, you were having calls with your friends about the project that would become Thumbtack. Can you speak about what was going on there and why you decided to work on this side project while you were presumably busy with law school?

Yeah, this is one of those other side projects that kept me happy and engaged and off the hamster wheel during law school. I kept in touch with my best friend from college and then another guy we had met afterwards. They were both working in Washington, D.C. at the time. Like me, they were also interested in public policy and politics. We all got together and said, "Hey, wouldn't it be fun to start something together? We all respect one another. We don't really know what starting something looks like. We've never done it before. But why don't we talk and see what we come up with?"

So we got on the phone. From there, for about one year, we had weekly phone calls where we explored the idea of what we could do that, if successful, would make a big, positive impact on people's lives. From a very early age, I felt very lucky for all the opportunities I'd been given. I knew that when I grew up, I wanted to do something to give back.

We brainstormed all kinds of different ideas. We brainstormed political advocacy groups, nonprofits, and potential tech products. We had come up with all kinds of ideas. This structured brainstorming process turned out to be a pretty good idea generator. We came up with a number

---

4   I'm referring to an article on Thumbtack's blog that highlights ten interesting things about Sander. You can find it here: https://www.thumbtack.com/blog/10-things-sander-daniels/

of ones that, in retrospect, would have probably worked out alright. But what we ended up on was this idea for Thumbtack.

When you're first starting to do this, where did the passion come from? Was it more of just you and a couple of friends exchanging ideas or did you have a longer-term plan in mind?

I'm trying to place myself back then. By that point, I felt like I had been in school for twenty-two years straight or something. I wanted to get out and start doing something practical. At the time, I was exploring many different paths. I was exploring consulting firms, finance, and politics. This was another thing I would say that I was exploring.

This brainstorming with my friends was more of a passion side project. I never imagined it would really turn into something real or that it would ever become a vehicle by which I could earn a normal income that I could raise a family on. I never imagined it would get to that point. This was more of just a fun thing to do with friends. We were also very idealistic at the time and truly believed that one, two, three, four people working together in a very motivated, dedicated way could make a big impact on the world. So that was another big motivator for us to try our hand at it.

We wanted to make something of ourselves. We wanted to be somebody. So we were motivated to come up with an idea or vehicle to make an impact.

How much time was this taking out of your schedule? Were you feeling stressed with your coursework and your other commitments?

It didn't take that much time out of my schedule. This was a one to two hours a week brainstorming exercise.

Oh, got it. So while you're doing this, you're also presumably looking for other jobs as well. You eventually decided to enter Big Law and work for Sullivan & Cromwell. What tipped the scale there? When you're looking at Sullivan & Cromwell, are you thinking of maybe joining Thumbtack full-time or maybe holding off and working on it on the side?

Thumbtack was incorporated on August 1, 2008, which was in the summer between my second and third year of law school. As my third year of law school progressed, I got a job at Sullivan & Cromwell. I had a really tough choice to make (which was actually imposed on me). The choice was to honor my offer and take the job at Sullivan & Cromwell after I graduated or go to Thumbtack. But it wasn't really a choice for me because I had to go to Sullivan & Cromwell. And the reasons I had to go to Sullivan & Cromwell were that I was married, I knew I was going to have a child soon, and I needed an income (Thumbtack did not pay an income for two or three years).

So Sullivan & Cromwell was obviously an incredible firm. I love the firm. I love the people I met there. I'm very proud to have been there. But it was also the way that I could quickly earn enough cash to save up money that would then allow me to go make the leap and work at Thumbtack for eighteen or twenty-four months with no income. On the first morning I went to work at Sullivan & Cromwell (in November 2009), I put a note on my refrigerator. The note said, "You will leave Sullivan & Cromwell by January 31, 2011."

Oh really?

That was the amount of time I had calculated I would need to work there in order to save up enough money to then go without an income for two, three years at Thumbtack. It was also a kind of defense mechanism that ensured that I would not be sucked into the high income, high-cost, Big Law treadmill that is easy to get sucked into. I would live in a very frugal way that would allow me to leave in fourteen months and go pursue this other dream.

Yeah, that's so interesting. You had the exact date. So did you leave on that date?

So I ended up leaving that week. It happened to be the same week my first son was born.

When you were at Sullivan & Cromwell, were you on the transactional side? Or were you a litigator?

I was on the transactional side.

Just to go back really quickly: if readers of this book are thinking of joining a Big Law firm, what are some things that you think they should be aware of—not only about a firm itself, but the Big Law environment generally?

I guess I would say just before you go to Big Law, do as much research as you can to know what this life really is and what you're getting into. Try to talk to as many senior partners as you can—preferably at different Big Law firms. If you're able to talk to anybody who's done this as a career and recently retired and is able to objectively look backwards and talk about it, I think that would be very helpful.

I think people should understand that Big Law is just a fraction of all the potential lawyer jobs out there. There are lots of people who have great, fun, successful careers who are not in Big Law. In fact, probably the most fun careers and happiest people are people who are outside of Big Law. They are practicing outside of the top two or three cities in the country, are at smaller firms, have their own practices, and have clients they have built over the years and have gotten to know well. They are parts of the legal community that offer business advice in addition to legal advice. So I would think long and hard before committing to a partner track at a top fifteen law firm in one of the top five cities.

While you're at Sullivan & Cromwell, your cofounders are still working on Thumbtack. Did you try to help them out in your spare time while you were at S&C (if you had any spare time)? Or were you just keeping tabs on what they were doing?

Yeah, I tried to help out as much as I could—on nights and on the weekends. It was funny. The period I was at Sullivan & Cromwell was right after the financial crisis. It was probably the lowest period of work that the firm had in many, many years. In addition to that, since I knew that I had an expiry date at Sullivan & Cromwell, I didn't ask for more work. I did great work while I was there. The work that I did was, from all accounts, seen as great. But I didn't ask for more work and it was a low work period. So my number of hours that year was actually pretty reasonable (even low) which allowed me to have a life outside of work and dabble around in Thumbtack with my friends.

Especially right after the financial crisis, I suppose an argument would be that maybe you'd think of sticking at Sullivan & Cromwell just due to the salary and the security—even though Thumbtack is growing. Were you feeling any sort of risk aversion to take the leap and leave the firm even though you committed to leaving by that certain day?

People often ask, "Wow, you took this huge risk, this huge leap. That's amazing. How did you think about that?" I say a couple of things. First, it wasn't as big of a leap as other people take. I knew that if I ever needed to earn cash or a salary, I could easily move back into the law and earn money for my family.

The other thing I thought was that the riskiest thing to do would be to stay at the law firm. This is because I knew that would probably lead to a life of dissatisfaction and unhappiness for me. I had to do something different.

Also, I knew that if there was ever a time to take a risk, it was early in my career before I had children, a mortgage, and a high cost of living. In your thirties and beyond, it's really hard to extract yourself from a high-income, professional track that you're on. So I knew that if there was ever a time, it was then.

All those things combined made it a pretty clear decision for me. In general, I'm pretty risk-averse by nature. I always did super well in school. I went to law school and then went to a private law firm, but this to me was a no-brainer decision. It was a life-optimizing decision.

For those readers that want to do something like you did (perhaps work in Big Law for a bit and then leave to start or join a startup), are there certain things that they should think about before they make the leap?

Not really. I would just do it.

Yeah.

People overthink it way too much. Your career trajectory is going to be determined not by design, but rather by opportunities that come up where you don't know what's on the other side. You just have to take those opportunities and hope for the best. It's almost like marriage. If you overthink about whether to marry someone, then you're just going to stall and not commit. At some point, you just have to take the leap and do it and trust in yourself and do the best you can.

Somewhat associated with that, do you generally think lawyers make good entrepreneurs? I'm sure you've heard the arguments that lawyers are risk-averse. They act too slowly. These critics say that lawyers should be very careful before they become entrepreneurs. Do you agree with that?

I think saying that lawyers can't be good entrepreneurs or aren't good entrepreneurs, is, obviously, a vast overgeneralization. It very much depends. I mean, on balance, sure. Lawyers are risk-averse and you need to be risk-prone in some respects to build a business.

But building a business takes a team. In our case, I would say we had three founders who all have very different, but complementary skill sets. One is a classic "entrepreneur's entrepreneur"—always taking risks in personal and professional life. You go to the beach with him and he's the first to jump off of a massive cliff into the ocean. The other is a fantastic visionary and verbal communicator to a large team. That's a massive asset—particularly in sales. And then the superpowers I have are operational expertise, hard work, and good judgment. I would say there are vast numbers of lawyers who are able to structure things well in their mind, who are able to make order out of chaos, who work hard, and who are motivated. Every team needs that type of person. I've played that role on our team and it has worked out great.

That's great. So if lawyers are non-technical and are joining a team, they can best contribute by leveraging those critical thinking skills, hard work, and skills like that.

Yes. Every business to succeed needs both technical and non-technical people—in equal parts.

If lawyers are looking to do something tech-related, do you think they should learn how to code if they're mildly interested?

No. I believe in comparative advantage. Let coders do the coding. You can do something else.

And if a lawyer wants to start his or her own business, whether they are a solo founder or joining a founding team, would you recommend they focus on an idea related to the law or the legal field? I suppose that goes back to comparative advantage. Or are they sabotaging themselves by trying to create the next photo-sharing app or something like that?

No. I used to think the world is efficient, that if there was a one-hundred-dollar bill on the ground waiting to be picked up, it has already been picked up. But that is not the case at all. The world is gigantic. The economy is gigantic. There are vast numbers of opportunities out there to start businesses in every single field. If anything, the legal field is probably oversaturated by smart people trying to build new businesses—just because lawyers are smart people. And somebody smart can become a world expert on any topic in three months. So I would, in fact, probably stay far from the legal field if you start something new (just because it's probably particularly competitive).

You stayed at Thumbtack full-time after leaving Sullivan & Cromwell. The company has obviously shown impressive growth—valuation-wise and otherwise. I'd like to discuss your role at Thumbtack and the lessons that law students and lawyers can take from your story. First, how did you handle the adjustment of shifting from an environment with legal assistants, paralegals, and people like that, to a startup where resources are inevitably constrained?

Oh, that was not a problem at all for me. I have never felt entitled in any way and certainly not entitled to assistants. I feel like I was lucky to be born where I was, to have the parents I have, and to have a good head on my shoulders. But you also have to work for everything you earn. So I had no problem working hard and putting in long hours to achieve a dream and launch my career. That was not an issue at all for me. In fact, I was happy with it.

Yeah.

Because the thing with a company that is very different from a law firm is that you get to harness your entire creative abilities. If it works, you get compensated for it. At a law firm, you don't get to harness your entire creative abilities, and if you're an outperformer, you really don't get compensated for it. It's just a flat compensation structure. There's a real disincentive to work more. When you build a company, you're basically rewarded for the value you create in the world. It's a huge motivator and one reason that I think working in a company is way more fun than a law firm.

Right. I think a lot of people would agree with you. Was there a situation in the early days at Thumbtack where you didn't know how to solve a particular problem, but your law school or legal training ultimately helped you solve it?

We had outside counsel in the early days. We would have been able to get by just fine had I not gone to law school. But having gone to law school helped on edge cases. I was able to translate a little bit between us and the law firm.

I also helped build our trust and safety teams in the early days (these are the teams that keep our marketplace safe). I was able to navigate a little bit of that more effectively than I would have had I not gone to law school. But I would say otherwise, having gone to law school hasn't had much practical use for my work at Thumbtack.

Or even your training at Sullivan & Cromwell? It hasn't contributed that much to your work at Thumbtack?

So the one thing that has been most useful is understanding that contracts can be negotiated. I learned that at Sullivan & Cromwell and it has been helpful many times over the years.

As a former lawyer in the startup world, how do you pitch yourself? Do you ever reference your legal training when pitching yourself to others? Does it ever come up that much?

It almost never comes up. At this point, my career is built on my success at Thumbtack, not my legal credentials.

Right.

So I got really lucky that we started a company and it turned into a huge success. The success of that company far outweighs the legal credentials that I have. My value-add to the world is now as a successful entrepreneur, not as a lawyer. It rarely comes up.

With your experience in the startup world, let's say a lawyer wants to become the general counsel at a startup. Or perhaps an attorney wants to work at a startup in a non-practicing role. Do you have any tips on how these sorts of people can make that transition? Separately, what advantages or disadvantages do those attorneys have when making that transition?

The best advice I have is to just start working on something else outside of the law firm—whether that's with friends or by yourself or independent projects. I was very surprised at how much progress and how much opportunity there was for a smart, hardworking person to thrive in the marketplace. I think a lot of lawyers have a hard time seeing the value that they can add to the world outside of the legal field. It turns out the world is very inefficient. There aren't that many super smart, hardworking, motivated people out there starting new things.

People often think the risk is much bigger than it is. So the best way to get out there and make the transition is just to start doing something. For example, build a portfolio of ideas or prototypes on the side. Then at some point (probably earlier than you are comfortable with), take the full-time leap into those things. You'll also want to emphasize saving—being as frugal as possible in your personal life to give yourself some runway and see where those one, two, three different ideas can take you. It's probably going to take you further and faster than you think.

When working on those ideas, should readers focus on their passion or follow their curiosity? Are you a believer in the passion argument?

No. I think you can be passionate about most anything. What you really need to do is just commit to something. You'll be passionate about most anything you commit to. So don't optimize for whatever your passion is beforehand. Optimize for finding something interesting and potentially a good idea or a market opportunity. Then just go after it like crazy. Say you had asked me, "What are your passions" when I was ten, fifteen, twenty, or twenty-five years old. If I made a list of one thousand things, local services would not have made that list.

Right.

But here I am. It's been my chief life passion for the past ten years. And that's because I built it into my passion.

Exactly. Do you have any books that inspired you on your career journey and that can help law students or lawyers who want to do something else with their careers?

I read a book called *Founders at Work*[5] when I was at Sullivan & Cromwell and about to make the transition to Thumbtack. It was super powerful. It has very raw, practical stories of how semi to semi-successful to successful entrepreneurs made the transition. That was just eye-opening and awesome and made me feel like I could really do it. It's probably a little bit dated at this point. But it can still be great.

---

5   *Founders at Work* is a 2007 book by Jessica Livingston. Livingston and her husband, Paul Graham, are most known for starting Y Combinator, the prestigious startup incubator in Mountain View, California. The book profiles some well-known entrepreneurs like Max Levchin, Steve Wozniak, Craig Newmark, and Evan Williams.

CHAPTER 13

Nelly Baksht

Artist

Lawyers, like most other professions, have their fair share of stereotypes. I'm sure you know many of them. Unfortunately, most of these stereotypes are quite negative. In the public's eyes, lawyers can be overly garrulous, unnecessarily aggressive, and way too expensive. These stereotypes, whether or not they are true, play some role in how we view the profession.

One stereotype held inside and outside the legal profession is that lawyers aren't creative. As the stereotype goes, lawyers are stringent, rule-based actors. The legal profession is also substantially based on precedent. Attorneys often need to color within the lines, whether they are drafting a merger document or citing Supreme Court precedence in a legal brief.

A key point in this discussion, however, is the definition of "creative." In the traditional lexicon, creative is synonymous with "artistic." It is about free-thinking individuals using their imagination in the arts. For instance, a musician taps into her creative spirit to make a Top 40 record. A chef combines two seemingly random ingredients to create a world-class dish. A photographer uses a lens in a new way to capture a stunning picture.

I would agree that these individuals are creative. That said, when evaluating our creativity as lawyers, I think we sell ourselves short. We say we aren't right-brained or that we weren't born creative. These side comments and internal monologues may seem insignificant in the moment, but they can make it more difficult to identify that creative side within us.

While we may not be the next Pablo Picasso or Julia Child, there *is* an opportunity to be creative in the law. Albert Einstein once said that creativity is "intelligence having fun." A good part of it comes from constraints the law imposes. It may not seem to fit the "traditional" view of creativity, but a lawyer can absolutely be creative if they articulate a novel legal argument based on an archaic statute. Creativity can also come in the form of juggling many different parties' interests to draft a key line in a contract. Better yet, lawyers *have* the skills to be creative. Problem-solving skills, critical thinking skills, and empathy can be learned in law school and legal practice. Any attorney can rely on these skills to develop creative solutions for their clients.

Nelly Baksht is a former attorney who can certainly be considered creative. After practicing law for several years in Russia, she moved to Canada and became a full-time artist. Nelly specializes in fine art and the burgeoning field of cryptoart. Cryptoart, if you haven't come across it, combines fine art and cryptocurrency. It celebrates the social, economic, and philosophical ideas tied with cryptocurrencies like bitcoin and ethereum. Whether it is in traditional or digital form, cryptoart is often sold on a blockchain through non-fungible tokens (NFTs).

Nelly is at the forefront of this burgeoning cryptoart movement. As she describes on her website, her cryptoart works "take technology, weave it with beauty, [and] drape philosophy in romance to present a whole image of something new and incredible." Her talent and interest in the cryptocurrency space have led to her work being displayed at places like the Blockchain Futurist Conference and the Malta AI and Blockchain Summit.

Nelly is one of the few lawyers who has navigated the transition from corporate lawyer to full-time artist. She graduated from Tomsk Pedagogical University and practiced law for a little less than eight years. Working at the municipal department of healthcare in Tomsk and for the legal department of a large construction company, Nelly practiced law amidst the changing legal and political landscape in post-Soviet Russia.

At the same time, Nelly couldn't shake her interest in art. Granted, it wasn't like she was picking up a new hobby. She spent eight years of her childhood studying art in an intensive program. There is, however, something much different in pursuing art as a hobby versus leaving behind a legal career to pursue it full-time. Even considering the risks, Nelly took that chance.

Nelly's story shows how lawyers can be creative inside and outside the law. Moreover, it shows the courage she had to take on so many life challenges within one time. Her passion for art is palpable, and she continues to share her work with many satisfied collectors and fans.

* * *

Nelly, I'm excited to speak with you about your path from law school to art. Generally speaking, what is it that an art career gives you that you can't find anywhere else?

So let's start off with the fact that I am not the first creative person who went through this interesting journey. It's worth remembering the names of greats like Henri Matisse, Wassily Kandinsky, Mikhail Vrubel, and the genius composer Pyotr Tchaikovsky.

In my opinion, art gives you a feeling of flight and freedom. However, it also has a flip side. You become a slave to it and you can't live without it like before.

That's quite a provocative statement. Can you explain what you mean by that?

I think the point is that when you are able to create a piece of art by yourself, it simultaneously inspires you and makes you look differently at the world around you. You are the creator of your own world.

In the world you create, only you decide how and what it should look like. You decide what mood or emotions it should create in a spectacular mind. You decide what impression it should make. And if your works are interesting to others, then you get the opportunity to broadcast your message to many people.

Through art, you give people the opportunity to see the beauty of the orchestrating world, its ugliness, or, in my case, changes taking place in the world. You transmit information through visuals, which is the most effective way to convey information.

By becoming an artist, you often begin to notice much more around you compared to the average person. You see nuances in ordinary objects and influences—most of which you would not have noticed before. All of this is a part of you. It is a kind of superpower and you cannot voluntarily refuse it.

So let's go back to the beginning. You gave an interview to The Next Web where you discussed your initial interest in art. You said how in your childhood, you participated in an intensive eight-year-long art program. While you had this passion for art as early as seven years old, you decided to study law. Why did legal studies sound interesting to you?

Russian art education is very different from its North American counterpart. It is also true for the entire education system—including the university system. I need to tell you a little about it.

To pursue art in Russia as a child, you absolutely must have talent. Starting at seven years of age, you need to paint classical art for eight hours per week. Naturally, if you don't have a passion for art, you won't be able to last in these conditions—especially at such a young age. During these years, art simply becomes a part of you. You dream of being an artist or an architect. You read books, visit museums, and dream of greatness (even if you are slightly naïve).

However, when the moment came and I needed to choose my future degree, my rational mind won. During that time in Russia, work as an artist did not guarantee anything. Looking back, if I had to make this choice right now—when people who can draw well are in high demand in the animation, video game, and film industries—I would have made a different decision.

Who really knows? But at that moment, becoming a lawyer seemed very promising. Moreover, I had all of the abilities and interests necessary to start doing that. The long-term plan was unambiguous. That plan was a career in the law and nothing else.

You studied law at Tomsk University in Russia. Many of our readers will be unfamiliar with legal education in Russia. Can you give them a sense of what it was like? Did you enjoy it?

Yes. It's worth exploring the education system in Russia and the legal system in general. It is dissimilar to the North American system.

You start studying legal disciplines when you are eighteen years of age. Among the subjects that you study include Latin, Roman law, and the theory of the state and rights. This immersion into the legal world happens right away. In effect, students are transitioning from a childish life to an adult life. It's amazing in that you become fully aware of your rights and responsibilities in society. In some ways, it gives you the feeling of being the almighty keeper of forbidden knowledge. You get all of this from five years of studying jurisprudence.

My legal education came easily to me. I was simply in love with jurisprudence. I remember those years with great fondness and gratitude. A legal education in Russia spans five years. It starts after students take exams to enroll at their universities. These exams—and a legal education in general—are extremely competitive.

Ultimately, I studied in a difficult time in Russia. It was after the collapse of the U.S.S.R. It was an era where a new legal system was being established. New legislation was constantly being enacted and the world was changing in front of my own eyes.

Besides this larger picture, another key difference is in the law itself. In Russia, the continental (Romano-Germanic) legal system is used. This is fundamentally different from the Anglo-Saxon legal system. The Russian legal system is characterized by codification. The main source of law in Russia, like the continental system in general, is the legal code (not precedent like in the Anglo-Saxon system).

Both then and looking back, it must have been such a fascinating time. Not only were you taking on this new challenge of legal studies, but the country as a whole was experiencing some dramatic changes. Were you still painting at the time? Did you have any second thoughts about whether a legal career was right for you? And if you did experience those second thoughts, how did you address them?

I did not experience even the smallest doubt that a law career was my calling. I knew that it was the correct choice. Every exam that I took in university gave me even more confidence. Learning about the judicial system brought me joy. Ultimately, I graduated university with high marks and almost completely dropped art throughout that period.

Just to provide more context for your readers, it is also helpful to understand what it is like working as a lawyer in Russia. After graduating from university, law graduates are able to work in any area or specialty, whether that is civil law, employment law, or administrative law. You can represent the interests of individuals or legal entities for all issues connected with legal encumbrance in any area. However, there is one exception here and it relates to the representation of individuals facing criminal charges. This work is exclusively done by criminal lawyers. To become eligible for a criminal law position, candidates must take the corresponding exams and work a few years as a lawyer.

There is also another characteristic of working as a lawyer in Russia. In medium and large-sized companies, there is an in-house legal department that occupies itself with absolutely every jurisprudential problem that may arise. This includes things like taxation, employment disputes, and even the actual representation of the company's interests in court.

How did you get your first job at your law firm?

After graduating from university, I went to work in the legal department of the municipality of Tomsk. I completed an internship there as a student. When I was working there full-time, I joined a team that focused on healthcare. I am very grateful that the legal department allowed me, as a fresh graduate, to obtain such a nice start to my career.

This was an extraordinarily interesting period in my life. Let me remind you that this was a time where a new government was being formed. While it was an unstable time, it was full of opportunity. At work, I was able to participate in the development, actual writing, and formulation of laws concerning the provision of medicine to certain segments of my hometown's population. I also helped in the creation and formation of new structural pharmaceutical units in the city administration.

After around a year and a half, I changed jobs. I went to work in the legal department of a large construction company. That company was tasked with the construction of water lines in all of Western Siberia. This was a completely different branch and field of activity. As a reminder, a lawyer in Russia relies on a system of codes and laws. Because of this, changing legal fields is slightly easier in Russia than it is in North America. The choice that you made at the beginning of your career does not completely determine your future path.

Working in a big company gave me a huge amount of experience. This was especially true in the fields of corporate law and arbitration disputes. All activities of construction firms are tied with huge risks and large financial flows. You must constantly be alert and be ready to solve any problem at the first request.

While you are gaining these professional experiences in the legal field, you also attended a university art program in graphic design.[1] You graduated in 2008. How did you find the time to attend this program? I think this is an important question because some attorneys struggle to work on hobbies or other things outside of their day-to-day work.

With time, I started to feel a pressing sense of tiredness. The rhythm of life became more difficult and I felt the need to shift my attention after the workday. At that point, I remembered that in my "past life," I was able to draw. I gave many years of my earlier life to this craft and thought that I could return to it.

Graphic design, however, was flourishing at that time. It became extremely interesting to me and it captured my attention. Because of this, I went to university for a two-year course in graphic design. Classes began at 7:00 pm and lasted until around 10:00 or 11:00 pm.

The course was extremely inspirational. After work, I would run to the university auditorium and listen to lectures on art history or advertising. Then, I would go to my tablet and draw. At that moment, I felt like it was an outlet for me to cope with the accumulating fatigue from work.

So even though you were fatigued at work, you made the decision to spend your valuable free time reigniting this passion. That requires a lot of discipline. When you were in that program, did you ever start thinking that you should take this path more seriously and maybe even leave your law job?

At that time, I was a lawyer for almost eight years. I did start to have thoughts about leaving my legal practice to draw cartoons or focus on design. However, I had to consider the financial aspects of the decision, as it is challenging to make money through drawing. The authority and status of being a lawyer in society also mattered to me.

However, those months of courses made something clear to me. That was the fact that I had lost something important in my life by giving up painting. I then began acquainting myself with artists in Tomsk. I began

---

1   Nelly attended the graphic design program at Tomsk State University of Control Systems and Radioelectronics (TUSUR).

immersing myself in the environment. Like in my youth, I grabbed a physical brush rather than an electronic pen. I participated in competitions. Art grasped at me and it no longer let me go.

So at this point, your passion for art and painting has reignited. You're obviously not a lawyer now. How did you make that decision to take a leap of faith and pursue your art dreams? When did you decide that it was time to leave and make this big career move?

In my case, the conclusion of my legal career happened by the will of fate. Because my husband had good job prospects in Canada, we decided to emigrate there. Making this type of move was scary for a number of reasons. The thought of emigration itself was scary, along with the uncertainty of how my legal background would be used in a new country. I was starting with a completely clean slate.

On the other hand, I was happy to make this move. Suddenly, the advantages of my art education became clearer. This was a skill that did not require me to start from scratch and find a job in a new country. In fact, I could go to any country in the world and start (or continue) to paint. To put it another way, you really don't need a diploma from some specific country or even knowledge of a specific country's language. Your creativity speaks for itself. It has its own language that everyone understands.

Did you have a plan of how you would deal with the financial side of your new career? Presumably, at the start of your art career, you would be making less money than you would as a practicing lawyer. As part of the same token, do you think you would have pursued art full-time if you and your husband did not move to Canada?

No, I didn't have a concrete plan. The end of my legal practice was directly related to our emigration to Canada. It doesn't make much sense to speculate on what would have happened if I stayed in Russia. Nobody knows the answers. But I am glad that once I arrived in Canada, I had the opportunity to discover myself from a new angle. I could fully devote myself to a long-standing passion.

In your *The Next Web* interview, you mentioned how joining a community of artists in Canada was a key part of your transition. Can you speak about that more and how your network helped when you dove headfirst into your art career?

Even though I had doubts in the beginning, my arrival in Canada put everything in its place. In the first weeks of my life in a new country, I met some wonderful artists. I entered into an amazing creative atmosphere. I was able to acquire the knowledge and skills in the commercial side of art that I lacked. Better yet, I learned new painting techniques.

Somehow, everything started to happen by itself. Participation in street fairs turned into exhibitions. Those exhibits then turned into the first sales of my paintings. Of course, what I was making at the time was not the money that even the humblest lawyer in Canada makes. But I was happy that I could unleash my potential (which had been dormant for many years). I could paint right away and whenever I wanted. There were no special conditions that stood in my way.

The further this direction developed, the more exciting it became. I opened a small studio where I taught children about drawing and painting. I also helped prepare them for admission to art programs. Of course, I continued to draw myself. I can't say that it was easy from the very beginning. I think a good part of it was a combination of both immigration and growing pains from my transition. There were more difficulties from the former. Having said all of this, I have always felt the support of my family.

So even though the challenges were quite stark, you showed grit and persistence.

Yes. While the difficulties were there, the feeling of the work that I created was indescribable. The fact that someone wanted to purchase my art and hang it in their home was amazing. Even better, this feeling does not diminish after several years. It feels like something magical and incredible.

At the beginning, I painted things that were more understandable for everyone. This included things like figurative paintings and cityscapes. Clients purchased these paintings to decorate all types of interiors. The artwork did not carry a strong message; rather, it simply decorated an interior and created a special mood or atmosphere. My wonderful collectors were people who absolutely loved art.

Then, there came a time where I started developing my first works in the field of fine cryptoart. Again, I'm talking about work that struck collectors on an emotional level. I remember when one of the first collectors told me, "For the first time in my life, I spent money on art. I just saw this work and wanted to buy it."

Upon hearing these types of things, I had a slightly different feeling than the feelings I experienced before. That feeling was that I, out of plenty of talented artists across the planet, was able to awaken an interest in art within another person. It sounds a little bit too self-confident now, but that's what I felt back then.

As you reference, your art career seems to have also taken a dramatic shift. While you focused on these figurative paintings and cityscapes in the beginning, you are now focused on cryptoart. Can you tell the readers more about cryptoart and how you made that transition within your art career?

So with fine cryptoart, there is a different story. Cryptoart attracts completely different types of collectors. These collectors are younger people. They often have a technical mind and many didn't intend to acquire works of art. Perhaps some of them hadn't even thought about this side of life before. They may not have thought about the need for art in their lives. They already have a lot of ideas and projects in their heads.

I had this desire to express incredible world changes on canvas. Artists are often at the forefront of change that occurs throughout the world. I wanted to reflect the harmony and beauty of the changes that were occurring in the cryptocurrency space.

Ultimately, I felt that my art was a great interrupting force. It made collectors stop for a moment in their crazy rhythm of life to admire something beautiful. It could inspire them to find new ideas or simply just bring some joy on a normal day. It brought me an indescribable feeling of happiness. Of course, you can find many talented artists who surpass me in technical art skills. But I don't aim to compete with them in painting technique.

Art should evoke emotions and associates. It should possibly induce action. I am grateful to my collectors that they experience these emotions and feel the inspiration to create positive change in the world.

What skills from your legal background gave you an advantage as you were building your art career?

Since I work in two different areas—art classes and fine cryptoart—I see advantages in both areas. As for the art classes, I can more easily explain, systematize, and identify cause and effect relationships. I can notice even the most insignificant nuances in an extremely clear and lucid way. These skills definitely came from my legal background.

As for my fine cryptoart, entering the world of cryptoart was largely due to my prior education. Being a former lawyer, I became interested in these novel ideas of smart contracts and decentralization. I began to follow these ideas and asked questions to family and friends who had any relationship with the cryptocurrency industry. It became interesting not just to "depict something on a given topic" as an artist, but to explore ideas that captured my attention. I wanted to unite modern intelligence and beauty in its traditional sense.

So in the beginning, a combination of maximalism, perfectionism, and high expectations of excellent results impeded me. I still struggle with it. I think that it is both a legacy of my past career and part of my character.

For lawyers that perhaps painted in the past and are thinking of proceeding with a dramatic career change like you, do you have any tips or advice?

I don't really like giving advice at all. Everyone has their own path. But if a lawyer came up to me and asked for that type of advice, I would probably tell the lawyer to just start drawing. Recall what happened in your past and start drawing for yourself or for friends. If time permits, try to take art courses. See what comes out of it.

While there is no guarantee, our past hobbies can ignite us with renewed vigor after five, ten, or even twenty years. If you have this spark and it flares up into a flame, don't hesitate to take the risk and start creating. Even if you don't succeed in becoming a full-time artist, you can still be an excellent lawyer and have a delightful hobby that provides rest to your soul and mind.

Would any of your advice change if you are speaking with a law student or lawyer with no experience (or virtually no experience)? Say this individual feels a burst of inspiration and wants to leave the legal field to do something much more creative.

Well, I would say that if a law student wants to leave their studies, then they probably are not interested in it. What can you advise here except for that law student to follow their interests? It is torture to study for many years at a college or university and not get any pleasure from it. But also, you need to listen to yourself and soberly estimate your capabilities.

As an up-and-coming artist, how did you get your name out there?

A lot of it came from social media. I learned from Reddit that my first fine cryptoart work (which is called "ethEra") was warmly received by the crypto community. I received a barrage of letters, purchase offers, and praise. It was an indescribable feeling.

If you had to do it over again, would you rely on social media as your predominant marketing channel?

Yes, I think so. The strategy worked well. Along with this, given the specific themes of my paintings, I don't think that traditional placement in galleries on a permanent basis is the right strategy.

I'd like to ask you about something that has been on my mind. Do you think you would have achieved the success that you did if you didn't have that early art experience? To put it another way, do you think you would have gotten to this point if you hadn't had that youthful experience in art?

To be honest, I do not know artists who haven't had any youthful experience, interest, or love for this kind of activity. Perhaps there are such artists, but still, most of them draw from childhood. The degree of involvement and intensity of classes may vary. However, the need for drawing mainly arises in childhood. In my case, I think my youthful experience helped me a lot.

Let's talk about some of your works. What is your favorite piece that you have created?

Undoubtedly, "ethEra." It was my first work in the field of fine cryptoart. It appeared from under my brush overnight and has not lost its relevance to this day. I think that "ethEra" shows the process of creation and genesis as something magical, but also quite logical.

In 2020, my work "Hope" also became equally significant. In it, I tried to express all the feelings from the possible impending danger of Covid-19 and the global lockdown. It was also very personal work. I painted "Hope" just after arriving home from a vacation trip to Spain. At the time, Spain was in one of the most difficult situations in the world because of the emerging coronavirus. Since I came from a country with a high risk of infection, I was the first among all of my friends to go through the procedure of taking a Covid-19 test and isolating at home. I was like a pioneer, telling everyone about my experiences and feelings. It was a little scary since there was so much unknown in the world. But this self-isolation also sharpened my sense of hope, which resulted in the artwork named after the same idea.

So with ethEra, you were able to both show off your talent and your passion for something that continues to make a huge impact in the worlds of finance and technology.

Yes. I painted ethEra in 2017 and it was dedicated to the creation of Ethereum. After this painting, everything changed. I felt that I had found my own way in art, where I could combine painting techniques with the ongoing changes in the world of high technologies. I realized that I could ignite an interest in art for people that are far from art in their daily lives.

Where do you see the art market moving in the next several years? How can new artists take advantage of it?

I'm happy to see how the world is changing for people who are both painting and drawing. There is an unlimited number of opportunities to demonstrate your art. There is practically no need to exhibit your work in physical galleries. The emergence of online and virtual galleries offers a great opportunity for creative people to gain recognition and earn money. Fortunately, the time has passed where an artist has to be poor and hungry. Today, there is an even greater opportunity to monetize your passion for drawing.

I can also see how the attitude of collectors is changing. People began to appreciate original art more than twenty years ago. The development of printing is helping to produce giclee prints for artists. There is significant demand for this. Those collectors who cannot afford to purchase the original work can get a perfect copy with the original touches by the artist. They don't have to simply go to a store and hang a fictitious poster on their wall. Of course, the virtual world will surely merge with the physical art world soon. This will open up plenty of new opportunities.

Should new or would-be artists think about making non-fungible tokens (NFTs)?

Yes. As an artist, I would consider NFTs a wonderful opportunity to confirm the copyright to your work. It also benefits collectors. NFTs are a proof of ownership along with a tool for provenance.

Let's move on to some tips for lawyers or law students that may be interested in a career similar to yours. There seems to be this stereotype that lawyers aren't creative people. Do you agree with that?

I think that there is a sufficient number of creative people within the legal community. But another thing is how much creativity is inside you. You have to consider how strong your desire is to create so that it becomes your main activity. As always, there is a difference between thought and actual action.

So even if you are a naturally creative person, you can't expect it to naturally show in your work.

It all depends on desire. With painting, you can start at any age and with any level of training. You can go beyond that and do things like study art history, listen to lectures, or subscribe to art critics' podcasts.

Nothing is guaranteed. Whether you will achieve outstanding results is unknown. However, you'll likely make some progress. You'll also experience pleasure. You will begin to see and feel the world in a different way. The effect varies. Some people will experience it to a large extent and others will experience it to a lesser extent. But these feelings are more likely to occur than not.

What can would-be artists or current artists do today to maximize their chances of success?

The more people know about you, the greater your likelihood of success. You need to be as representative of your potential collectors as possible. While what you paint and your audience may be different, you need to keep this point in mind. Of course, social media plays a huge role today. Perhaps tomorrow, there will be new opportunities that artists need to pursue.

I think the world of law and the world of art are two beautiful worlds. They are far from each other. To make the transition from one world to another, you need to feel an urgent need. If you feel this need, then you can actually take your existing skills from the first profession. Doing this can significantly help in achieving success in your newly-chosen direction.

CHAPTER 14

David Hornik

Venture Capitalist and Educator

Whether you are a transactional associate at a commercial law firm, a public defender, or a lawyer that just hung your own shingle, several things will likely influence the trajectory of your career.

One of them is your knowledge of the law. This relates to those technical skills that I mentioned earlier. Experience is the best teacher, especially since you probably won't learn the nuances of your specific practice area in law school. Through your day-to-day work and conversations with your colleagues, you start to develop technical expertise in your chosen area of law. Although the law is always changing, putting in your metaphorical ten thousand hours gets you closer to mastering your practice area.

Legal writing skills are another huge factor. Focusing on oral advocacy might be easy, but the practice of law is primarily based on the written word. Many of us trace our legal writing skills to law school, where we learned some type of legal writing framework. At its core, legal writing is formulaic. We learn the formula in law school and rely on it to best represent our clients. While we learn the foundations of great legal writing in law school, our writing skills improve as we gain more experience as practicing lawyers.

Then, there are interpersonal skills and building relationships. After all, legal practice is a service-based business. You need to find new clients and continuously provide value to your existing clients. If you are a junior lawyer, your *real* client may be a partner or other senior attorney. If you work as a public defender, your client might be someone who could be imprisoned for years (or even decades). No matter who your client is, you need to provide sound legal advice *and* manage their expectations.

This ability to build relationships and connect with others is highly underrated. While technical skills are important, the ability to connect with and provide value to others will give you a huge edge, whether you practice law or leave the law to do something else.

David Hornik has mastered the art of building relationships. He is a venture capitalist who has worked with technology entrepreneurs for the past twenty-five years. David is currently a founding partner at Lobby Capital, a self-described "venture capital firm that is all about the people." Lobby Capital traces its roots to the Lobby Conferences. Organized by David, the Lobby Conferences have brought together over two thousand founders and investors to build relationships and discuss the future of the digital economy over the last sixteen years.

Before his current role at Lobby Capital, David spent two decades as a partner at August Capital. He has funded many well-known startups throughout his career, including Splunk, Bill.com, Fastly, Evite, Ebates, and Gitlab. He was the first venture capitalist to create a blog (Venture-Blog) and podcast (VentureCast) that specifically discussed the venture capital industry. David is also busy outside of his day-to-day work as a venture capitalist. For instance, he has taught courses on venture capital and entrepreneurship at Harvard Law School and Stanford Business School.

David wasn't destined to become a venture capitalist, however. Before that, David was a practicing lawyer. After graduating from Harvard Law School, David began his professional legal career at Cravath, Swaine & Moore. It was catching up with a law school roommate that led David to the world of startups. While he stopped practicing years ago, David continues to rely on his legal training to work with hungry founders and see what's next in the digital startup ecosystem.

The venture capital universe is extremely competitive, yet David has achieved significant success. While there are many reasons for this, one could argue that it comes down to his giving nature and his focus on building strong relationships. David's positive personality, willingness to meet new people, and focus on helping others are so well known that he was an example of a "giver" in Adam Grant's bestselling book, *Give and Take*. As Grant describes, givers tilt reciprocity in the other direction. They are more focused on what other people need from them. On the surface, it may seem like givers obtain poorer results than takers, but as Grant argues in *Give and Take*, givers like David are more likely to be top performers in their companies or industries.

Throughout his career, David has been energized by his work. Moreover, he seeks to collaborate with others who are *also* energized about their work. From clerking on the Second Circuit right out of law school to leaving a Big Law firm to work with startups, David doesn't sit still. He follows his interests even if they don't lead to a "traditional" career arc. Ironically, by following those interests and building strong relationships with others, he has unlocked career opportunities that he may not have found if he'd followed a well-trodden legal path.

* * *

David, you have a really unique educational background. You obtained a computer music degree and then a Master of Philosophy. From there, you decide to head on over to Harvard Law School. Looking back from where you are now to, say, college, how do you think about your career arc? Is there any underlying theme or can you tie it together in a cohesive way?

Nope. I guess what I've always said is that I have pursued the things that struck me as exciting and engaging. I have always taken on things with incredible vigor. When there's something that strikes me as more exciting or engaging, I'm happy to contemplate it. I have never been afraid of change, but I haven't been searching for it.

It isn't the case that I have gone through my career growing impatient and looking for the next great thing. I've mostly gone through my career trying to find the best and most interesting and engaging group of people to work with.

So that's the litmus test for you. You're not afraid of change. But how do you know when it's time to change? I'm sure people and relationships are one aspect of that.

Yeah. Absolutely. I think of all business as people first. Your experiences are only as good as the people that surround them. You spend a huge amount of your time in your profession and your job. To do anything but be surrounded by amazing people who you love spending time with during that giant chunk of your day would be insane. If you're faced with the opportunity to work with a new and exciting group of people in a way that strikes you as at least as compelling (maybe more compelling) than the thing you're doing at the moment, pay attention -- I have always taken that seriously and it has served me well.

That's very interesting. But before we dive into that, I'd like to travel back to a little before you attended college. When did this idea of law school or becoming an attorney really enter your mind? When did it become something that you seriously considered?

Probably elementary school.

Oh, really?

I was an argumentative little Jewish kid. There was no other profession that struck me as more appropriate. Also, I have always been someone who thought that the justice system was amazing and important. I went into college assuming that I would go to law school.

You're also the son of a computer scientist. Were you envisioning combining your legal education with technology in that way?

Not necessarily. I grew to find intellectual property fascinating. It was certainly a combination of having a passion for language and a passion for the law, but also a passion for technology. That all led me to that space and helped me appreciate how interesting it was. But I certainly didn't go into college or even law school thinking that I was going to combine computers and the law as my profession at any point (never mind for the foreseeable future).

I see. So like I said, you graduated with a computer music degree. When readers see that, I'm assuming that some of them may be wondering what that is and what you were planning on doing with that type of degree. Can you discuss that?

Yeah. It's a great example of me leaning into those things that I found exciting and interesting. When I got to Stanford, I knew that Stanford had an amazing Center for Computer Research.[1] I was a kid who was already fascinated with synthesizers and with synthesis. In many ways, I chose to attend Stanford because of this unique program.

Having said that, I didn't go to Stanford thinking that I was going to be a music major or that I was going to be a computer science major. I certainly didn't contemplate being a computer music major because there was no such thing at the time. But when I got to Stanford, one of the first things I did was go up on the hill to a place called CCRMA (the Center for Computer Research in Music and Acoustics) and meet one of my heroes. His name was John Chowning. John Chowning was the inventor of the Yamaha DX7 synthesizer. In many ways, it was the instrument that changed the sound of pop music in the 1980s. It was this absolutely iconic synthesizer that every synthesizer nerd had huge respect for and coveted. The guy who invented that synthesizer was the head of the computer music department at Stanford.

So when I got to Stanford, I went marching up the hill to the old president's mansion that now houses the Center for Computer Research in Music and Acoustics. I knocked on John Chowning's door to say hello and introduce myself. That resulted in me getting a tour of CCRMA and getting to know what they were doing up there. I started to take classes around computational music and acoustics and psychoacoustics and psychophysics. I found it completely fascinating. At some point along the way, I realized that I had taken as many computer music-related courses as I had taken political science courses.

At that stage, you were just following your curiosity and passions. But in the back of your mind, law school was still something you were aiming for. Is that correct?

Yeah, absolutely. I did have one possible path that would have led me to a very different life that would have been related to computer music. Most of what I was doing was very much focused on my intention to not only go to law school, but to be a public defender.

---

1   The Stanford Center for Computer Research was founded in 1975. It describes itself as "a multi-disciplinary facility where composers and researchers use computer-based technology as an artistic medium and as a research tool."

Right. So when you graduated from Stanford, you went to Cambridge for one year and then Harvard Law School. Do you think or maybe wish you had taken more time off before you went to law school? Now, it's easy to say that everything worked out. But if you had to go back in time, would you have taken some more time between college and law school?

No. I actually would have taken more school.

Oh, would you have?

I had two different opportunities. One was presented to me. The other never struck me, but it would have been interesting. The first (which was presented to me) was that one of my computer science professors during my undergraduate studies asked me to stick around and do a master's in computer science. This was not a professor who was teaching some high-level computer science class. It was introductory computer science. And I said to him, "Why would you even ask that?" He said, "Well, musicians have a long history of being some of the best computer scientists in the world." And I said, "Oh, that's super interesting. But no. I'm not going to do that." I then applied to graduate school to go study overseas.

In retrospect, I would have been incredibly well-served to have spent one more year and gotten a master's in computer science—not necessarily because I would have been a computer scientist but because it would have been fascinating and would have been fun. But I didn't do it and I moved on.

As for the other one, in retrospect, I would have been extraordinarily well-served having done a JD/MBA instead of just a JD. But to tell you the truth, I had no idea in law school that I was interested in business. I actually thought that business was kind of a dirty word. I very begrudgingly took corporations in law school (and only because the judge I was clerking for was on the Second Circuit). He said, "We see a lot of corporate cases. It would probably be a good idea if you took securities regulation and corporations." I said, "Oh my God, that sounds awful." I begrudgingly took those courses. I could say with some certainty that I attended fewer securities regulation classes than any other class that I took at law school. I found it so profoundly boring that I could not even bear to go to class.

And ironically, in many ways, it is the single most relevant class to my profession today.

That's right. You just never know how things are going to turn out. I would like to ask you about HLS. You graduated magna cum laude. In law school, everyone is working hard. Everyone is looking at essentially the same outline. Everyone is intelligent, yet you thrived. You also had to battle through dyslexia. How do you think you separated yourself from other students, say, on exams? What can current law students learn from that?

I don't have a great answer to that. Today, I would tell you all aspects of the law are just about storytelling. The reality is that, given the opportunity, I'd rather tell a story than do something else. I think that served me well in law school. Ultimately, law school exams are really about how you think about a set of facts and how those would interact with the things that came before them. I just never got too caught up in the things I didn't know because I was aware, as someone who is dyslexic trying to get through all of this stuff, that I would never have all the information. So I just made the most of what I had -- it was all I could do.

And I learned to predict what would be asked of me. I think that turned out to be the single most powerful tool I had in law school. It also ended up being a really powerful tool as I've gone through being a lawyer and ultimately a venture capitalist.

When you're saying, "predict what they ask of you," it just really comes down to empathizing with them and standing in their shoes?

Yes.

I would like to ask a specific question for readers who are in law school. Specifically, how can law students, particularly 2Ls and 3Ls, make the most out of their law school experience?

Take classes that you're interested in. Also, take classes from professors who are amazing. It turns out law schools can pretend all they want that they are trade schools, but they are not. If you practice law after law school, the people with whom you work will teach you the skills you need to engage in that particular law. And I can tell you that because I started out my career as a litigator. I then became a corporate attorney. Then, I ended up doing a huge amount of licensing and M&A work in an extremely short period of time.

I practiced for six years and I did all of those things. I hope I did them competently, despite the fact that I was inexperienced in each of those disciplines. It had nothing to do with the fact that I had been well-trained by the professors of Harvard Law School to be a great technical lawyer. What I had been well-trained in was the ability to be thoughtful and apply logic and write well and speak well and tell a good story. In the end, those things not only will serve you well in any aspect of the law, but they will actually serve you well in any potential career you enter into.

There's a reason that there are so many incredibly successful non-lawyers who attended law school. It is because law school is really great training for being an articulate advocate. Being an articulate advocate is the single most important skill you can have in nearly every profession.

Sure. That's really interesting. So this idea of storytelling has been applied everywhere in your career thus far. I'm happy you brought that up. But before I move on, at least at HLS, is there anything you wish you would have done that would have prepared you for your career in venture capital or startups generally?

Well, no. Here's the thing that I think is also incredibly important. The people you meet in any given situation are probably more important than the things you learn. I met amazing people at Harvard Law School. I am good friends with dozens of them still. They are all doing interesting stuff. I enjoy catching up with them and hearing about what those things are. I think all of that benefits me, but more importantly, benefits the planet.

So one answer is to do things that allow you to build deep relationships. That is not likely a big lecture class on a particular topic. If you're excited about that topic, then by all means. But if you have the opportunity to do things that will allow you to meet other people, engage with them as humans, and build real relationships, that will serve you really well over time. I think that's exciting. So one is I would have taken more classes that allowed me to branch out more and meet a bunch of interesting people.

The second thing (and I think this is actually extraordinarily important and I so wish I had thought about it at the time) is that at Harvard Law School (and I suspect at many law schools), you can actually take classes outside of the law school for credit toward your law degree. Harvard has amazing classes that would have been fascinating, fun, and exciting. I wish I had taken them. I wish I had taken more undergraduate classes. I wish I had taken classes over at the business school. I wish I had taken classes at the school of architecture.

I think that if I were to do it again, after my first year of law school, I would have absolutely taken a class somewhere else every semester. That would have been amazing.

For those classes, it's more about following your interests or passions, right? It's not about having a set in stone path on how you would use those courses after graduation.

Exactly. Because if we all knew what we were going to do after school, then taking courses that informed that would be a great idea. But it turns out that the vast majority of us end up doing things that we hadn't intended to. So whatever things we did to support the thing we thought we were going to do will actually prove to have been a waste of our time. Whereas if you just take classes with great professors teaching things that are fascinating to you, you'll extract the tools and the ability to articulate and reason while still enjoying the time to the greatest extent.

That should have been my philosophy. I was too young and I wasn't aware that that was a possibility. So if I were to go back again, I would do that.

Very interesting. From Harvard Law School, you had a brief career as a public defender. Like you said, you begrudgingly took your securities course and didn't think you would be doing what you're doing now. But before that, you had this experience in a public defender's office. I read that you were focused on brokering deals rather than actually going to trial. Can you explain more of the work that you did there?

Yeah. I mean, again, I was just a student, right? I took the public defense clinic. I went into it with the expectation that I would go and be a public defender after graduating from law school. It struck me as the most noble calling imaginable. It still strikes me as the most noble calling imaginable. I had spent time in law school working with the Prison Legal Assistance Project. I had seen the ways in which the system was not serving humans well. I believed that everybody deserved the most vigorous defense imaginable. I entered law school expecting to make that my calling.

So I took this amazing clinic with Professor Charles Ogletree, who was one of the great thought leaders in the space.[2] I worked with wonderful clinical professors. I wish I could remember Abbe's last name – it was Smith, Abbe Smith – she was just a force of nature and someone you had nothing but huge respect for. After you study, you go and pick up cases in Roxbury. Those cases are sort of low-level misdemeanor kinds of cases because you're new to defense and new to the law. They want to make sure that your level of expertise is appropriate for the cases you're working on, et cetera.

You go to court. They give you a client. You go to the back of the courtroom. You call out their name. They would come to you. You would ask them about the charges. You would ask them about their history. You would get to know them. You go through this process and then you are off to the races. Now, I have to represent you in a bail hearing in ten minutes.

It instantly became clear to me that the practice of criminal law was all about negotiation. There was a huge volume of cases. People were coming into the system, and the thing that the system was interested in doing was being done with the cases—not in coming to some ideal around justice. It was simultaneously heartbreaking and empowering because it made perfectly clear to me that I had only one job. That job was to vigorously represent my clients and get them out of the system as quickly as possible.

Now, what I observed was that I had a number of classmates who thought that the practice of being a defense attorney was to engage in the law. They would move to exclude evidence. They would make a bunch of motions. It struck me that those things were not going to result in the best possible outcomes for my clients. The thing that was going to result in

---

2   Professor Ogletree is the founder and executive director of the Charles Hamilton Houston Institute for Race & Justice at Harvard Law School. Among his many accolades, he is well-known for representing Anita Hill during Justice Clarence Thomas's confirmation hearings to the U.S. Supreme Court.

the best possible outcome for my client was negotiating a great outcome. Offering the prosecutor some way to be done with my client (and that was advantageous to my client) was the best way to represent them.

That's what I did. In all but one case, I settled quickly, efficiently, and got my clients very good outcomes relative to the circumstances of their criminal behavior. That was in particular the case because each of them had actually done the things that they had been accused of doing. I knew that because they told me.

And what was interesting is that I thought to myself, "Gee, I'm probably not going to get a great grade in this class because I'm not doing the things that we were taught. I'm not engaging with the law in the ways that one would think of as the calling of a public defender." It turned out that the reaction of my supervisor was exactly the opposite of that. She essentially said, "You obviously understand how this works and I hope that this will be your profession."

In the one instance where I couldn't settle, it was because they had made a mistake. The court gave me a client who had been accused of a crime that already was a fairly serious crime and probably should not have been on my docket. But worse yet, my client had a previous suspended sentence where if I were to fail to resolve the current claims against her, she would go to prison for five years. There was absolutely no way that they had intended to give a brand new student a case in which someone was in jeopardy for a minimum of five years. But it was too late. I had been assigned to this case. I started representing her and I did so zealously. My client was a transgender woman at a time when transgendered clients were not terribly well understood, nor were they taken care of in any reasonable way. It made the potential of her going to prison all the more concerning.

So that was a very tricky set of circumstances. She was a wonderful human and she made me rethink my desire to not be a public defender. I continued representing her after I graduated. I couldn't settle her case and there were real issues at stake. I had to do real work and it gave me some faith in the system. But in the end, I decided that I was not a good enough human to take on this job (which I felt was such an unbelievably thankless job). I have nothing but the most monumental respect for public defenders because I think it is the most difficult and thankless job in the law. I wasn't a good enough human to be willing to take that on.

Well, from there, like you say, you moved on. It sounds like after this matter, you began working at Cravath, Swaine & Moore. From there, you also moved to a couple of firms in California. A good part of this book is about transitions, whether a reader is making a transition from one firm to another or from legal practice to something else. My understanding is that when moving from Cravath to the firms in California, your wife noticed you were unhappy and recommended that you make a decision. Can you talk about how you made that decision to leave Cravath and move to California to presumably work with startups?

Yeah. Let me start by saying that as a general matter, I really enjoyed my time at Cravath. It was an incredible postdoc and I went into it thinking of it that way. Here was an opportunity to learn litigation at the very highest level while representing some of the most important corporate clients in the country on matters that were of major consequence to them. The result is that you got to approach those cases with the greatest possible seriousness. Any effort that could potentially influence the outcome was pursued, which is an astonishing gift. Right?

That was amazing. More importantly, I got lucky. When I arrived at Cravath before my clerkship, I worked for an attorney named Frank Barron.[3] Frank Barron is also a Harvard Law School graduate. He was not only an astonishingly good attorney, but he was also an extremely lovely human being. Those two do not necessarily go hand in hand. I just had lunch with Frank Barron and his wife Eve (who is another Harvard Law grad) a month or so ago. This is around twenty years after I left Cravath. It was such a wonderful chance to catch up with Frank and thank him for having been such a thoughtful mentor and such a decent human in the face of a job that requires an unbelievable amount of commitment and time to be done at the level that was expected at Cravath.

Sure.

---

3   Frank Barron had a multi-decades career as a litigator at Cravath. He retired from Cravath's litigation department at the end of 2014.

So I worked for Frank for nine months. I went off and clerked for Judge Frank Altimari on the Second Circuit. I got to experience a lot of what the appeals world had to offer.

I'll tell you this story because it may serve the students well. I actually was supposed to return to take a job at the end of that time at Arnold & Porter in Washington, D.C. I had clerked at Arnold & Porter in the summer after my second year of law school. I had worked with a really wonderful attorney named Cary Sherman. I had done intellectual property work with him which I enjoyed. I thought it was fascinating and ultimately decided that I would return to working at Arnold & Porter. I would work with Cary Sherman and move to Washington, D.C.

As my clerkship came to a close, I went with my wife to Washington, D.C. to look at neighborhoods. I had one small child at that time (possibly two). We looked around the various neighborhoods and talked about the central places to live. At the end of that weekend, my wife said, "I have no interest in moving to Washington, D.C. I have a community here in New York. I have friends. I can parent in a way that I think is healthy. I would rather continue doing that than moving to Washington, D.C., so I think you should tell the people at Arnold & Porter that you're not going to go work with them."

I said, "That's an interesting problem because I have a job in Washington, D.C., but I don't have a job in New York." My wife said, "Yeah, well, I guess you need to solve that problem." So in any event, I said, "You know what, that's fair enough." I called Frank Barron up and I said, "I know I had told you that I was not going to work for you and that I was going to go to Washington, D.C. to work for Arnold & Porter. But I've had a change of heart, and if you would have me back, I would like to come to Cravath." Frank said, "That sounds great. We would love to have you."

Then, I had to have the tough conversation of calling back the folks who were expecting me to join them some number of months later and let them know that I would not be joining them. They were incredibly gracious. I certainly have a soft spot for Arnold & Porter because they treated me with so much humanity in the face of what was assuredly a problem for them. They had an expectation they'd have a certain number of attorneys and now, one of them had withdrawn.

So I didn't go to Arnold & Porter. I went to Cravath and had two big trials in a row. They were fascinating, but a huge amount of work. I was truly working tens of hours in ways that truthfully, I had no problem with.

I think there are lots of complaints about the scale of work and the volume of work. My view is if you're working on things that are interesting and you're working on them with people who you like, who respect you, and who you respect, working long hours is a perfectly reasonable ask in the name of doing the best job you can do.

Interestingly, as a side note, one of the associates with whom I worked was a guy named Tom Shakeshaft. Tom and I worked really closely together for Frank Barron. We became very good friends. I left and he left and he ultimately became the deputy in the U.S. Attorney's Office in Chicago. He was the guy who ultimately indicted El Chapo.

Really?

He was the guy who went to Mexico and met with the informant who ultimately led to El Chapo's conviction.

To give you a sense of why I think relationships matter and why the people with whom you interact and work are important, I was on the phone with Tom the day that El Chapo was convicted just to catch up with him and talk with him about how incredible that was. He called me just to check in and say hello. We talked about this amazing outcome and that he was going to be on TV talking about it. And this was a guy who I haven't worked directly with since 1997. I think that's telling. You build these relationships when you work in these intense environments that matter.

In 1997, I was having a conversation with my wife and she said, "I wonder if there's a better opportunity or better place for us to live." She's a Californian and she would have been excited to move back to California. It would have also been a different place to practice the law. So it got me thinking, "What am I interested in doing? What is a good fit?"

I started talking with friends about what they were doing and how they were doing. One of those friends was my law school roommate. He was a guy named Steve Boom.[4] Steve lived across the hall from me in my freshman dorm at Stanford. He and I were friends with Jerry Yang, who was the founder of Yahoo. Jerry lives in our freshman dorm and one of our mutual friends joins Jerry to help build the company. He was a fantastic

---

4   Along with his work at Venture Law Group, Steve Boom was a senior vice president at
    Yahoo! He is currently the VP of Amazon Music.

guy named Tim Brady, who was the COO of the company. As Yahoo was emerging, Steve joined the law firm that represented Yahoo. It was called Venture Law Group and was strictly representing startups.

When I talked with Steve, he said, "Well, why don't you come out here and work at Venture Law Group and represent Jerry and other startups? It's actually a really fun job. We're working with smart people who are trying to build really cool stuff." I said, "Well, that's super interesting except I'm not a corporate attorney. I'm a litigator." Steve said, "Yeah, that's a fair point."

I actually contemplated switching to the corporate group at Cravath to get some corporate experience before I would start interviewing with other places. The only problem is that when I talked with my friends at Cravath who were doing corporate law, it sounded terrible. It was giant corporate finance. It was just big transactions that didn't sound appealing to me at all. Whereas what Steve described, where he was representing these little companies of ten, twenty, thirty people who were creating new technologies, that sounded fascinating to me.

So I said to Steve, "You know, I think it actually doesn't make a lot of sense for me to practice corporate law here in New York. It won't give me any better training for what you do than being a litigator. Would the partners at Venture Law Group consider interviewing me to be a corporate attorney and training me?" Steve said, "I don't know. Let me check." He literally put me on hold and walked down the hall to the partner for whom he worked (a really smart guy named Jim Brock).[5] And he said, "Hey Jim, I've got this friend. He was a buddy of mine in college and my roommate in law school. He's currently at Cravath as a litigator. Would we consider interviewing him for a corporate job? Jim said, "Yeah, sure, just have him talk to our recruiters and fly him out."

Wow, that's how it happened?

Yes. So Steve said, "It sounds like it's no problem. I'll connect you with the recruiters." Luckily, they were extraordinarily busy. They just needed more attorneys. So days later, I flew to California and I interviewed. To

---

5   Jim Brock led the internet practice at Venture Law Group. Now, he is the chief product officer and founder of Joinder.

tell the truth, what I said (in a hopefully not quite as obnoxious way) was I don't know anything about corporate law, but how hard could it be?

To my point earlier: the law is not about knowing anything about the law. The law is about being thoughtful about how to apply the rules that you learn on the job to the circumstances of any given case. In this instance, there were a bunch of startups. The corporate law was not very different from case to case. I felt like it was something that they could train me in quickly. Truthfully, they kind of said, "Yeah, you're right."

I did have the incredibly good fortune of being Steve Boom's friend. Steve was about as good an associate as they ever had. He was deeply technical. He had an engineering degree. He was an excellent lawyer. He was polished and thoughtful and charming in ways that I was not. But I got the benefit of the doubt because of Steve. Steve was willing to vouch for me. They were like, "Alright, fine. We'll give you a job."

So they hired me. And they said, "Welcome. We're happy to have you and we'll teach you how to do this job." We moved to California a very short time later and I started working with startups (literally knowing nothing about startups). My first client was this little company that was being started by four gentlemen who had a consulting firm together. They wanted to incorporate because they had an idea about creating an online calendar. The first thing I did was I had to incorporate the company, which meant I had to figure out who the founders were and what founders' stock was. That was pretty interesting.

And then one of the first things that we did for this particular company was meet with one of these four founders. His name was James Joaquin and he was the Vice President of Business Development.[6] James was probably in his twenties at the time. In that meeting, we spent all of our time discussing data. Would it make sense to license calendar data? Or would we be better off creating it and licensing it to others? Would we get the calendar of Red Sox games from ESPN.com? Or would we be better off creating all baseball game calendars and selling them to ESPN.com?

It was a fascinating conversation for a couple of hours. Maybe it was twenty minutes, but my recollection was a couple of hours. I left that meeting, first of all, thinking, "Wow, this guy James Joaquin is such

---

6 James Joaquin has a multi-decades track record of building early-stage technology companies. Currently, he is the cofounder of Obvious Ventures, which focuses on investing in companies that combine profit and purpose.

a lovely, energetic, and thoughtful person. I'm so excited to be lucky enough to work with him." And two, I thought, "I can't believe that this is what we call doing the law. I can't believe this conversation (that's really a business conversation) ultimately had some legal implications around how you would license data or sell data, et cetera, and that I could sit in this meeting, have this conversation, and recognize it was my job."

It was just a revelation. I describe that meeting as the moment I became addicted to startups. It really was like the first hit of startups. I was a complete addict and I quickly learned that these startups were being started by a bunch of genuine, hard-working, and engaged people. The very best thing that I could do for them was to be the most responsive person they'd ever met. The biggest gift I could give them was speed – when they asked me to do something, I did it as quickly as possible so that I was never the bottleneck. In many ways, the lawyers were the bottle-necks in these companies. They were creating all sorts of challenges and I wasn't going to be that. So if you needed something ASAP, I'd stay up all night and do it. That actually meant that my clients relied on me a lot more.

I also ended up becoming a licensing attorney because a lot of what my clients needed were contracts. And they needed them quickly. I could give those contracts to my licensing partners and associates, but then it would slow down the process. So I quickly came to the conclusion that the better bet was for me to draft the contracts myself and run them by the licensing people, rather than have the licensing people draft them and run them by the client. So suddenly, I was doing the licensing and all the corporate work for all of my clients. I was doing it as quickly as human-ly possible. That meant that I was working immense hours during this period of time. It was not an unusual thing for me to pull an all-nighter (maybe a couple of weeks).

But the byproduct was that my clients trusted me. They liked me. They relied on me. So I got to know the business better. I got to spend more time with them. The more deeply I understood their business, the better job I could do for them and the more likely they would trust me to play a role in the decision-making for that company.

So between 1997 and 2000, I worked with a bunch of really smart, young entrepreneurs and helped them build big, interesting businesses. Because I was working as hard as I was working, they trusted me to be a part of the team instead of just being a service provider. That made a huge difference. It gave me much more motivation and much more opportunity. It served them well and it served me well.

I would like to ask for those readers who are current attorneys or perhaps even law students that would eventually like to transition into venture capital. It sounds like from your story that it's essentially about building those foundations with your clients (or perhaps non-clients). It's about building that trust and those long-term relationships that will help them transition to the other side. Is that correct? What advice would you give to a current attorney—whether they are on the transactional or litigation side—if they want to transition into venture capital?

Yeah, I think that's right. Relationships matter. Provide value and be helpful. It was definitely the case that by being helpful, engaged, and responsive, I got to build real relationships with my clients—not just as a service provider, but ultimately as a friend. It turns out if you spend a lot of time with people, you get to know them. You get to know them as people.

I've had a long relationship with James Joaquin. He ended up selling his company maybe a year after we incorporated it for hundreds of millions of dollars. He then became the CEO of a new company called Ofoto, which was one of the first digital photography companies. He hired me as the attorney to represent that company. He offered to hire me into Ofoto, which I ultimately did not do but could well have. I would have happily worked for him.

One of his employees who worked with him at When.com (that first company) went off to another company called Evite and convinced Evite to hire me as its attorney. Luckily, I had the opportunity to work with them and built a really deep relationship with the founding team and then ultimately the management at Evite. Evite was actually the path that led to me becoming a venture capitalist.

So I think you have an opportunity to build real relationships with your clients. There is an opportunity to be seen as someone who is not just helpful, but who is a great advisor and a smart and helpful human. The stronger those ties, the more value you create, and the deeper the relationship you build, the more likely that you'll be considered a member of the team—not just a service provider that can be plugged in and unplugged.

Right. And then perhaps they'll vouch for you as well, whether you want to work at a venture capital firm or another startup.

Yeah. When my now-firm[7] was contemplating hiring me as an investor, I gave them a list of every one of my clients. I said, "Here's everybody I worked with. Call any of them. They called a dozen of them, which is a little bit of high-stakes poker when you're representing them.

Yeah.

And I wasn't a partner at the firm at that point. I was an associate. But my view was, "Even if I don't ultimately become a VC, my expectation is that they'll have a good conversation about me and they'll feel good about the work that I've done for them. So feel free to talk with them and ask them whether I'm the kind of person they want to work with." That proved to be really mutually reinforcing. All of those clients are still friends of mine. I'm still interacting with them. I probably see James Joaquin monthly. This is twenty-two years after I first met him and incorporated his first company.

So for those lawyers who are looking to join a VC firm, would you recommend that they work at a startup before moving into VC? Is there any way that they can make a direct transition into VC?

Well, I think that the opportunity to go straight to a VC firm is minuscule to non-existent. There are very few people who have gone directly from the law to venture capital. It's not impossible. There are some great attorneys like Ted Wang, who is now a VC. He was one of the best-respected startup attorneys in Silicon Valley before he left to join Cowboy Ventures.

But as a general matter, if you're someone who's excited about the venture business, then you need to be excited about the startup business as well. You almost assuredly will be better served by finding your way to a startup than trying to find your way directly to venture capital.

For those readers who are lawyers and thinking of starting their own startup, what would you recommend? What are things you've

---

7   Here, David is referring to August Capital. He cofounded Lobby Capital in January 2021.

identified as a VC that they should know before they start their business?

Nothing. You don't need to know anything to start a startup. You have to be passionate. You have to be excited about the idea of creating something from nothing. You have to understand that it almost assuredly will not work because it almost never does. But you have to be totally fine with that.

Beyond that, you have to have a problem that you want to solve. It's not enough to say, "I want to be an entrepreneur." You need to either join other people who are building something that you believe in or you have to have some big problem that you think requires a solution. You need to be willing to put aside all other things to solve it.

Does that require domain experience for that entrepreneur? Or if they identify some problem in the market that they don't necessarily face themselves, would you have a problem investing in them?

Domain expertise is a great asset when you're trying to solve a technical problem. When you're trying to solve a general problem, it isn't necessary. In some instances, it is an impediment. I funded two twenty-two-year-olds (maybe they were twenty-one when I funded them) that were building a payments company and they had no experience in payments. One of them had attended law school (I believe for one week) before he dropped out.

They were not domain experts by virtue of having performed the tasks associated with money transmission. They were experts because they took the time to understand the ecosystem. They took the time to understand the risks, the opportunities, the failures of the existing solutions, and came up with a great opportunity to build something big and interesting.

So I funded them because they were spectacularly thoughtful individuals, not because they were financial services experts. Ten years later, we sold that company to Chase for hundreds of millions of dollars. Now, I would say they are experts. If they were to form a second startup in the payments space, you would be very wise to support them.

Absolutely. So just to reiterate: if a lawyer wants to work in venture capital, those opportunities to go directly into VC are few and far between. Because of this, you would recommend that this lawyer works for a startup or enters the startup world in some other way. Is that right?

My recommendation is, first and foremost, to go do something you love. Don't take a job that will propel you towards the job you want to have if that job that you're taking isn't the greatest job you've ever had. History suggests that the thing you think you might want to do you won't ultimately do. That is particularly true in venture capital.

There are an innumerable set of people who have put their sights on being venture capitalists. They have engaged in a set of tasks that they thought would make them more likely to be a venture capitalist and never ultimately become venture capitalists. It was either because they found things they were more excited about or because it's extraordinarily hard to become a venture capitalist. There's a very small number of jobs available in the industry. The requirements for being a VC are very broad. So to do anything to prepare for being a venture capitalist that isn't the thing that you really want to be doing is a mistake.

And then the second piece of advice is that there are a million things that one could do that would make one a good candidate for venture capital. They're not only in the startup world. There are bankers who have become venture capitalists. There are consultants who have become venture capitalists. There are journalists who have become venture capitalists. So it's non-limiting.

What I would say is do something that you love that allows you to meet a lot of interesting people and build deep relationships with people. Ultimately, that will increase the likelihood that you happen to be in the right place at the right time when a venture firm is looking for help.

I would like to ask: what great legal startup (or any startup in the legal space) hasn't been built yet and perhaps one that a lawyer should build?

I guess what I would say is that's not really something I do.

Oh really?

I think that the job of a venture capitalist is to be open-minded about opportunities. It's far more likely that you would fund someone with the right idea that you'd never thought of than you come up with an idea and find that opportunity. I'm much more interested in meeting amazing people than I am in coming up with ideas about what the future will look like.

So when you're analyzing a potential investment, the team is the most important thing. Is it more important than the targeted market or the initial idea?

Yes. My approach to venture is that I look at team, team, TAM,[8] team. I care first and foremost about the team, but ultimately, if they're not building something big and interesting, it's hard to build a big and interesting business.

That makes sense. You have taught at Harvard Law School and Stanford Law School. As a teacher, what are some of the more significant insights that you've gathered, whether that's related to careers or life in general?

I think that it is a lucky position to be able to spend time with smart, young people. I think it's a privilege to be able to interact with them as they are making their way towards their first jobs or a profession that they are excited about. It will come as no surprise that the thing I always echo to them is that life is too short to work with people you don't love. Life is too short to do a job you don't love. Life is too short to pursue an opportunity that you don't think is important and valuable and will change the planet. That doesn't mean you have to be working on the next solar cell or some not-for-profit opportunity. I think that everything I fund makes the world a better place.

My advice is to find the way in which you can make the world better than the world you entered into. Do it with people you care about.

I'm sure you've seen law students who are thinking of building businesses or going into venture capital. What are some of the inherent

---

8   TAM means "total addressable market."

advantages or disadvantages that you see for law students (or even lawyers) trying to enter that world? How do you think about that?

It took me a lot of years to realize that the measure of me as a person and of my life was not my resumé. I had done all of the things that one would expect to try and make sure that I had that golden resumé. At some point, I realized, "Look, my happiness is not tied to the pedigree of that particular thing I'm doing. I should really focus on the question of what will make me happy."

I think that was important. I think it takes a long time for you to figure out what it is that will make you happy. I ultimately was able kept an open mind about the opportunities that have been put in front of me independent of how they would look on a resumé. I have had the great fortune of doing a bunch of things that have proven to be fulfilling and engaging (and they weren't bad jobs either).

And what general advice would you give to a lawyer who feels some inertia in their career path, whether that's Big Law or something else? They may want to transition into another field but they are scared. Maybe their fear is overtaking any action. How would you recommend that they break out of that inertia and make the change?

The first question is: can you afford to do something different? The reality is that it is not fair to assume that everybody can simply take on this kind of risk. If it turns out you are not yet in a position to be able to take additional risk, I would say don't. I wouldn't break out of that experience. You might be able to go from a great firm to another great firm where you're not taking on additional economic risk, but you're changing things up.

But in those instances where people are truly looking for something transformative, there's nothing one can do other than go and have those conversations. If you start talking with people about other opportunities, one of two things will happen. You'll either find yourself drawn toward those things (like an extraordinarily strong magnet) or you won't. If you aren't, then there's no reason to engage. If you are, truthfully, you'll have no choice. But in every instance where I started speaking with a new firm or facing a new opportunity, it really was like the breaking of a logjam. There was no going back.

The last law firm I worked at was Perkins Coie. I joined Perkins Coie when they were just getting their Bay Area corporate practice going. I really had an amazingly fun time working to help create that environment and build that team. I worked with a really wonderful young attorney named Buddy Arnheim. He and I had little kids and they were growing up at the same time. It was a fantastic experience. But when I started talking with companies and venture firms about the possibility of joining them, I was never going to be able to go back. It captured my imagination in ways that were not being captured by the legal work I was doing.

So once I started having those conversations about these exciting opportunities ahead of me, there just wasn't a circumstance in which I was going to end up remaining in a law firm. But I've talked with others who have entertained leaving the law — they've had a bunch of conversations and thought to themselves, "Those jobs sound terrible." For them, stepping away from the law would be a bad idea and they shouldn't do it. For me, it was the best decision I ever made.

Exactly. Are there any blogs or books that lawyers should read if they're interested in working in startups or venture capital?

Not really. There are lots of great things that have been written. When I started as a venture capitalist, I helped create the first venture capital blog. It was called VentureBlog. It started in large part because I felt like nobody was talking about the venture business and someone should. So I created VentureBlog and it was great fun. I wanted to share my point of view about the venture business.

Shortly thereafter, two other venture capitalists started blogging about the venture business. One is a guy named Brad Feld and he has a thing called Feld Thoughts. It is a great resource and he continues to write it. The other venture capitalist is a guy named Fred Wilson, who has a blog called AVC. Fred has written with huge consistency over lots and lots of years. It remains one of the great sources of information about the venture business. As for mine, I stopped after about one decade. But between Feld Thoughts and AVC, there is a lot of wisdom to be gained.

Chapter 15

Angela Saverice-Rohan

Management Consultant and Privacy Expert

One of the many interesting things about legal practice is the way it is portrayed in films, books, and television. While we may think that we rationally and independently come to our career decisions, humans are mimetic creatures. We see what others are doing and want to be like them (even if they only exist in fiction).

A classic example is Atticus Finch. If you survey any incoming law school class, you'll likely find at least one person who traces their law school inspiration to that attorney from the fictional Maycomb County, Alabama. Atticus's courage, wisdom, and commitment to justice are things that we can all admire.

Some fictional attorneys take it to the extreme. Think Harvey Specter, Alan Shore, or Ally McBeal. These attorneys make it seem like legal practice is about delivering perfectly crafted arguments to an infatuated jury. These garrulous attorneys win in the courtroom and win in life. They may drive fancy cars and have glamorous social lives. It's almost as if *they* are the ones in charge, rather than their clients.

Whether intended or not, those portrayals play at least some role in convincing us that we are meant to be lawyers. We are the protagonists of our own stories, yet we are surrounded by stories of others living the lives we want to live. Even if those stories are fictional, they play a part in painting the picture of our future legal careers.

With all of that said, almost every practicing attorney recognizes that legal practice is often unlike what is portrayed in movies, books, and television shows. This is especially true at larger commercial law firms. Less time is spent arguing in the courtroom, and more time is spent reviewing documents or researching case law. M&A attorneys—especially those at the junior level—are spending less time hammering out the actual terms of a deal and more time completing due diligence.

New commercial lawyers quickly discover that there is less glamour than they expected. In fact, it's easy to feel like a cog in a corporate machine. Work needs to get done—often on short notice—and attorneys are tasked with quickly responding to decisions their clients make.

For some lawyers, including the talented woman profiled in this chapter, the realities of being a commercial lawyer get old. By making a change, she found work that spoke to her passions, which included helping her clients navigate tough business decisions.

Angela Saverice-Rohan is a Partner at one of the Big Four consulting firms. As a leader in her firm's privacy practice, she helps her clients navigate a whole host of challenges related to privacy and cybersecurity. From privacy strategy to advising clients on new product offerings, Angela provides immense value to her clients and colleagues.

Angela attended William Mitchell College of Law (now called Mitchell Hamline School of Law) while working at U.S. Bank. After graduation, she remained at U.S. Bank for several years before working as corporate counsel for Digital River, WellPoint, and Spokeo. At Spokeo, she worked on landmark privacy litigation that eventually made its way to the U.S. Supreme Court.

After thirteen years of legal practice, Angela switched to management consulting. As she describes in her LinkedIn post on how she left the practice of law,[1] she enjoyed her earlier years as a practicing attorney. After starting "hot and heavy" with the law, she felt herself stagnating. She loved helping her clients avoid "The Pain," whether that was a financial loss, business interruption, or even reputational harm. That said, as she described it, her status as a lawyer prevented her from obtaining insider status and helping her clients make tough decisions.

In effect, she wanted to move beyond solely focusing on black letter law to helping her clients accomplish their business goals. She wanted to be similar to Tom Hagen, Robert Duvall's character in *The Godfather*. As the consigliere to the Corleone family, Hagen was the calm, cool, and collected voice that played an important role in the family's decisions. He was less of a corporate janitor and more of a trusted advisor whose voice was respected by all key decision-makers.

---

1   Angela's LinkedIn post is a fantastic introspective of her decision to quit legal practice and her initial impressions of the consulting world. You can find it at https://www.linkedin.com/pulse/my-transition-from-lawyer-consultant-what-past-2-have-angela/

With that in mind, Angela took a leap of faith. She entered the management consulting world and didn't look back. In our conversation, Angela spoke about things like her earlier years at William Mitchell College of Law, how she combatted imposter syndrome in her career, the ideal time to make the switch from legal work to management consulting, and some of the subtle yet important differences between legal practice and consulting.

* * *

Angela, you work in management consulting and have a specialty in privacy and cybersecurity. For those law students or lawyers that aren't familiar with consulting, can you describe what you do on a day-to-day basis?

I have two roles. The substantive consulting role is truly about advising clients on how to operationalize privacy into their business. Doing this, we architect privacy from cradle to grave—the full lifecycle of the customer journey. Alternatively, it may be the full lifecycle of the employee experience. Within that, there's a lot of accounting for law and regulation, but there's also a lot of accounting for aspects of data management and technology.

My job as a consultant in this space is to bring all those pieces together and have a layer over the top with respect to risk management. It's about figuring out how to create what I call a reference architecture for a client to manage against a multitude of requirements. That's the day-to-day big picture.

Then there's the other side of my work. Because I lead the practice, I have responsibility for about one hundred eighty people within the firm. A big part of that work is strategy, creating the go-to-market for the firm, interfacing with many policymakers and regulators, and keeping the firm's brand top of mind when it comes to privacy. So that's all about the market aspect, building the practice, thinking about the solutions and partnerships, and, truly, revenue management. To be very honest, I love that part. In part, that is what was missing for me in my legal career. I truly like creating a solution from the group up, trying to bring it to market, and seeing if I can innovate with it. It's no different than an innovator that creates a product or service.

My role requires me to be very entrepreneurial. A Big Four firm is generally very large, very complex, and with many different teams supporting various aspects of our clients' agendas. To be successful in these firms, you need to be a connector. You need to bring together different solutioning and teams to maximize the value proposition. You also have to hustle. It's a very competitive landscape for consultants, so you need to be thinking about how to constantly deliver value and exceed client expectations. I love all of these challenges.

Well, even what you were describing resembles some aspects of working at a corporate law firm. The partners and practice group heads have their day-to-day lawyering work, but they also need to focus on business development and marketing tasks.

As a Partner, I'm committed to the long-term success of our firm. Hence, I see the relationships I develop with clients as a key asset to ensuring that success. Having said that, I've had to learn to balance my personality with the expectations of a Partner. Similar to law firm life, there's a need to network and build relationships that support a continued pipeline of opportunity in your practice area. Prior to Covid-19, there was lots of socialization. I was just admitting to my team the other day about the cerebral nature that I have. I'm a bit of an introvert. People never believe it, but it's true. So I manage my client and team social functions in the right way to make sure I meet the goals of the firm while being true to myself.

Like you're saying, you have to juggle so many things. Do you know many people that have made this similar switch from law to consulting?

It's an interesting question. I don't know many people, to be very honest, that have been terribly successful with it. I know more people that have tried it after they had extensive practice experience. It was too challenging, and they wanted to leave consulting.

I think there are a couple of different reasons behind that. We'll get into this in a moment when discussing my specific experience. However, the longer that you are in law practice, the more difficult it becomes.

When you move into consulting, consulting firms won't often take someone at a senior level who hasn't had experience in consulting. It's similar to trying to get an in-house role. Many lawyers that transition into consulting are hired at a more junior level. So they're not getting the deference that they're used to. Initially, they may be working on projects that may feel like a step back for them. I think this part of the transition can be challenging.

I have found in my own work experience (and also when speaking with others) that there is some bias in favor of people that grow up in consulting. There's a respect for how hard they've worked—across so many different engagements, clients, and partners along the way. When someone is hired as a direct admit at a senior level, they don't automatically get the same level of respect. They will need to earn it, which can be harder for senior lawyers as they are back in a position of having to prove themselves and their value.

Now, the opposite of that would be juniors right out of school. Because of my urging and leadership on this, we are one of the only Big Four firms (that I am aware of) to create a law school recruiting program. I have targeted certain law schools in the United States that have a privacy curriculum. Then, I'm bringing in attorneys right out of school who already know they don't want to go into traditional practice. We're grooming them to become consultants.

I think they will do well because they're growing up in the firm. They have some of the challenges of transitioning into what it's like and what they believed they would be doing post-law school. But we manage for that. Like everyone in their career, we all probably had an interesting first day when we started working after law school.

How long would you say the window is? Like you said, it's harder once attorneys get older and more established in the legal industry. Would that window be something like three to five years out of law school?

Three to five years would be a good time. I think once you hit between the five to seven-year mark, as a lawyer, you probably have been on a number of projects that have given you an opportunity to learn and demonstrate your fastball in a particular area. You likely don't have your own book. You're starting to support a senior partner. You have great relationships with the clients. I think it's going to be much harder for you to jump into a new environment at that point.

You've also started to train your brain to think like a lawyer. When I moved into consulting, I had to do some refinement of how I thought. For me, it wasn't a huge hurdle. That's probably why I was successful. I realized I was slipping away from traditional legal thinking anyway. I was much more of a businessperson, so it was okay. But I've seen other lawyers (and I've actually had them work for me in the firm) where it is much harder for them to undo their thinking after about five years.

I can imagine. In your LinkedIn article, you also mentioned how one of your favorite parts of legal practice was helping your clients avoid "The Pain." I think it's a great way to put it. Legal practice obviously isn't just about researching case law and writing legal briefs. It's about helping your clients solve business challenges.

Absolutely. It's about being part of the discussion as they're making decisions, rather than being told later. Also, just to be honest, it is kind of shirking off the naïveté of our careers as young lawyers. We get out of law school and believe all of our clients want to achieve compliance for the sake of compliance. That's a very naïve thought. I've had to explain that to my team. Our clients need to succeed in business while managing for their compliance obligations, but compliance doesn't drive growth.

I don't know if I noted this in my LinkedIn article, but I share this story pretty openly with people. One of my best clients taught me this right out of law school. I'll never forget it. I went in thinking I was going to be this adviser to the senior bank executive. I sat in a meeting and I gave advice on whatever the law or regulation required. After the meeting, he pulled me aside and said that one of the best things he could teach me as a young lawyer (he was not a lawyer) was that I did not own his P&L. I was an adviser. He was ultimately the decision-maker. He had to bear the financial consequences and the personal consequences of his decision. The role of the lawyer should be, of course, to advise and be part of that. But the lawyer must also remember that their clients are dealing with a multitude of decisions and risks. They are not always going to comply with the law in the strictest sense.

I never forgot that. He was a very, very challenging client, and he was perhaps one of my best clients. He taught me so much about the partnership with a client and how to become a trusted adviser. So once I got through and broke into that inner circle, I was much more involved. We would think through the impacts together and acknowledge different risks. This experience made me realize that I have to change lawyers' thinking when they come into the firm.

I would just like to circle back for a moment. You are a consultant with a focus on privacy. I'm assuming that wasn't the original vision when you were thinking of going to law school. What was really the catalyst for law school? Also, why did you choose the Mitchell Hamline School of Law?

Well, it was originally called William Mitchell. It has since merged with Hamline University School of Law.

I think there were a couple of reasons why I went to law school. First of all, my undergrad degree is in philosophy. I considered pursuing that further and becoming an academic. Alternatively, I could maybe make a little money and go to law school.

I grew up in a very conservative family. My father was a surgeon. He said to me, "Angela, it's really important to me that you are able to financially support yourself. I don't ever want you to have to get married." That was his phrase. "So I want you to pursue the professions of doctor or lawyer. If you do that, you'll be fine." I think we realized very early that pursuing medicine would have been extremely challenging for me (although he pushed me in all of the science classes he could). I tried, but it just did not come naturally to me. Because of this, I went into law.

With respect to the school, the reason I chose it, very simply, is that I needed to work full-time. I had gotten a job at U.S. Bank. After working there for a couple of years, I knew I was going to go to graduate school. I got married young (I was twenty-three) and we had bought a house. However, I was moving up at the bank and wasn't in a position where I could quit. Financially, we had to afford that mortgage and figure things out as a young married couple. To be honest, that made the path for me.

I'm happy to say we've been married twenty-five years and we have children. It has all worked out well. But there were times in my life where I wished I could go to school full-time. But I had been moving up at U.S. Bank. Eventually, I moved into the trust department and was the youngest trust executive that they had in the company. I got really good support from senior executives there. The bank also helped pay for some of my law school.

Oh really?

Yes. That was another reason why I got the in-house job after graduating from law school. I had a contract where I had to stay at the bank. If I didn't, I had to come up with $20,000 the day I left. My husband was like, "Well, I guess you're staying."

The opportunity to get into the law department, though, was still very challenging. I was on another team, but I had such support from really esteemed senior people. They made some recommendations, and when an opportunity came up, they made sure I got an interview.

So I was terribly lucky. The right circumstances existed. That client I was telling you about (the bank executive) had gone through something like four attorneys in two years because he was just really tough. I think they were looking for somebody wide-eyed and eager. That's what happened.

You were working and going to school at night. A big theme of this book is time management. Time management can be difficult for law students, but it can be even more difficult for practicing attorneys. If you want to make the transition from legal practice to something else, you have to find some time, whether that's time to work on a side project or time to meet other people that can facilitate the transition. Do you have any good time management tips or habits that served you well in law school, legal practice, or your current work?

They're probably not the best habits. I'm a complete workaholic. I'm a complete study-aholic. I think that all stems from a feeling or a need to feel very prepared. You should have a whole separate book on imposter syndrome and perfection.

I can't tell you that I managed time that well in school. It wasn't like I would say, "Now is the time when I'm going to do this and only this and then cut it off." I would get up, go to work, go to class, and then get home and read until I fell asleep. I would wake up the next morning and do it again. I don't know if that constitutes time management.

The weekends were what all of them are for law students. There's just a lot of work. My husband jokes that looking back, he's never been on a vacation with me where I haven't been working. I've always had my laptop. A couple of years ago, I reflected on how I could be better. I realized that it's partly because I don't want to be. I enjoy all of the daily reading and learning that is required for my current work.

To me, it's not work. Sure, there's the answering of emails. But I enjoy reading about the big challenges that my clients are facing. To properly advise them on privacy, I have to get very smart on the issues they're managing for on a global basis. I'll spend hours reading things that are ancillary to my clients' challenges. From there, I can bring that information back and advise them. But I love it.

And it's about curiosity and loving what you do, which you clearly do.

It truly is.

You went to law school. You obviously succeeded. Then, you returned to U.S. Bank. When I was in law school, I was thinking about doing different things with my career. Like many other law students, I thought a general counsel position sounded interesting. It was interesting in terms of the work itself and the lifestyle. You very quickly became a general counsel, though, and many attorneys don't make that jump immediately from law school—even if that is their goal.

Oh, gosh no. You see it more on the West Coast—particularly with startups. But you saw in my career that I moved to several different institutions.

Can you share some tips or advice for law students that are interested in a general counsel role right after law school?

In my opinion, the best thing you can do is get exposure to as many different regulated industries as possible. That's what I did. For example, Digital River was an ecommerce company that had the global privacy landscape that was really starting to evolve at that point. You also need to get as much exposure as possible to different C-suites.

When you say, "getting exposure to different industries," what does that look like in practice? Is it simply reading up on those different industries?

No. I mean going and looking for jobs. Alternatively, if you're going to stay in private practice, you need to expand your scope so that you get an opportunity to represent those different sectors. Having not had the background in financial services, I probably wouldn't have gotten the job in health care. Had I not had the background in health care, I probably wouldn't have gotten the job as a general counsel in tech.

I also had this history. I don't know what happens—it's kind of a running joke that when I come to a company, something bad happens and I'm there to solve it. I had a good run with companies that had data breaches.

Also, when I took that job at Spokeo, a huge part of me thought I wasn't ready for that job. Even though I thought that I shouldn't take the job, I did it anyway. At the time, I had a good mentor. I asked, "Should I do this?" He said, "This will make your career. Just jump in it." So that was intentional and why I took that GC role. If I had taken a GC role for a company that didn't have much going on just so I could call myself a general counsel, I would have been terribly bored. I am very strategic and actually want troubled clients. The problem-solver nature in me wasn't satisfied by working on day-to-day legal issues.

Your mentor was really encouraging you to take the position at Spokeo. But at the same time, you had those internal reservations. In this situation, how did address them before making the leap?

First of all, the founders that run the company are great guys. They are engineers. Although I was probably suffering from feelings of insecurity and the thought of whether I was ready for this role, I brought a significant level of experience and maturity coming out of corporate America. The company needed it in a very desperate time. I realized that after spending time with them.

Shortly after I arrived, the company became involved in a Senate investigation.[2] At the time, I'm thinking, "I may be out of my league right now." But I had excellent external counsel. I found myself in meetings with people that were on the Senate committee. At the end of the day, we're all smart people. My internal nature also helped. I'm pretty authentic and grounded, and I tend to bring it out in people.

Then, as I moved into consulting, there was another opportunity to think, "Am I ready for this?" It was a completely different challenge. It felt very different. There was a different feeling of imposter syndrome that I had to get over.

Sure. But it sounds like the bottom line is that you needed to be yourself and take action—even if you were nervous or anxious.

That's exactly right. There's no other magic answer to that. I think it's something that all of us struggle with.

So before talking about your consulting work, let's dig a bit deeper into your legal practice. What were some of the things that you really liked about it?

I actually really like the rule of law. It's why I went to law school. I appreciate any area of law that is very rule-based and prescriptive. In fact, I thought I was going to go into tax law. People said, "Tax law, really?" I think I loved the certainty around it. However, I also loved some of the grey. It kind of was the perfect mix and sufficiently complex. I like things that are complex.

The same was true when practicing in-house. The more complicated an issue and the more multidisciplinary impact it had, the better. I had to think through how that particular issue was going to impact six different things within an institution. For instance, it would impact the

---

2   Spokeo, which describes itself as a "people search website," was one of several companies being examined by the Senate Committee on Commerce, Science and Transportation. The Committee was seeking information on the companies' privacy and data collection practices on their websites.

institution's go-to-market strategy in this jurisdiction, whether it could sell a particular product, and whether it could buy certain technology. I liked having all of those touchpoints to consider.

When I got to Spokeo, for example, we dealt with an Article III standing issue. Looking back, part of the reason I loved that was that it was so unclear. I liked that ambiguity. It gave us an opportunity to advocate for something. It was the attitude of "Let's take a stand on this." That's what I really liked the most.

Otherwise, with respect to the law, I would enjoy issues where the circuits were split. In privacy, we didn't have a huge body of U.S. litigation to draw upon. It was only under certain limited privacy regulations.

It seems like you have a somewhat similar experience in consulting. At the very least, you have taken those elements that you enjoy and you've crafted your career around them.

I think consulting in the privacy area is the true intersection of law, technology, and policy. I was talking to someone this morning about the position that Apple has recently taken. As you may have seen, Apple's new operating system will ask you whether you want to be tracked on the Internet. You are going to say "no." We kind of know this. You are still going to get ads, but they aren't going to be targeted. Of course, most companies that have significant ad-based revenue are negatively reacting to this.

Yes, like Facebook.

It's a complete attack against Facebook. And that's the other thing. Privacy is truly this weapon. It's not really about what people think it is about. It is something that governments use against each other and companies use against each other. I love that because there is this whole separate layer that's happening up here while people think what's happening is down there.

This morning, we were discussing the impact of Apple's decision. Why would Apple take this position? Well, Apple's taking this position because they get a significant cut of all of the apps in its App Store. Once you have to start taking free apps and charging for them, their revenues are going to increase. Then, you start talking to companies and ask, "Well, what are you going to do to manage for this when it hits your ad revenue?" I love the different pieces and angles. Then, you start having really interesting conversations with clients.

Definitely. So you quit legal practice in 2014. You practiced for thirteen years. Can you walk readers through your thinking at that time?

So Spokeo had submitted its petition for a writ of certiorari. I got to work on that with external counsel and it was so much fun. I was functioning at that high level with these very esteemed lawyers who had previously argued in front of the U.S. Supreme Court. I did all of the amicus curiae briefs. It was great work. Then, I realized I had kind of a letdown. I thought, "What happens now? That's about as good as it's going to get for me."

As we were waiting to hear from the Supreme Court, I went back to the routine work of a general counsel in a technology company. I think that was such an anticlimactic moment. All of my feelings about wanting to leave the law came in.

I had met a number of consultants and started reaching out to some of them. I realized that at that point, I was highly sought after with my resumé. A number of people were watching my career and knew who I was. They were trying me out a little bit, too. They didn't know how I would be as a consultant. Like, was I going to come in and just be a lawyer in a consulting firm? Because that doesn't work. That doesn't sell. However, they were delighted that that wasn't my style. It really worked out well.

Interesting. People were monitoring your career. They were thinking, "Hey, if she is maybe interested in doing something else, we should contact her."

Privacy was an up-and-coming area for the Big Four. There was privacy consulting, but if you were to look at the revenues at that time, they were pretty minuscule. I got in at a time when some consulting firms were going head-to-head to build privacy into their cyber practices. They recognized that something was going to emerge from the European Union. It was a couple of years out. They knew they needed some senior practitioners that had credibility in the market. I hit it at just the right time.

The opportunity was there, but you still needed to take the leap and actually pursue it. Were you really nervous about making the switch? At the last moment, were you having any second thoughts?

A little bit. I was afraid to not identify as a lawyer anymore. Do you know what I mean? So much of our identity is built into the hard work to become lawyers and what we did thereafter in our practice. To not be considered part of that anymore was challenging.

Now, clients would still know that I was a lawyer. But I felt a little strange at first. I got distracted because I was so busy trying to understand the intricacies of a Big Four firm. But after speaking with my friends that were still in practice, I felt like I was just living this very different life. So there was this awkwardness. I felt like I didn't fit in anywhere for a while.

Speaking of that, when moving into consulting, you had to quickly pick up different types of skills and knowledge. How did you do that? Was it essentially about returning to your roots by putting in the hours and studying this new industry?

A lot of it was trying to understand how privacy fits within the context of risk services that the firm would sell and discuss. From there, it was taking everything I had done as a lawyer and looking at it through a different lens. I had to look at it through the lens of a chief security officer (CSO). I had to look at it through the lens of the chief audit executive. I had done some of that as a general counsel, but not in this way.

I had to start learning all of the other domains that these executives manage. When I go in and convince prospective clients to work with me, I can more easily understand how privacy fits into their agenda. This is different from legal advice, where you're coming to me with a problem. In that case, I know the law and I'll advise you on that.

It is very, very different. It's very competitive in consulting. I have to convince prospective clients that I understand everything that they're working with so that they'll choose me.

That's not easy.

No. I did a lot of reading, but it is also a personality game. Consulting is much more personality focused than it is in legal practice. I think this is because people will work with lawyers that they don't necessarily like. Those lawyers are excellent or their firm has a fantastic reputation. In consulting, if they don't like you, they will not work with you.

Lawyers also get deference from a client. They may put you in a box and say, "I don't want to talk to you about anything other than this, Adam." That's fine. But they still called you. They need you and they are deferring to you.

Did you find that there were any strengths or weaknesses that you had as an attorney that made your transition easier or harder?

I'd have to think that one through, Adam. My professional skepticism in consulting is the same quality that most lawyers have. I challenge my own thinking and I challenge the client's thinking. That's what I would say is probably the most important attribute to bring over to consulting—credible challenge.

It's always difficult to give advice to individuals that are on the verge of making a substantial career decision. That said, if a law student or lawyer is seriously thinking about pursuing consulting, are there any first principles or general pieces of advice that they should keep in mind?

In terms of general advice, I think I previously shared this thought. I don't think that law school effectively teaches the consensus-building that professionals need in this space. As part of our routine assessment work, we spend a lot of time interviewing our clients. That's what all consultants do. It's different from the practice of law in the sense that yes, you are doing client interviews, but you're often using the rule of law to bump something up against.

In our work, it's much more amorphous. Privacy has evolved so much that there hasn't necessarily been a definition of what "good" looks like for a company that manages challenges in this space. It is based upon a lot of other practices that we bring to bear. For example, it is about having a mindset where you're looking outside your current discipline to bring information in. I spend a lot of time thinking about models for things that have nothing to do with privacy. Then, I can apply those models to the lens of privacy to help the client achieve what it needs to achieve.

**That makes sense. I'm reminded of Charlie Munger, who frequent-
ly talks about the importance of knowing many different mental
models. From there, we can apply them to all types of situations in
our personal and professional lives.**

Absolutely. And they don't teach us this in law school. We had to learn
that on our own. So I think that's a key thing.

I think most lawyers are intellectually curious. But also, your reference as a lawyer comes from the principles and concepts that you are
taught in law school. They kind of become your guide and your North
Star. But sometimes, what happens is that you don't think outside the box.
You think inside the box. In consulting, the most successful consultants
are not thinking in a really limited way. They have to think much more
broadly.

Again, it's not something that you can necessarily pick up in law
school. It's a mindset that you have to work on and develop. I also think
that in consulting, you have to get over this desire to be deferred to. I
talked about the different ways that clients look at lawyers versus consultants. There's more ego management in consulting than in law.

**How do you practically do all of this? You mentioned earlier how
important it is for clients to actually like consultants. Things like
managing client expectations are also critical. These are soft skills
that lawyers-turned-consultants will need to perfect. If attorneys
are starting from scratch and want to become consultants, how can
they build up these softer skills?**

You hit it quite well. They lack the soft skills. We were just talking about
this in my practice the other day. How do we help accelerate the soft
skills?

I think it's practice. I'll give you two great examples. First, I was talking
to a junior lawyer this morning about an engagement. The client directly
said that the reason they hired us is that they want us to push them and
challenge their thinking. We were hired to re-architect an entire process
and drive out $2 million worth of cost in their business. They know that
to achieve that, they need people to push.

Now, when I went to my team (some of them are lawyers and they
are junior), I said the client expects that you will push on them. One of

the junior lawyers said, "How do we do that in a way that doesn't cause abrasion to the client relationship? Will they also respect our perspective if they see us just as lawyers who have been on the outside and in an ivory tower versus in the organization and running it?"

These are excellent questions. There aren't easy answers. I would say it's working with more of the senior consultants and prepping before you enter the meeting. This is to make sure you know the points you want to make. But it's also about determining a way to put it in front of the client and say, "The way you've been doing this isn't the best way to do it."

Usually, lawyers don't have to do that as much. They give advice and then they can sit back. If the client wants to do something different with that advice, that's on them. Consultants are right there in it, so you have to have that soft skill.

We are often in a position where we're competing with law firms for work. This is a really interesting aspect of the job. Just yesterday, I went to orals for a client where we were the only consulting firm that bid on the work. I could tell that the client probably gave us the opportunity to bid because of some relationships we had. So the game for that meeting was the following: how do we present the value proposition that consultants bring over lawyers?

What did you say?

I shared my perspective on what they were trying to achieve. Very few clients come to us saying, "Just give us advice on the requirements under the law." That's one part of the story. The reason that clients come to big firms is that they're usually undertaking some big initiative to grow their business. Other times, they have a retrenchment strategy to cut back on things. Either way, these are big, big initiatives. The work that we are doing is part of it.

In consulting, we want to come in where the lawyer would have left off. We want to see the bigger picture. We ask questions like, "How do we take current legal requirements and convert them into technical requirements that the client can embed into a data and analytics platform to support a brand new offering and achieve a twenty percent incremental growth rate? That's the difference in thinking.

Now, it means that on the front end, the legal advice (or what we say as lawyers) can't be so constrained that it doesn't anticipate what needs to happen down the chain. That's what often happens with lawyers. They don't see it because they say, "That's not my job." So somebody who moves in this space and wants to be successful must see the full chain as theirs.

It's easy for young associates to focus on that one discrete legal question that they are asked to answer. At the same time, they may not know the bigger picture, so it makes it tougher to complete the best possible work for their clients.

That's right. I think that's generally a challenge for people in a junior role. That's the other thing. Lawyers ask me, "When is it best for me to get into consulting?" As I said, I hire junior lawyers because I want to shape them and bring them in right away. But if you're at a law firm or in-house and transition too early, you're not going to have the experience to make yourself credible in these meetings. When consulting firms hire you and you're an experienced hire, they believe that you have a broad understanding of business operations. They see you as an asset because you're bringing that knowledge and experience with you. They also believe that you have this huge network. Most junior in-house practitioners (and even private practitioners) have a limited view just based on the type of work we do. Also, their network isn't that huge.

I've seen many situations where consulting firms thought they were going to get certain value from the lawyer. However, the lawyer gets into the consulting firm, fails, and then has to leave the firm. To succeed, you have to be sufficiently senior and have done enough work in business operations with many types of clients. But also, you can't be so senior that you are unwilling to retrain your brain. You need to look at it like a beginner.

That was that gap we were talking about. Do you think lawyers with a litigation background can transfer into consulting? Or is it better if they come from a transactional background?

I've seen them try. In consulting, I have seen a couple of litigators go into our forensics practice. Those types of groups support operations related to legal investigations and cybersecurity breaches. Therefore, some skills from these substantive areas can be helpful. That said, a litigator's personal traits will not be helpful in consulting.

By personal traits, do you mean the traits that make up the adversarial nature of litigation?

Yes. The way in which we present ourselves—both internally and to the client—makes the litigator style a harder one.

What about some of the harder skills that lawyers should acquire when making the transition into consulting? As just one example, would lawyers or law students need to have a math, science, or STEM background? Would getting those types of skills help or not?

Not in the practices that I've seen. I don't think math is necessary, but it depends on the area. I focus on cybersecurity and privacy. Within that particular area, I would certainly say that understanding technology is important. Also important is the understanding of data, systems, and applications. I think a lot of the skills and knowledge they teach in Master's in Information Management programs or Information Science programs are transferable.

At our firm, we have recently split into tech consulting and business consulting. On the business consulting side, I think you really need to understand risk management and how it works in an organization. For example, what does it practically mean when a company has mandatory reporting on various control-related issues so the board can meet its fiduciary duties? A lot of people don't know those things. They read about them at a high level, but they don't know how these things actually get implemented.

If you want to enter high-tech consulting, it's really good to understand things like how cloud technology works. How does data lake technology work? These are things that you can study if you're a lawyer. If you're not representing clients in this space, you can learn them on your own. The more substantive things that you're able to bring to the conversation, the more that you will move ahead.

One of my favorite insights (again, from Charlie Munger) is when he talks about Berkshire Hathaway's success. He basically says that both he and Warren Buffett weren't necessarily brilliant. Rather, they avoided the stupid mistakes that they could have made. They were just trying to be less stupid than other people. That obviously

got them far. So as far as lawyers that are transitioning into consulting, what obvious or not-so-obvious mistakes should they avoid?

That's an excellent question. I have had to coach many lawyers when I see their work product. I realized they were advising a client just like a lawyer. We can't practice law in the United States. First and foremost, from a liability perspective, we're not giving legal advice. Now, there's an art to doing what we need to do to make sure we don't do that. But more than that, there is this limited view. Like I said, they're just giving a perspective on this issue. They're not talking about the broader implications of what the client wants to achieve. That's something you have to overcome very quickly.

The other thing is humility. I was posting about this today on my LinkedIn. I spend a lot of time talking to the team about lessons in ego management. I truly believe it is at the heart of most problems that all companies have. We all have egos. We all have to manage them. Lawyers have the worst egos. We just do. It's a constant management and taming of the ego.

There are basic things that I think we all can learn—no matter what our profession is. But I feel like in consulting, there are so many opportunities to practice this. It's just a real, constant practice. Even at the highest levels, we're all doing it.

Have you read *Ego is the Enemy*?

It is one of my favorite books. It's one of the books that I quoted this morning on my LinkedIn post.

It's a great one. Just one final question from me. You said that you basically created a recruiting program at law schools. If someone is interested in entering consulting right out of law school, how can they maximize their odds of doing so?

There are some consulting firms that are better about looking at law schools. The reality is many consulting programs that recruit consultants right out of school don't go to law schools. They go to business schools. Big Four firms target people from CPA and audit programs. That's feeder.

So first and foremost, reach out to your career services office and see if consulting firms are coming. If they're not, I would directly reach out. Also, you have to think about where you'll be most wanted as a lawyer in consulting. Privacy is an easy connection because it is driven by law. Over the last five to seven years, I think it's an area that has become more of a focus within law schools. There is more curriculum that is specific to it. The same is true of cybersecurity.

But that's not the case for everything. For transaction advisory services, most big consulting firms have a transaction team. They support clients in big M&A deals (in addition to law firms). That's also an area where, as a lawyer, you can come in with these skills and be considered an asset. We also talked about forensics.

So think through what you want to do. A consulting firm has plenty of opportunities. Name your service and we provide it. But it's thinking about where you'll be seen as a differentiated candidate because of your law degree or law experience. If you can think that through, then you won't be perceived as equal to just any other candidate. That's what you want. You don't want your JD to be like, "Well, that's just another few letters after my name." You want it to be viewed as a real value proposition.

CHAPTER 16

Mia Dell

Policy Director

If you sampled a group of prospective lawyers with liberal arts back-grounds, you would undoubtedly find a few who want to use their law degrees to eventually enter politics.

It makes sense. Looking at American history alone, some of our most celebrated politicians and leaders studied or practiced law before reaching elected office. You can pick among Abraham Lincoln, Barack Obama, John F. Kennedy, Kamala Harris, Hillary Clinton, Mitt Romney, and more. On an international scale, there are legendary figures like Nelson Mandela and Mahatma Gandhi. The pipeline from law to elected office doesn't just occur at the absolute highest offices in the world. In the current Congress, for instance, one hundred and seventy-five members have law degrees (equaling around thirty-three percent of the total number of congress-people and senators).[1]

Both in modern and not-so-modern history, there are plenty of examples of lawyers entering the political world. Like many other things, these examples can power our own ambitions. Even the American Bar Association recognizes this common desire to leave the practice of law and become an elected official. It created a dedicated website that explains how lawyers can run for office.[2]

Ultimately, the practicing lawyer to elected office pipeline has existed for hundreds of years. In all likelihood, it will continue. Still, I think the focus on elected office sometimes overshadows many other outstanding

---

1   A list of all current members of Congress with law degrees can be found here: https://www.americanbar.org/content/dam/aba/administrative/government_affairs_office/117-congress-jds.pdf

2   You can find that website here: https://www.americanbar.org/groups/young_lawyers/publications/tyl/topics/getting-into-politics/

opportunities in politics and policy. There are positions where you can keep practicing law (like a counsel position for a congressional committee or a government agency), but there are also plenty of non-practicing positions. This includes everything from communications directors and legislative directors to policy analysts and public affairs managers. While these may not be the "headline" roles that uber-ambitious lawyers strive for, they offer great opportunities to use our core analytical, writing, and communications skills.

Moreover, it is easier to get these positions. Getting elected to office involves a whole host of variables, with timing and luck being some of the strongest. Even if you are the most charismatic or knowledgeable candidate in a race, there is no guarantee that you will be elected. On the other hand, if you are looking to leverage your legal training in a new way and make a difference in the world, it may be better to bypass the elected office route and find a practicing or non-practicing role in policy or politics. Who knows? You may be able to parlay that experience into an elected office position down the road. In the meantime, you could do some great work for a cause, agency, candidate, or committee you are passionate about.

That brings us to Mia Dell. Mia is the national policy director at Service Employees International Union (SEIU). With her colleagues, Mia works to represent SEIU members' interests in state and national politics. From working on the 2018 Florida gubernatorial race to lobbying the Biden administration on the American Rescue Plan, Mia and her colleagues work to build relationships and influence policy on a state and national level.

Mia had an interesting path to her work in politics and policy. After graduating from New York Law School, she practiced at several nonprofits in New York City, including Eviction Intervention Services and Bronx Legal Services. Upon moving with her husband to Washington, D.C., Mia decided she wanted to take a slightly different direction in her career. She found a position in Congresswoman Nydia Velazquez's office, and after spending several years on Capitol Hill, she moved into the policy world. There, she has worked for organizations like the Center for Science in the Public Interest, United Food and Commercial Workers, and now the SEIU.

Mia's career shows that you can do all types of interesting work in the political and policy worlds. While there is no guaranteed path, keep doing great work in your early career. Make it a point to meet interesting people—especially in these two worlds. Whether you pursue these opportunities right out of law school or several years later in your life as a practicing lawyer, they are there for the taking.

* * *

Mia, thanks for taking the time to speak about your law school experience and your work in the politics and policy worlds. To start off, I think it's common for prospective or current law students to think they can use their law degrees to get into politics or policy. This is especially true for those with political science or history backgrounds. They think they can use their law degree as a natural way to become a staffer on Capitol Hill or even run for some sort of elected office. So when this cohort approaches you (or even prospective law students generally) and they say they want to work in politics or policy, do you have a typical response? Is there anything that they should know before trying to pursue this path?

Whenever anybody is interested in policy, I always encourage them to do it. I've done a lot of different things and I think this is so interesting and exciting. Policy is the opportunity to identify a problem, come up with a solution, and create a strategy to implement the solution by putting together all of the different pieces. It's incredibly satisfying and creative. You actually get to see the results. So I always encourage people who are interested in going into policy.

I also tell everyone (it's usually young women who ask me about this) that I am so glad that I went to law school. I think it really helped me be better at this job. But you don't have to go to law school. I think it has to do with your background and your confidence. I started law school when I was twenty-one years old. I graduated at twenty-four. I was young, so law school gave me the confidence to advocate and do the things I needed to do. Some people start off with much more confidence than I did.

I graduated from law school in 1995 wanting to practice law. I didn't know how many Master of Public Policy programs there were in the early 1990s. Now, there seems to be this actual option to really develop those skills and relationships and be targeted in learning about policy analysis and creation. You can do it in two years instead of three and for less money. So if you know this is what you want to do, there is an option now that I didn't have.

So while it isn't necessarily a prerequisite now, you did get that benefit of going through the pressure cooker of law school. It helped you gain that confidence and learn some of the softer skills that serve you well in politics and policy.

Yeah. Do you know who Jerry Seinfeld is?

Yes.

So Jerry Seinfeld once said, "Lawyers are like when you play a board game with people who read all the rules on the back of the box cover. That's what a lawyer is." I do like knowing all the rules. There is a confidence that comes with understanding how things are made and their history. So I found the content of the law to be very interesting.

Let's go back to the early days when you were first thinking of law school. When did you think it was an interesting idea? Did you have an overarching vision of what you would do with your law degree?

I went to a Quaker college in Indiana. Most of my classmates were becoming teachers and were joining the Peace Corps. I was in a space where people weren't going on to business school. People weren't going into finance. That just wasn't the community. So I wanted to go to law school to become a public interest lawyer. That was my plan and that's what I did for a while.

Before entering politics, where did you practice?

I practiced at Bronx Legal Services for about three years.

Before that, you attended Earlham College. What did you study there? Like you said, you were thinking of law school at the time. Did you select your major to help prepare you for the law school path?

I was a political science major. I grew up in Washington, D.C. before we moved to Florida. Both of my parents worked in government. So I was surrounded by politics. Both of my parents were political scientists so I was not going to study political science.

I was a Japanese studies major. I was a philosophy major. I did all of these other things. Then, I took one political science course and was like, "Oh, right. This is the coolest and most interesting thing." I don't think that's an uncommon journey for a young person. Then, once I started studying political science, I knew I wanted to practice law.

Did you take any time off between college and law school?

So I went to college when I was seventeen. I went to law school at twenty-one. That is one thing that I would do differently. It would have been to take a gap year at some point because that was very young to be going to law school.

What do you think you would have done in that gap year?

Well, maybe I would have traveled through Europe. Then, maybe have done something like being a camp counselor. Just anything. It would have been something different and some experience of being out on your own. By just going from home to college to law school, I was entering the workforce at twenty-four without having really been a member of the workforce. I did summer programs as a law student, but it's not the same.

I'd like to talk about that in a bit. But just going back. You said there are many more MPP programs out there. Knowing what you know now, as you are graduating from college, would you have done that instead of going to law school?

Maybe if I knew I wanted to work in Washington, D.C., I would have gone straight to Washington, D.C. But I've also learned after spending time on the Hill that a great thing to do after college is to work on Capitol Hill. You make $21,000 a year. You live in a group home five hundred miles from Capitol Hill. You learn so much and that's the time to do that. I missed the window. I didn't get to Capitol Hill until I was twenty-eight years old.

Before getting there, however, you enrolled at New York Law School. Why did you select it over others? Was there anything in particular that was attractive to you?

Well, I wanted to go to New York. We didn't have the internet, so I had to go to the library and take off the shelf this big book of law schools. I had to go through it and figure out where to apply. I looked at Seton Hall in New Jersey. I was looking at a bunch of schools that were in my tiers. I had taken the LSAT and I could get into a second-tier law school. I could have gone to CUNY. I could have gone to a lot of places that maybe were more focused on public service (which is what I wanted to do).

New York Law School is a good law school. I passed the bar the first time I took it. I learned how to be a lawyer. But most of the people going to law school with me were interested in getting a legal degree to make money. A lot of them still lived at home on Long Island with their parents and commuted. It was just a different vibe than what I was going for. I think it's easier to research things like that now than it was back then. In 1992, it was hard to pick.

Can you take the readers inside your law school experience? Is there anything that was particularly memorable? And looking back, do you have any tips for current law students on how to make the experience easier?

I really enjoyed law school. It was really fun to learn the things that we were learning. I was not on law review. I was not in the top ten percent. I think there's a whole different level of competitive engagement that some people thrive on that I do not. One thing that is hard is if you are not someone who wants to be pitted against your peers in constant competition. You just have to get over it in law school. It's hard. You succeed if others don't do as well as you. That doesn't appeal to me.

But what I did love was a civil law clinic. That was great. I participated in some of the moot court competitions. When you do a law clinic, you actually get to represent clients. You get that sense of whether or not this is something you want to do. I feel like now, a lot of law schools have more of those than we had back then. My niece is a third-year law student at the University of Maryland. She's doing a couple of those. Her experience is very much what I experienced twenty-five years ago.

I couldn't agree more. I did a clinic during my 3L year. It's great because you get the best of both worlds. You get to actually engage in legal practice, but you also have someone there to guide you. Also, I prefer the practical to the theoretical. Clinics are more hands-on compared to the theoretical underpinnings of your traditional law school class. Looking back, is there anything that you would tell yourself in your 2L or 3L years (especially related to finding a job after law school) that would put you at ease?

It's such a time of uncertainty. That is really, really stressful. During my summers, I worked at law firms. But during the school year, I got work-study jobs that placed me in New York City Mayor Dinkins' office. It was so cool.

I would say that you should pay attention to the thing that you're getting excited about. That was the job I was looking forward to. It was the work in politics and dealing with constituents. I worked in the Office of Constituent Services and I was responding to inquiries from people who lived in New York City. I also worked in the Office of Immigrant Affairs. New York City was one of the first cities that had basically sanctuary status. So dealing with policy got me a lot more excited, but I didn't notice. I was busy doing everything else to become a lawyer.

At the time, you didn't think, "Well, maybe I would work there after graduation?

That never crossed my mind.

So your priority was public interest work throughout law school?

Yeah.

How did you find your first job after law school? You said that you were working at law firms during your summers. Were they public interest law firms?

No. For the first summer, I clerked for a judge. For the second summer, I worked for a patent and trademark firm. I realized that someone else could represent the interests of Rolex and Stanley Tools. They did not need me. I wanted to do something else.

The first law job I got was with a not-for-profit called Eviction Intervention Services. It helped people who were threatened with eviction. We worked out of a church basement on the Upper East Side. Every night, the lawyers had a milk crate. We would put our files and stuff in these milk crates and lock them in a closet because the church basement was rented out to Alcoholics Anonymous meetings after our office closed. It was that level of grassroots advocacy.

Because I did that, I was in court within one week. It was all just very scrappy. We made very little money, but I learned so much and it was hands-on. So that was my first job. I went from there to Bronx Legal Services, which felt like the big time after working out of a church basement. I was a tenants' rights attorney.

Can you take us back to that time? Your first job at Eviction Intervention Services must have been such an eye-opening experience. You graduate from law school. You do have some of this practical experience working in clinics, but now you're a practicing attorney. You passed the bar and it's all up to you. I'm assuming you didn't have much help around you. You had to do everything yourself. Can you talk more about how you did that?

There was a senior attorney who basically was responsible for teaching me. Quickly after hiring me, they hired two other recent law school graduates. We were all incredibly young and he just had to teach us. We were like his little ducklings.

As far as things I learned, there were assumptions that I had made about the cause of people's problems. There was a certain amount of addiction that I saw in my clients. But a lot of it was just bad luck, liking the wrong guy, and trusting the wrong people. And there was no safety net. Basically, if they got the flu and missed an appointment, they would stop getting their checks. Therefore, they would fall behind on their rent and they would be evicted. If they are evicted, they lose their kids.

You just watch it go. It was eye-opening to me to realize that there was something systemic about it that I, with my middle-class background, had never been aware of before. Nobody taught me about how unfair it all is.

It's eye-opening on that front and also eye-opening because you have to represent them. They're relying on you to do the best work that you possibly can. How did you get that first job at Eviction Intervention Services?

So in order to pay the rent, my first job when I left law school was at Gay Men's Health Crisis. I don't know if it exists anymore, but it was a fundraiser for AIDS research and treatment. They did two big events per year: one was a big bike ride and one was a dance-a-thon on New Year's Eve. I was hired to go walk around and get storefronts to agree to put a little plaque on the counter with the fliers for the Gay Men's Health Crisis dance-a-thon. That was my job, and they paid me $10 per hour, which was an incredible amount of money. I could pay my rent.

I was doing that job for a while. I was temping as a secretary. Also, in 1995, there was a glut of attorneys in a city of top-notch law schools. And I had gone to New York Law School. So until I passed the bar, I wasn't going to get a job as a lawyer. I found out I had passed the bar in December. So that whole space between September and December, I was working at Gay Men's Health Crisis and I was working for another six months as a secretary.

I got my first law job after that. That was at Eviction Intervention Services. I got it because I would make a call to New York Law School's job line every Friday at 4:00, where they would post new jobs on an answering machine in career services. Alumni would call up and listen as the woman who worked there read job descriptions out loud. So you had to sit there, listen to the whole thing, and write it down. One of them was this job. I applied for it and they hired me. When I went in to interview, they said, "We like you" and they hired me. I was so happy.

That's a great story. It shows grit and determination to keep calling into that phone line and actually reaching out for that opportunity. From there, you get to Bronx Legal Services. You said you felt like you were in the big leagues and that you had made it. Can you share some of the cases you were working on and what you did or didn't like about that experience?

Our offices were in a building in the Bronx. It has all been gentrified now. But at the time, it was rough. I would walk down the street and people thought I was a social worker. They would be yelling out to me from windows and street corners and I would explain that I was a lawyer.

The housing court was in the basement of the civil court building in the Bronx. It was right next to the old Yankee Stadium. So we would go every day into this basement. We were signing court orders in stairwells. It was incredibly messy. At the time, it was like we were the least important thing that could possibly be happening in civil court (and we were keeping people from being evicted). Then, while I was working there, they built a new housing court. Now, there is a beautiful courthouse. It was much more appropriate for the significance of the matters.

I had to learn many things on the job. I studied Spanish. My husband was in graduate school and I took two years of college-level Spanish so that I could talk to my clients and coworkers. That was really cool. But I also had to learn when my clients were lying to me. I had to have conversations with them where I said, "That makes no sense. And if I don't believe you, the judge won't believe you." I did bench trials and they were great experiences.

The best part was if I could slow an eviction and stop an eviction. People kept their homes, their jobs, and their kids. After around three to five years of working in New York, I would every once in a while run into old clients who would come up to me and ask, "Do you remember me? I have a job now." We changed some lives. Clients would give me thank you cards. I wasn't writing an *amicus* brief in the Supreme Court, but I was helping this one person and everyone they love make it to the next step so that they don't fall apart. That was the best part.

You're seeing all of the output of your hard work. That's in contrast to working somewhere like a commercial law firm. The work is more siloed off, so it can be tougher to see your impact on a human level. But where you were working, you saw it every single day. At the same time, however, you made the switch and worked on Capitol Hill. Why did you decide to make that change?

My husband went to graduate school and worked in the environmental movement. Washington, D.C. is where the jobs are. When he graduated, he got a job there, so we moved to D.C. I had a realization about the work that I was doing. I was burning out emotionally and I wasn't necessarily as good at it as I wanted to be. I was going to get better. But there is a confrontation aspect to it—especially in a job where you're dealing with low-end landlords and low-end law firms. A lot of it is screaming in your face. It's just part of it and that's just not my strength.

So when I came to Washington, D.C., I thought I would try working on Capitol Hill or getting a job in policy. I interviewed at some not-for-profits. It was interesting. Then, I met someone who had previously worked for a Republican Senator (he was a friend of a friend). He took me out to lunch and he said, "All you have to do is print out your resumé, go through a map, and make a list of every single place that you could claim as your own." So I could claim Naples, Florida, and then Florida as a state. I could claim Montgomery County, Maryland (I lived there as a child) and then Maryland as a state. I basically made this list of twenty members of Congress where I had some sort of connection. Then, my friend of a friend said, "Go in there (it's an open building) and drop off your resumé." I'm like, "Really?" He was like, "I swear, you can just do it."

So I did. And that night, the chief of staff for Congresswoman Nydia Velazquez of Brooklyn called me to set up an interview. I was a housing lawyer from New York and she was on the Housing Subcommittee for the House Banking Committee. She needed someone who was a housing policy expert. It was just one of those random things. If I hadn't dropped off my resumé, that never would have happened. And I got the job.

That's so cool. It was basically about pounding the pavement and putting yourself out there. I think that's a great lesson for readers, as they may need to do this type of work to find their ideal job or position. So you worked for Congresswoman Velazquez, but you also worked for Congressman Bill Pascrell, Jr. Is that right?

Yeah. So I started with Congresswoman Velazquez and then went to Congressman Pascrell pretty quickly. I stayed with the Congressman and became his legislative director.

As a legislative director, what were your responsibilities? What did you do on a day-to-day basis?

Every office is different, but a personal office for a member of Congress is an intimate thing. You'll have six to eight people with their desks jammed into a room that is the size of a dining room. It's really cramped. Everybody has to do a little bit of everything. There isn't a lot of hierarchy. It's very flat.

Members of Congress differ. Some of them are lovely, easygoing people. But as you stay, you become more and more reliant on your staff. I'm not speaking specifically of the Congressman. But just in general, the care and feeding of the member of Congress is part of the job. It's picking them up and dropping them off. It's making sure they have lunch. It's escorting a constituent who's visiting over to where the member of Congress is voting so that the constituent can get a photo taken with the Congressperson. A lot of the mechanics of that are just part of the job because all of those things matter.

Then, you have to respond to constituent mail. You organize meetings with interest groups and stakeholders. The strategic part of it is getting your member onto the committee that is most helpful to them. Congressman Pascrell is now on the Ways and Means Committee, which is a very important committee. That happened right after I left. When I was working for him, he was on Small Business, Budget, and Transportation and Infrastructure, which is an entirely different ball game. Once you're on Ways and Means, you get more money and more attention.

Were you practicing when you were a legislative director?

No. I keep my license, but I haven't practiced law in twenty years.

Looking back, do you think it would have been helpful in both the politics and policy worlds if you kept practicing law?

No. It's not as much fun. That was the thing. I just told you that when I was making the decision to try something new, it was the realization that maybe it didn't play to my strengths. When I started working on Capitol Hill, everything I did had the response of, "That's a great idea" or "You wrote that so well." I was getting that feeling of, "Oh, this is a much better fit." That's why I stayed. It was a better fit and it just made sense.

Let's say that a law student or lawyer wants to follow a similar path and work in a Congressional office. Maybe they want to become a legislative director or something else. Is there anything they can do

to increase their odds of successfully making that switch? On the surface, it seems like networking is the most important thing.

Relationships really matter. For instance, when I was a legislative director, a woman came to my office who was a practicing lawyer but wanted to transition to Capitol Hill. She was from New Jersey and her mother knew a friend of the Congressman. I met her and she was smart and cool. I offered her a non-paying internship. She took it and was incredible. She then went on to work for Carolyn McCarthy and wound up on the education subcommittee as permanent staff and is now at the Department of Education.

If a young lawyer comes to Capitol Hill and takes a job as a legislative assistant, within a certain number of years, they will be a legislative director.

What about a practicing role? Say a counsel position on one of the committees. Do you have any tips for lawyers looking to make the transition to those types of roles?

Not so much. When I was in New York, if you went to law school, you became a lawyer. If you weren't a lawyer, we called you a non-practicing attorney. We didn't necessarily say that because it was cool. Then, I moved to Washington, D.C., and every third person here is a non-practicing attorney. Everybody has a law degree. It's very common in this world that I'm in now to be a non-practicing attorney. So the practicing attorneys have their own language, groups, and hierarchy. They all know each other and I'm not really a part of that.

I've been in three labor unions now and we always have a general counsel's office. They've got their own thing going.

But going back to what you said, if a reader is seeking out a non-practicing role, networking and building relationships is critical. Once you get your foot in the door, it's game on.

Yeah.

So you worked with Congressman Pascrell for a while. Then, you ended up transitioning into policy work. Can you talk about that

transition and why you chose the Center for Science in the Public Interest?

Well, I loved working on Capitol Hill and I loved working for the Congressman. But I had a child and that changed everything. I wanted to be home. So I wound up going home and being a full-time mom for about three years. Then, I decided it was time to go back to work. But I knew I couldn't go back to the Hill because you are beholden to the floor schedule. At that point, I had two children.

I had done some work in nutrition when I worked for the Congressman. So I ended up at the Center for Science in the Public Interest. It was a wonderful experience. The woman who ran the nutrition department was Margo Wootan. She taught me everything there was to know about being a lobbyist.

We called one of our initiatives "menu labeling." That was where calorie information had to be placed on menus. Today, when you go into Starbucks, you can see that the scone has twelve hundred calories. We did that. We took the joy out of eating out. That was one of our big projects. When we were working on it, it was revolutionary. People were like, "No one will do that" and they do it and it's fine.

We worked on really great issues. That was where I learned how to build a coalition and what a coalition meant. You agree on what you agree on until you don't. I was doing a lot of work trying to get funding for obesity research at the NIH. So I was partnered with Nestlé and Kellogg and all of these big food institutions who were supporting the research into what causes obesity and how to stop it. I organized and lobbied with them. Having an experience like that and learning about the different bedfellows was interesting.

Can you discuss some of the major differences between working on Capitol Hill, lobbying, and policy work? You are building coalitions in these arenas, but are there any major differences that the readers should know?

What's fun about working on Capitol Hill is that you're sitting on that side of the table. Everyone is coming to you and asking you for things. But once you have that line of sight of what people are looking for, when you're on the other side of the table and you're coming in as the advocate, you can message it better. You understand what you can do in your messaging to make it easier for the person you're trying to persuade to get to "yes." I feel like one really informed the other. You don't have to have worked on Capitol Hill to be a good Capitol Hill lobbyist. But it was very helpful because I had that background.

Being an advocate is really fun. My favorite part of the law is getting the chance to convince people of your point of view. That's what being an advocate is. We used to have to explain what obesity was and how we could stop it. It was fun to bring people in that moment where you see them coming over to your point of view.

Definitely. If I can ask you something related to what you said a few moments ago. You took some time off to be with your children. You then came back into the workforce and found your first job in policy. Can you describe how you actually did that?

Well, I've done it twice. I did it then and then I did it again. I found that it wasn't as hard as I feared it was going to be. That was very satisfying. The warning to give future parents who perhaps want to do something like that, though, is that you do lose time. I am not a vice president. I'm not a chief of staff.

There were choices that I made along the way. I decided to spend time with my children when they were young. I had a moment when I came back to work the second time where I just had to say, "It's not going to bother me that my boss will be younger than I am. My boss will probably be younger than I am from this point forward. You can be younger than I am and be a seriously mature adult. I just can't let that bother me. You just have to let it go." So there's a certain amount of ego that you have to set aside.

Sure. So re-entering the workforce and getting that first job was about mining through your old contacts and seeing what opportunities were out there. Is that right?

This might be somewhat specific to Washington D.C., but once you've had Capitol Hill experience and worked in a Congressional office, it's like you're in the club. No one cares anymore—especially since the Congressman is still in office—that I haven't worked on Capitol Hill for eighteen years. I did it once, which means I understand the game. That has opened so many doors for me.

So with that job and the job I came back to the second time, my Capitol Hill experience was a big part of it.

That's definitely good to know. You've worked in three labor organizations now. So when you were evaluating opportunities to go from one to the other, what factors did you consider? Did it come down to things like certain people you wanted to work with or more responsibility that would be allotted to you?

I worked at the Center for Science in the Public Interest and then my husband got a job overseas. We went away for two years. That's why I left that job. When we came back, I started working for the United Food and Commercial Workers. I think I was there for about seven and a half years. How familiar are you with labor unions?

I have some familiarity, but I'm definitely not an expert.

The leadership of a labor union is elected. They are politicians and there can be complete turnover. I was hired by one president. I was close to him and did a lot of work for him. He later retired. The next president entered and wanted to bring in his own people. Things change and that's pretty common with labor.

Now, you're a policy director at the SEIU. What does a typical day look like for you?

SEIU is wonderful. People don't know a lot about labor. I think only six percent of the private workforce actually belongs to labor unions. But SEIU represents people who work in health care. We represent people who work in janitorial work, security in airports, and public sector workers. Most of those people that I just named were essential workers during the Covid-19 crisis.

It's hard to say what I do every day because everything is always evolving and changing. I started at SEIU in 2018 and one of the first things I did was I went down to Florida and ran the Tallahassee office for Andrew Gillum's campaign for governor. Then, I came back and we immediately had five hundred people running for president. So I was doing policy work to try to get all of the candidates to include my institution's priorities in their campaigns. We succeeded in getting almost all of the Democrats to include our priorities.

I spent a lot of time doing that. Then, I spent the next nine months trying to get Joe Biden elected. SEIU's president was on the platform committee for the Democratic National Convention. We had specific language that we wanted to get into the platform. I had to do a lot of work with the DNC staff. We had to do a lot of coalition building to try to get other people to support our language as an amendment in the platform. Post-election, now we get to govern.

What does that look like now?

It's the best part. The American Rescue Plan had just passed. We worked very hard to try to keep the fifteen-dollar minimum wage in the American Rescue Plan. It was booted out of the Senate version for procedural reasons. But that's an example of one of the things that we were pushing for. There is more money for Medicaid in that bill. There is the child tax credit expansion. There are all of these social changes that will stop suffering and help people who are in the situation they're in because of Covid.

There's a lobbying team that goes to the Hill and talks to people. I am coordinating meetings with all of the incoming Cabinet members and their teams to make sure they understand what our priorities are and to try to get them to put those priorities on their agenda. With the American Rescue Plan, $350 billion is for state and local governments. I represent people who work for state and local governments. So we're also doing briefings for our leaders at the local level so they know who they need to talk to, what levers they need to pull, and what language they need to make sure is included in whatever the state rollout is. I'm also talking to the Treasury Department, where they are drafting guidance for how that money will go out. I want to make sure it is done in a way that my members can use it.

So I'm doing that right now. But in a month, I won't be doing that.

How big of a team do you manage?

My total department (which is policy, research and capital stewardship) is fifty people. Of that, policy is about eight people.

There are many moving parts that you have to monitor. What are some of the biggest challenges in your work? On the other hand, what parts of your job get you most excited?

One of the biggest challenges (and I think it has been made worse under Covid) is that there's too much to do. I've got a family and children at home. How do I create that boundary between the work I'm responsible for and my home life? The job is big and fun and exciting, but it can take up more room than the work necessarily deserves. I think that's a constant challenge. That's my biggest challenge with this job.

But the thing that gets me most excited is when we win. We hadn't won in a long time. This win was really satisfying. Doing something that's going to help people is really great. That's the best part.

Is there anything that you do that you didn't initially foresee when you took on this role with SEIU (or even your prior advocacy work)? Was there anything that was on your plate where you thought, "Oh, I didn't expect this and I have to do it now?"

I would say that since I've been working in the labor movement, I have very rarely worn one hat. Policy is a term of art. It could mean so many different things. I find myself being responsible for writing talking points, a letter, or something that's going to be used in a press statement. Sometimes I think, "Isn't there someone else who could be doing this?" But I'm the person who knows the subject matter. So that is the secret: policy can be whatever the person who is giving you something to do wants it to be.

You just have to be adaptable.

Yeah.

For law students and lawyers that are thinking of getting into political or policy work, I'm assuming that there are some first principles that they should generally follow to increase their chances of getting their dream jobs. If you have someone that comes up to you

and says, "Hey, Mia, I want to work on Capitol Hill" or "I want to work in public policy," what general advice would you give to them?

We've discussed networking. I would say informational interviews are great. Whenever anybody asks for an informational interview, I'm someone who almost always gives it because it is so important. I've recently hired someone on my team that I met through an informational interview. So I think that is a great thing that a lot of people aren't necessarily familiar with or don't feel comfortable asking for. If people don't think you're asking for something, they'll give you some of their time. I always advise people to do that.

So this informational interview is something like, "Hey, I'm interested in SEIU. Can you tell me more about it?"

Yes.

Are there any mistakes that many prospective candidates make? This is both in the politics and policy worlds.

I guess the thing to know is that so much of this is about clicking with people. Also, it's important not to take it personally if you don't get a job. It can be a bad fit. It doesn't mean that you weren't qualified. It means there was somebody else that said it differently and they liked it more. Knowing that this is part of it is just something to accept.

And when those candidates get into their jobs, do you have any tips on how they can be more effective and make an impact?

I think they should always be positive. Also, don't think something is beneath you. This is especially true if you're right out of college and have been treated like you're really smart and special while you were in school. Then you get out and discover that you're not really smart and special (or rather, everyone is). That is an important and humbling step to go through. Some graduates don't manage that well. But if you're positive, upbeat, and a good team player, people respond to that.

Do you think law students or lawyers have any advantages or disadvantages in getting these roles?

Oh, definitely. Like I told you, I have not practiced law in twenty years. I went to a law school that no one has heard of. I get one hundred percent credit for being a lawyer everywhere I go. It opens doors for me. Even now, people will defer to me. People will say, "Now, I'm not a lawyer like you, but..." It's a real value that I didn't know would travel with me for this long in my life.

Interesting. It's the prestige factor of getting a law degree and becoming a lawyer. Just to wrap up: can you share some of the best career advice that you've received? This can be from anyone like a mentor, friend, or family member.

I did not have a mentor and I didn't get a lot of career advice. Something that I have experienced in this part of my career is young women being assertive in seeking advice from me and wanting me to play a mentor role for them. I don't have any of my own to share because I didn't realize that it was something I was missing. But I encourage people to find those mentors and seek them out.

Chapter 17

Twenty-Five Key Takeaways

According to legend, Mark Twain once said, "Keep away from people who try to belittle your ambitions. Small people always do that, but the really great make you feel that you, too, can become great."

If you want to do something non-traditional with your legal degree, you'll inevitably come across naysayers. They may cast doubt on your ambitions and make you seriously question whether you can reach your career goals. Granted, there may be some truth to their statements. You should soberly evaluate your capabilities and financial circumstances, especially if you are leaving a great job or gig to do something new.

However, if you are set on doing something beyond traditional legal practice, it is important to surround yourself with positive influences. Having a collection of relationships that focus on the possibilities, rather than the impossibilities, gives you a greater chance of transforming your ambitions into realities. Even though you may not personally know these fifteen individuals, I hope you can think of them as unofficial mentors. They have gone on to have stellar careers outside the law. It's not impossible.

When creating this book, I wanted to hear from impressive law school graduates who have had fascinating careers outside the law. All of their stories are unique, ranging from Melinda Snodgrass's journey to Hollywood to Daron K. Roberts's experience in the NFL. I found their stories to be extremely inspiring. I hope you have as well.

However, I think these interviews go beyond pure inspiration. After reviewing more than twenty hours of audio, I came up with twenty-five key takeaways from these conversations. To be clear, these are *my* key takeaways. You may disagree with some of them or find others that are more relevant to you. Nevertheless, I believe these insights are helpful for anyone who wants to take on a non-traditional career. At the same time,

I encourage you to go back to these interviews as necessary, especially if you want to move into a sector or industry covered in this book.

Whether you read this chapter alone or read all fifteen interviews in this book, I hope your journey doesn't end here. With a book like this, it's all too easy to get inspired but fail to act. I can speak from experience. The great news is that you don't need to take a gargantuan step. It can be as small as having a conversation with someone outside the legal industry or taking a ten-thousand-foot view of your finances. Action begets further action. Often, the hardest step is the first step.

* * *

The best opportunities often come from relationships.

If I had to select one key insight from all fifteen interviews in this book, it would come down to two words: relationships matter.

Strong relationships are vital if you want to have a non-traditional career. However, they are arguably just as vital if you want to have a traditional career in legal practice. Whatever you are trying to accomplish, you will have a much greater chance of accomplishing it if you can rely on a solid and diverse network. As David Hornik told me, the people you meet in any given situation are probably more important than the things you actually learn.

Nonetheless, if you are trying to game the system and develop relationships solely for your benefit, you'll likely be disappointed. Relationships are a two-way street. You can't just be initiating relationships to get what *you* want. On the other hand, by giving back and genuinely investing in your relationships, you'll find that some fascinating career doors begin to open.

Throughout this book, you have seen how professional and personal relationships can change the course of a career. Keith Rabois was able to join PayPal because the person who hired him (a former college classmate) believed Keith could quickly pick up the necessary skills to thrive. In part, Richard Hsu found his first job out of law school and a job at a venture-backed company because of his connections at Caltech. Jessica Medina had plenty of great relationships with lawyers at the SEC and lawyers who used to work at the SEC. That substantially increased her odds of getting a new job at the SEC Division of Enforcement.

To be clear, these don't have to be "professional relationships" that are built at the office. You can see this in Melinda Snodgrass's story, where she regularly played role-playing games with Vic Milán, George R.R. Martin, and other renowned writers. Building real, authentic relationships with these talented individuals helped Melinda improve her craft and enter Hollywood. She wasn't trying to game the system and use these individuals to advance her career. Rather, she was there because of the community. The career benefit was secondary to the genuine relationships she created.

Your technical skills are important. As Ayelette Robinson said, whenever you are starting, you need a craft. In your chosen line of work, you must know what you're doing. But once that basic threshold is met, you'll find that your relationships will be a key driver in achieving your career goals. In other words, the odds are that you aren't going to find an enticing non-practicing role by blindly submitting your resumé on job boards. It is going to come from your network and the personal relationships you've built over your life.

If you remember one thing from this book, I hope you remember the power of relationships. Not only do they make life better, but they can help you build the non-traditional career you desire.

Identify mentors, whether they are inside or outside the legal industry.

While relationships matter, there is one type of relationship that is especially important. It is the mentor-mentee relationship. If you look through history, many of the best performers in any given field trained under an older, wiser, and more experienced individual.[1] A master-apprentice relationship is beneficial because you, the apprentice, get a first-hand account of the wisdom and knowledge that the master has gained. Moreover, you get direct feedback from an experienced sage.

Throughout this book, you have seen how these talented individuals cultivated mentors in their careers. Those mentors gave them priceless

---

1   To further learn about the importance of mentors and apprenticeships, I encourage you to read *Mastery* by Robert Greene.

knowledge and helped them pursue their goals. For instance, as Daron K. Roberts worked to break into the NFL, he sought out Mike Leach, who was a law school graduate and coach of Texas Tech University's football team. Daron received some priceless guidance about football, breaking into the NFL, and more.

As Melinda Snodgrass said, mentors are huge. So how can you identify helpful mentors? Richard Hsu gave some helpful advice. He said the best mentors are those who have a vested interest in your career and who had a great mentor themselves. While these individuals are hard to find, they *are* out there. It is your job to find them.

Beware the identity trap.

Unlike many other professions, lawyers must make a significant time investment before practicing their craft. As I described in the first chapter, there is a long, expensive, and time-consuming path before our first day as practicing lawyers.

The problem emerges when we suddenly discover that we are on the wrong path. While that initial realization may be a relief, a new problem can emerge. We invest so much time in becoming lawyers that the profession becomes tied to our identities. When we self-identify as lawyers, there can be a real sense of loss when we leave the legal field to do something else. As Angela Saverice-Rohan said, it was difficult not to identify as a lawyer when she moved into consulting. I also experienced this feeling when I left legal practice to do something else.

I'm not sure if there is a quick and easy way to address this issue. Simple awareness is a good start. Taking up hobbies or interests outside of work can help you recognize that there is more to life than your work as an attorney. You can even try to join clubs or other groups outside of your industry. The goal is to look beyond your job title and understand that your identity doesn't need to be congruent with "practicing lawyer."

It's easier if you can somehow avoid this identity trap in the first place. For instance, Jay Bilas said he didn't have his identity attached to how he performed at Duke Law School. He credited it to being out of school for some time and recognizing that the layperson doesn't really care about a lawyer's law school grades. Whether or not you're like Jay, don't forget about this identity trap as you proceed through law school and your legal career. It is a real thing and something that many attorneys must navigate.

A step back isn't negative if you're on the right path.

One of the scarier things about making a career switch is the feeling of stagnation or regression. It's easy to think that our career paths will be like a hockey stick (up and to the right). This is especially true for lawyers. As just one example, many Big Law firms compensate their associates through a lockstep model. Your base salary is dependent upon the year you started at your law firm. You and other attorneys in your class receive the same salary increase each year. While bonuses are discretionary, the lockstep model gives associates the feeling of incremental progress toward that final goal of partnership.

This appeal of up and to the right growth isn't just in Big Law. Many of us with high goals tend to focus on our potential successes instead of the trials and tribulations that may emerge. The reality is that most of our careers aren't linear. This up and to the right framework doesn't account for the complexities of life.

For lawyers, one of the challenges in leaving the legal field is the fear of getting off a set track and starting over. By choosing to pursue a career in some other sector or industry, you may need to initially find a role with significantly lower pay. Your starting role may not have the prestige that you had as a lawyer. You may have significantly fewer responsibilities or oversight over others. Recognizing this reality, it is tempting to think twice about making the move—even if you are unhappy with your current work.

In this sort of situation, I think it's critical to take a long-term view. As Anthony Scaramucci told me, the greatest thing that ever happened to him was when he went from a job at Goldman Sachs that paid $110,000 to a job at Goldman that paid $56,000. Even though it was a step back in pay, he was placed into a role that better fit his skill set. A temporary pay cut resulted in Anthony dramatically increasing his earnings throughout his career.

I heard a similar sentiment from Ayelette Robinson. We must keep our long-term career trajectories in mind. If you are spending one hundred percent of your time heading in the wrong direction, it doesn't matter how quickly you travel in that direction. On the other hand, if you know exactly where you want to be in five to ten years and are taking some sort of gig that helps you get closer to that ultimate destination, you will probably find that it is time well spent.

If you are considering a move out of legal practice into a role that pays less or offers less responsibility, you probably don't want to dismiss it outright. In fact, that role may be just the thing you need to build your new career outside of the law.

There may be an optimal time to leave legal practice for something else.

This book is about non-traditional careers. I hope you've seen that you don't need to be shoehorned into a legal career that you're "expected" to have. While it certainly isn't easy, you can craft a non-traditional career on your terms.

That said, the interviews in this book have shown that certain principles can make your work much easier. There may be exceptions to these principles, but generally speaking, they will steer you in the right direction. One of those principles relates to timing. Depending on what you want to do outside of the law, there may be an ideal time to take the leap and pursue that craft.

For example, Angela Saverice-Rohan said that the optimal time to switch into management consulting is three to five years after law school. After five years, it becomes harder to reverse the habits—both analytical and otherwise—that we develop as practicing lawyers. In other industries, that ideal transition window is different. I think the best way to discover it is to speak with experienced individuals in your new sector or industry.

Sure, nobody is forcing you to adhere to these transition windows. It isn't impossible to succeed in a new sector or industry if you enter it outside these windows. Nevertheless, keep this in mind as you contemplate a career shift. Sometimes, the best time to make a major career move is right now.

Monitor and combat inertia.

All of us know what inertia is. Essentially, the idea is that an object in motion tends to stay in motion unless some external force acts upon that object. While Newton's discovery revolutionized the physics world, we can apply this idea of inertia to our careers, both inside and outside the practice of law.

Simply put, inertia can take us to places that we may not necessarily like. If you are dissatisfied with your legal career but don't actively combat inertia, it could be several years before you make the leap and leave the law behind. If you just let inertia run its course, you may not leave at all. By refusing to make tough decisions or interrupt an unsatisfying career path, inertia will automatically make career decisions for us.

Several individuals in this book alluded to this idea when speaking about law school recruiting. Many of the top law schools make it extremely easy to pursue associate positions at commercial law firms. As Keith Rabois said, many graduating law students end up at Big Law firms for economic reasons *and* because it is the path of least resistance. Sander Daniels noted that it was hard to go in an independent direction during law school. He told me that law school funnels you into very specific career paths and that there is incredible social pressure to follow those paths. That social pressure is real, and inertia can take over if you don't actively resist it.

You can also experience inertia in legal practice. Jessica Medina said that if you intend to work at a Big Law firm and then leave to do something else, you must plan. If you don't aggressively plan, you may get sucked into default mode, making it much more difficult to leave.

The antidote to inertia is action. Sometimes, you need a dramatic change of environment to get some clarity on your current career trajectory. For Tiffany Duong, this came from a trip to the Galapagos Islands. The insights she gained on that trip helped her recognize that she was on the wrong path. She needed to leave legal practice and start with a clean slate.

You don't necessarily need to go to the Galapagos to combat inertia. Search for those moments where you can break out of your routine and think about the trajectory of your career. Whether it comes from an impactful trip, a conversation with a trusted mentor, or an experience in a non-legal field, you may discover something interesting about yourself and your current career path. Then, take action.

Know yourself.

When speaking with Tiffany Duong, I noticed she was especially attentive to gathering "data points" in her career. As she explored her new career outside legal practice, she tried many different things. Embracing this exploratory mindset helped her discover what she enjoyed and didn't enjoy.

While you don't necessarily need to create a large spreadsheet containing every data point in your career, I think her practice speaks to a larger point. Whether you try to get a new position in law or leave entirely, you must know yourself. You have to get introspective and be honest about what you enjoy. Further, knowing what you don't want to do can be priceless as you build your career outside legal practice.

There are plenty of examples in this book. For instance, Jessica Medina recognized that she is not an adversarial person. Even though she loved her colleagues at the SEC, she was tired of the inherent conflict that comes with being a litigator. Mia Dell felt the same when she represented her clients in housing court. A good part of her job involved confrontation (which she didn't particularly enjoy).

Sit down and think about what you enjoy in your work. If you want to leave legal practice to do something else, understand your preferences and find a gig that caters to those preferences. In some instances, you may discover that leaving legal practice itself is *not* the problem. As Richard Hsu told me, many attorneys don't consider why they want to leave their law firms. It's a question of fit. Sometimes, legal practice itself may not be the problem. Rather, it could be a specific boss or a particular organization. To best gauge that, honestly recognize your likes and dislikes. Be true to yourself. The answers are there if you look within.

When moving out of the law, exercise humility.

No matter which type of law you practice, lawyers like you have tremendous amounts of responsibility. Your clients depend on you to exercise your best judgment when representing them. In some cases, your work directly impacts your client's liberty. These are high-pressure situations and your clients and colleagues are looking for you to make the best possible decisions.

As much as the general public likes to criticize or make fun of lawyers, they tend to see lawyers as intelligent, hard-working individuals. Like Anthony Scaramucci said, people are impressed with lawyers and a legal education. So when you want to leave legal practice to do something else, there can be some culture shock. Depending on your new role, you may not get as much deference and respect as when you were practicing law.

You may be asked to do things that seem to be below your pay grade. It can challenge your ego, especially if you have been practicing law for some time.

If you are seeking to leave legal practice for a non-traditional career, it's critical to stay humble. As Mia Dell said, nothing is below you, especially if you are early in your career. There's real value in saying *yes* to show your work ethic, humility, and willingness to help your new team. A great example comes from Daron K. Roberts. Simply put, the NFL didn't care that he graduated from Harvard Law School. Daron had to run "as fast as humanly possible" to prove his worth to the Kansas City Chiefs. He took on all sorts of tasks to show his dedication to the organization. His humility and hard work paid off.

Humility is a great attribute in many situations; however, it is especially helpful when you are leaving legal practice to do something new.

Hustle.

You have read how talent and relationships can propel you toward your career goals. This is true whether you have extremely high goals outside of legal practice or are looking for a more fulfilling role outside of the law.

What happens if you are earlier in your career? What if you don't feel confident in your craft or have a smaller-than-desired network? In that case, there is real value in hustling toward your goals. By hustling, I mean being scrappy and relentless. I mean doing things that others won't do. Clearly, I'm not saying you should break any legal or ethical boundaries when doing this. Having said that, embracing a hustler's mindset can open some doors that otherwise wouldn't be open.

Anthony Scaramucci cold-called fifteen Wall Street law firms to find a job before law school. When Daron K. Roberts was trying to break into the NFL, he treated his NFL dreams like a political campaign. He wrote letters to nearly every head coach and assistant coach in the NFL and college football, hoping someone would take a chance on him. Mia Dell called New York Law School's jobs hotline every day, which led her to her first legal job at Eviction Intervention Services. Tiffany Duong literally took on eighty-nine interviews to find a job amid the Global Financial Crisis.

Hustle isn't a dirty word. It can be your competitive advantage should you choose to embrace it. As just one example, if you are trying to expand your network, consider sending cold emails to interesting people in your industry (or even an industry that you eventually want to enter). While there is an art to this, I am a huge fan of targeted cold emails. In fact, I had no prior relationship with every individual I interviewed in this book. Every initial contact came from cold emails. The key word, however, is *targeted*. While you certainly don't want to spam people, a well-crafted and targeted cold email can open doors.

Your work ethic, creativity, and persistence are key traits here. Don't hesitate to tap into them when you are making a major career move.

Take advantage of opportunities created by macro events.

I have found Stoicism to be a fantastic guide when navigating the challenges and vicissitudes of life. Even though there is a public perception of Stoics being cold and constantly thinking about death, I have found Stoicism extremely empowering. One of the key principles of Stoicism, which is particularly relevant to this book, centers on control. That principle is to focus on the things we can control rather than what we cannot. In other words, we cannot control how certain things occur, but we can control our reactions to them.

As a law student or practicing lawyer, it can be frustrating to have events outside your control impact your career path. However, these macro events can also be outstanding catalysts for change. As Jessica Medina told me, the 2008 Global Financial Crisis ended up being a net positive for some graduating law students about to enter Big Law. Those graduates ended up taking their stipends and finding fellowships, clerkships, and public interest work. They enjoyed their new work so much that a good number of them didn't return to their firms. They couldn't control the fact that they graduated during a worldwide economic crisis, yet they could control their effort in pursuing new opportunities.

Even a layoff can be an outstanding catalyst for change. This may not be as "macro" as a global financial crisis, but layoffs or firings can be positive turning points in a career. Just look at Michael Bloomberg, who was fired at Salomon Brothers and built a gargantuan business empire. Ayelette Robinson experienced an unexpected layoff, but instead of being paralyzed by doubt and fear, she aggressively pursued her acting dreams.

I encourage you to adopt a similar mindset when you navigate your post-law school career. Adopt a glass-half-full perspective when you are reacting to substantial macro events. Control what you can control and focus on your reaction to events outside your control.

Be careful about following your passion.

Search Google for any type of career advice and you will undoubtedly come across the question of whether you should follow your passion. If you dig deep enough, you'll find compelling arguments on both sides.

I think it's fair to say that every individual in this book is passionate about their work. If you look at someone like Melinda Snodgrass, you can see how passionate she is about writing. She told me that she literally could not write. A "cosmic cheering section" of characters in her head is imploring her to write about them. Nelly Baksht spoke about an indescribable feeling of creating artwork for her collectors. Speaking with all fifteen individuals, I could tell how much meaning their careers provide them.

That being said, it isn't necessarily true that they were passionate about their work *before* they took on that work. Sander Daniels, for instance, didn't grow up being passionate about local services. When he started working on Thumbtack, the passion gradually arrived. Working in local services is his life passion because he built it into his passion. Keith Rabois shared a similar thought. He told me that passion comes as a result of experience and success. Having a lifelong passion or obsession over a particular area or sector isn't a requirement for working in that particular area or sector.

This "follow your passion" debate will continue for the foreseeable future. Nonetheless, I don't think you necessarily need to take a side. There are other signals that you'll want to closely track when you're considering alternative career paths. For instance, Mia Dell told me that people should pay close attention to what excites them. Following your excitement can lead you to some interesting gigs or opportunities that you may not necessarily be "passionate" about. Keith Rabois also said people should pay close attention to their skills. By finding a role that lets you leverage those skills, you will find that the passion eventually arrives.

The bottom line? I don't think you necessarily need to be passionate about a particular sector, industry, or opportunity outside of the law before pursuing it. Asking whether you are passionate about it is too simplistic. Instead, canvass your skills and see where your interests lie. By tying both of them together, you may come across a specific opportunity that ends up being your lifelong passion. When you get that opportunity, aggressively pursue it.

Experiment during your law school summers.

This is an important takeaway for prospective or current law students. Your 1L and 2L summers offer outstanding opportunities to get first-hand experience in all types of offices and organizations. You want to take advantage of these summers, as they represent some of the few data points on what your early professional life could be.

You may have an idea of what you want to do before arriving in law school. You may have a better idea as you're proceeding through your first semester. However, it is tough to know what the actual work is like unless you have personal experiences. I'm not saying you can get a complete picture in just two or three months, but you can get a clearer picture than you would *ex ante*.

As Richard Hsu told me, it is helpful to get the widest breadth of experiences that you can. Your 1L and 2L summers are there so you can combine legal theory with actual work. The summers are especially valuable if you are debating between two distinct career paths. You have two great opportunities to get first-hand experience in the practice areas or domains that excite you.

Now, there are some nuances here. For instance, if you are interested in a summer associate position at a commercial law firm, you probably want to pursue that opportunity during your 2L summer. If you like the work and receive an offer, you can accept the offer and go into 3L year knowing that you will have a job after graduation. It can be harder to find those types of opportunities if you don't work at commercial law firms during your 2L summer. Putting that aside, your 1L summer is an excellent time to find some opportunity that interests you—even if you aren't certain whether you want to take on that type of work full-time. If possible, keep experimenting outside your 1L and 2L summers. Depending on where you attend law school, you may be able to find externships or internships during the school year.

In the end, don't take these opportunities lightly. By pursuing them, you may find an awesome gig that you may not have necessarily considered before entering law school.

Avoid premature optimization.

Premature optimization is an idea that originated in software development, yet I believe it is relevant when you are trying to do something
different with your career. Essentially, premature optimization is the
idea of spending significant time to make something great (even perfect)
before verifying whether your initial assumptions are true. A simple
example of this is making a dinner reservation before realizing that your
spouse can't make it. You assumed that your spouse was available, but
without testing that assumption, you ended up wasting time.

By avoiding premature optimization, we mitigate risk. We evaluate
our assumptions upfront before investing more time and effort into a task,
project, or career path. Granted, you must have the self-awareness to
identify the assumptions you are relying upon, but if you can do it, you'll
be in a better position to make good decisions.

One great example comes from Tiffany Duong. She never mentioned
the term "premature optimization," but we can see the value of this idea
in real life. Tiffany left legal practice and thought that she would be
interested in becoming a marine biologist. Before fully taking the plunge,
however, she wanted to see if she really enjoyed fieldwork. Tiffany literally went to the Amazon rainforest to test that assumption. After around
two to three weeks, she discovered fieldwork *was not* for her. Instead of
discovering that perspective after completing her science prerequisites
and attending marine biology school, she tested it head-on. It helped her
find work that spoke more to her interests and preferences.

Premature optimization is something that all of us should keep in
mind. One natural connection to this idea is the law school decision itself.
As you've seen, I asked nearly everyone in this book whether they would
encourage prospective law students to work in the legal field before
attending law school. There were convincing arguments on both sides.
There's also the question of whether you should get some type of tangible
experience in your preferred non-legal field before making the switch.
We've seen some individuals who had prior experience in their chosen
field while others made the transition with literally little to no experience in their field.

So what do I think? Tangible experience is a great way to avoid premature optimization; however, I still believe you can get the benefits if you
don't become a paralegal before law school. You can identify the assump-

tions you make before a large decision and stress test them. For example, you can speak with individuals in the legal field and determine whether your assumptions are gauged in reality. If you want to leave legal practice and work in a totally unrelated field, read about that field and have as many conversations as possible. The goal is to collect data points, stress test your assumptions, and avoid poorly-fitting paths that may initially seem exciting.

Take action—even if you end up failing.

As Daron K. Roberts told me, time is a finite resource. It's easy to ignore the ticking clock when we are in the early stages of our careers. We are constantly incurring opportunity costs. Every day that we forgo something we've always wanted to try is one fewer day we have to do so.

All fifteen individuals in this book have a bias for action. They are willing to enter the arena and bet on themselves with the risk of falling flat on their faces. Sure, they are thoughtful individuals. However, they aren't overly contemplative. They understand that even if they are slightly off course, their consistent bias for action will lead them in the right direction.

Diahann Billings-Burford also articulated this idea. Especially for individuals that are earlier in their careers, it's important to do *something*. While you may fear failure, it is much easier to recover compared to someone who is later in their career. When I asked Sander Daniels about leaving Big Law to do something new, he said that people tend to overthink the decision. You simply have to take opportunities that emerge and hope for the best.

As Nelly Baksht told me, people interested in art should just start drawing. Tiffany Duong said if you want to get into journalism, just start writing. Ultimately, action can cure many of the fears and anxieties about doing something new, whether that is a new skill or a new career. If you fail, don't take it personally. Pick yourself up, recognize the mistakes you made, and avoid making those mistakes in the future.

There may be hidden risk in not making a move.

When we consider major career moves, it's easy to focus on the risks that come from taking that leap of faith. The future is largely unknown. Our minds come up with all sorts of scenarios—most of them negative—about leaving a safe and secure job for something new.

Yet just because the future outside the law is daunting doesn't mean your future in law is less daunting. By staying at your current gig or position inside the law, your career may be on a rockier trajectory. If you aren't interested in your work, your colleagues will notice. If you forgo an opportunity to follow a mentor to another firm, you may miss out on a chance to advance your legal career. If you are nervous about pursuing that one nagging startup idea, it will just remain an idea.

Sander Daniels understood this principle. He recognized that the risky thing was staying at his law firm instead of taking a leap and making the most out of Thumbtack. As he told me, staying at his legal job would have probably led to a life of unhappiness and dissatisfaction. Even though he had a great career as a practicing lawyer and was financially secure, he understood that standing pat was the wrong long-term decision.

Sander hit a home run with Thumbtack. In retrospect, he undoubtedly made the right move. While we don't have the benefit of hindsight, we must recognize the risks of inaction. Yes, the security and comfort of a job are enticing—even if you don't necessarily enjoy your day-to-day work. But by zooming out and projecting your overarching career timeline, it may become obvious that your biggest career risk is going through the motions in your current job.

Stay in touch with your old contacts.

No matter what you want to do after law school, you'll find it much easier if you keep in touch with your old contacts. This not only includes your law school classmates but your classmates in college and high school. It also includes your professional contacts, whether they are from internships or jobs inside or outside the legal industry.

As Tiffany Duong told me, there is much more to law school than class. Creating real friendships with your law school colleagues makes the experience much more enjoyable. Among many other things, your friends can help you manage stress during the thick of exams and open doors after law school. For instance, David Hornik's law school roommate helped him find a practicing role at Venture Law Group, which catalyzed his career in the startup world. There are other situations where some of your classmates could become some of your future clients. In the end, you just never know.

Another great example comes from Diahann Billings-Burford. When she was ten years old, she participated in Prep for Prep. It was a profound life experience. Even before attending law school, she thought about returning to Prep for Prep and finding a full-time role at the organization. However, she decided to go to Columbia Law School and work at Simpson Thacher & Bartlett. When she was at Simpson and looking for opportunities outside of Big Law, Prep for Prep came calling. Its founder was leaving, and the organization had a new position for her. Without her early experiences and effort to stay in touch with the organization, she may not have found that particular opportunity.

I'm not saying you should make these connections solely for your professional benefit. This "me first" approach is the wrong way to look at it. However, by building authentic personal relationships with your contacts, maintaining those relationships, and giving back, you will be pleasantly surprised at the doors that open. Arguably, your second-degree contacts (the contacts of your contacts) can provide even more opportunities that you don't initially expect.

While the value is obvious, that value doesn't automatically arrive. It takes work to build and maintain your contacts—especially when you are out of law school and are in the thick of your legal career. It can be much easier to focus on the work in front of you. That said, there are simple things you can do that can go a long way. Share an article that your contact may find interesting. Try to schedule a Zoom call or coffee meeting where you can catch up. Ultimately, provide value where you can, even if it is in the form of advice or words of encouragement.[2]

Don't underestimate the value of preparation.

As lawyers, one of our strengths is preparation. Whether we are getting ready for a high-stakes oral argument or a meeting with an important client, we put in the work to give ourselves the best odds of success. This great habit is arguably strengthened in law school, where we read hundreds of pages per night and prepare for a grilling from our professors.

---

2   If you are looking for more ideas, I recommend you read *Never Eat Alone* by Keith Ferrazzi. It is a classic book on how to build strong relationships that last.

The great news? You can take this strength and use it to unlock new opportunities. For example, Jay Bilas has recognized the importance of preparation throughout his life. He identified it as a basketball player, as a law student, and as an assistant coach for Mike Krzyzewski. By being prepared, he seized opportunities in his career, whether he was in the courtroom or in the broadcasting booth.

Sander Daniels also made sure he was prepared before leaving the law to work at Thumbtack. As he told me, he put a note on his refrigerator saying he would leave by a specific date. To get ready for that date, Sander ensured he had enough money saved where he could work at Thumbtack for two years without an income. He did this preparatory work about fourteen months before he left to pursue his dream.

Critically, there's a fine line with preparation. You don't want to prepare *so much* that you end up not taking any action. Preparation can be a tantalizing excuse for procrastination. That said, whether you are looking for a way out of legal practice or just want to increase your chances of reaching your career goals, embrace the preparation skills that you've developed.

When taking a role outside of the law, leverage your "soft skills."

In this book, I have mentioned how law students and attorneys over-whelmingly focus on improving their technical craft. In law school, it is about understanding case law and doing well on exams. In legal practice, it is about marrying our knowledge of the law with our clients' problems. Legal practice is a craft at its core, and we spend much of our time work-ing on that craft.

At the same time, we develop other soft skills. We may not recognize it at the time, but these soft skills can serve us well after we leave legal prac-tice. As former practicing attorneys in non-practicing roles, these skills help us stand out. They help us become better practitioners in whatever craft we're pursuing.

In these interviews, I frequently asked about the advantages and disadvantages that lawyers have when moving into a different field. I did so because I think the question can lead to some helpful insights. To increase your odds of success in your new sector, I encourage you to rely on your soft skills. At the same time, you should try to avoid some of the habits and tendencies that may play well in the law but hold you back in a non-practicing role.

So what are those soft skills? Some of them include:

- **Analytical skills:** Anthony Scaramucci mentioned that lawyers have outstanding analytical and critical thinking skills. They can hold two ideas at the same time and rely on nuanced thinking to make better decisions. Diahann Billings-Burford also repeatedly referenced critical thinking skills as extremely valuable whenever lawyers work outside legal practice.

- **Problem-solving skills:** As Angela Saverice-Rohan said, lawyers have great problem-solving skills. Daron K. Roberts agreed. While we develop these problem-solving skills in law school and legal practice, these skills are certainly transferable outside the law.

- **Oral advocacy skills:** Even if we don't appear in court every week, we naturally develop oral advocacy skills throughout law school and legal practice. David Hornik said that law school is a great training ground for effective oral advocacy. Being an effective oral advocate, according to David, is the single most important skill that you can have in any profession.

- **Research skills:** Research skills are critical for almost every job in legal practice. Even if you aren't researching case law in your new job, your research skills are certainly transferable. For instance, Tiffany Duong told me that her ability to research and distill information quickly is extremely helpful as a journalist.

- **Time management skills:** As law students and practicing lawyers, we need to protect our time. The great news is that time management skills help us become more efficient in our non-practicing lives. While you don't need to keep tracking your time in six-minute increments (like Tiffany Duong does), you can rely on your time management skills to get more done.

- **Grittiness:** As lawyers, we are gritty and persistent. We proceed through three years of law school, pass the bar exam, and face challenges in our day-to-day work. Through all of that, we survive. As Diahann Billings-Burford referenced, our ability to be tenacious can literally change our clients' lives. We can apply the same tenacity and grittiness to our careers outside the law.

As Tiffany Duong said, don't sell yourself short. No matter what you are doing outside the law, you aren't starting from scratch. You have plenty of soft skills to apply in a new career. Use those skills.

Beware the golden handcuffs.

This is a specific concern if you work—or intend to work—at a Big Law firm. As you read in this book, the "golden handcuffs" is the concept of being unable to leave your high-paying job because it would force you to take a dramatic pay cut. No one is physically stopping you from leaving. However, it can be tempting to stay in a high-paying job (even if you don't like it) because leaving would force you to adopt a lower standard of living. It is especially difficult if your standard of living includes high fixed costs.

Several individuals in this book warned about the golden handcuffs effect. Tiffany Duong experienced it when she increased her expenses as a way of coping with the difficult workweek. Anthony Scaramucci also mentioned the golden handcuffs as a reason why some attorneys don't leave large commercial law firms.

The most obvious antidote to the golden handcuffs effect is controlling your spending. Tiffany knew she wanted to leave her commercial law firm, so she dramatically cut her expenses around two years before her departure date. While there are some expenses (like student loans) that you can't necessarily cut, there certainly are some expenses that you *can* cut. Being aggressive on this front can help you avoid the golden handcuffs syndrome and make it easier to leave a high-paying practicing position for something else.

Don't ignore financial planning before making a substantial career move.

Non-traditional careers involve different types of risk. Whether you are thinking of dropping out of law school or leaving legal practice to head in a completely different direction, we need to at least acknowledge—and seriously consider mitigating—those potential risks.

For instance, there is career risk. Choosing to pursue a craft or vocation outside the law can make it harder to return to legal practice (especially if you spend years pursuing that craft). You've already heard about opportunity costs and how you are constantly incurring them—no matter the path you're pursuing. Beyond opportunity costs, you will certainly want to acknowledge the financial risks and consequences of leaving your current gig to do something else.

Quite obviously, not all career moves are the same. Moving from one Big Law firm to another Big Law firm is much different than moving from a practicing role to a non-practicing role. Moreover, giving personalized financial advice in a book like this is virtually impossible. It's a sensitive subject and one that is slightly different for every person.

That said, I think an important first principle involves planning. No matter the move you're pondering, it is worth your time to complete some sort of financial audit or plan. It's an obvious step, yet it can be surprisingly easy to ignore or put to the side. The value is abundantly clear if you have substantial student loans and are stepping away from legal practice. But even if you don't have loans or are in an extremely healthy financial situation, spending some time on financial planning is a net positive. It can help set your expectations and make it more likely that you achieve your financial goals.

If you're looking for an in-depth discussion of finances and leaving legal practice for a non-traditional career, I encourage you to review my conversation with Jessica Medina. For starters, she encouraged lawyers to look at where their cash is going. It's an insightful exercise that can give you some good ideas about where you can cut unnecessary spending. Then, think about what life will look like after leaving legal practice. Even if you are making less money, you may not have to support the same lifestyle (and the associated costs that come with that lifestyle). As Jessica told me, this exercise can reveal many different possibilities. It can provide some perspective and give you more confidence to make a move.

You can also go one step further. Before becoming an Accredited Financial Counselor, Jessica aggressively tracked her spending. Sander Daniels looked into the future, determined how much cash he would need to save to join Thumbtack full-time, and lived frugally to reach that financial goal.

In the end, planning can help you identify your financial vulnerabilities. It can help you mitigate financial headaches and set your expectations for your life outside of the law. Frugality can't hurt either. As Sander said, you want to give yourself some runway, especially if you take on a risky endeavor like launching a startup. Whatever you choose, embrace financial planning. Your future self will be grateful.

Sometimes, you simply need to pay the bills.

When contemplating a move outside of legal practice, it's easy to underestimate how much time it takes to reach your goals. As I mentioned, careers aren't linear. A smooth transition to your dream job likely won't be instantaneous. There are going to be twists and turns that you may not necessarily anticipate. In those situations, there's nothing wrong with taking a job that helps you pay your bills as you are pursuing your long-term goal.

After Melinda Snodgrass quit her law job to become a writer, she still had to make a living. While she worked on a large science fiction trilogy, she wrote romance novels under pseudonyms. Even though she wasn't necessarily passionate about romance novels, they paid well, and she could finish them quickly. Her science fiction trilogy was her priority, but she needed to delve into the romance market *so that* she could finish her science fiction books.

For Ayelette Robinson, her training as a Pilates instructor helped her earn cash and have the flexibility to pursue her acting dreams. Before she left her knowledge management job, she had taken a Pilates certification course. She had always loved Pilates and never planned to teach it. However, her Pilates certification acted as a bridge when she started pursuing acting full-time. She could both earn cash and have a flexible work schedule to go on auditions as they came up.

Don't be ashamed or annoyed that you need to take on some side job or gig as you pursue a larger goal outside the law. So long as you are making tangible progress toward your long-term goals, this interim work can be extremely valuable. The same is true if you remain in legal practice before making a more substantial change. If you have a large amount of student debt and don't see how you could financially pursue your dream job outside the law, you may need to stay put, do great work, build your savings, and then make a move. While this isn't specific financial advice, it goes back to the point of preparation. You can't prepare for everything, but you can manage your expectations—both before and after you make your move.

Listen to your hobbies and interests.

I mentioned the importance of hobbies and interests in the introduction to Jay Bilas's interview. Jay, however, wasn't the only individual in this book who had an interest or hobby that transformed into a unique career opportunity. There's obviously no guarantee that'll happen, but the odds may be better than you think.

For instance, Jessica Medina didn't have a decades-long plan to become an Accredited Financial Counselor. Instead, when she was at the SEC, she spent some of her personal time running spreadsheets and projections to plan her financial future. She subsequently recognized that she could help others with their finances, which led to her new career outside legal practice. Nelly Baksht pursued her interest in art and graphic design by attending a two-year course in graphic design. Sander Daniels and his friends wanted to work on interesting side projects, eventually settling on the idea that would become Thumbtack. While he never imagined Thumbtack would turn out the way it did, he actually entered the arena. He took action.

Even if you aren't leaving the law, carving out time to pursue those hobbies and interests can make you better at your craft. Keith Rabois referenced this idea in the context of diversifying your knowledge. By pursuing your interests and reading things that others in your field aren't reading, you can stand out amongst your peers. Daron K. Roberts also mentioned hobbies as great ways to provide perspective while in law school. They help you understand that there is more to life than your grades in Civil Procedure or Contracts.

There's no need to be extremely calculated with your hobbies or interests. To this day, Melinda Snodgrass is an equestrian rider. She does it because she loves it. The benefits naturally flow from the pursuit of her hobby. It helps clear her head, thereby allowing her to write compelling stories that her fans love.

By solely focusing on your work, you easily become dull. However, pay attention if your hobby or interest opens up more serious career opportunities. It can be a blaring signal in a world full of noise.

Take advantage of clinics in law school.

I asked all fifteen individuals about their general impressions of law school. Their experiences varied, but I think one of the more notable insights is related to an activity that you can leverage in your 2L and 3L years. I'm talking about clinics.

Clinical opportunities are great for so many reasons. First, you get to move beyond legal theory and work on real legal problems. As Mia Dell said, you get to actually represent clients. Working underneath a skilled and experienced professor, you start developing practical skills that you can use in legal practice. Sure, you gain a better sense of a particular area of law. But beyond the technical aspect, you learn priceless skills like active listening, managing client expectations, how to best craft a legal argument to accomplish your client's goals, and more.

You're also able to get outside your comfort zone. Diahann Billings-Burford said clinics represent a great chance to "get out there, be scared and be nervous." These early experiences can be intimidating because you are learning the practice of law *and* representing real clients. However, you still have a professor or attorney supervisor to back you up.

I found my clinical experience to be one of the best things in law school. Many others feel the same. If you are interested in one (or several) of your law school's clinics, don't hesitate to take a closer look. You may be on the cusp of one of your favorite experiences in law school.

Have a totem to motivate you during tough times.

Law school and legal practice can be stressful. This is true whether you are in the thick of law school exams, trying to find your first job after law school, or are dealing with an extremely difficult client or colleague. The stress can also come when you leave the legal field to try something else. These situations can strengthen our tenacity and grit, but in the moment, they can feel overwhelming.

In those tougher times of law school, legal practice, or your post-law life, it helps to rely on a totem. Essentially, a totem is a symbol (a thing or person) representing a larger concept or idea. It can be your *why* as you are aggressively pursuing your goals. Thinking about that totem in difficult times or situations can help you maintain perspective. It can even provide you with some extra energy when you feel like giving up.

Several individuals in this book alluded to this idea. Melinda Snodgrass spoke about her love for her father and how he wanted her to finish law school. She told me that she couldn't bring herself to disappoint him—even though she wasn't entirely enthused with the law. Jessica Medina thought of her children as she went through some of the more challenging times in law school. As she said, it didn't feel like a choice. She had to finish so she could support her children for the rest of their lives.

You can also create and rely on a totem in your professional career. If, for instance, your new career outside of the law isn't going the way you expect, keep going back to your totem. Your totem doesn't have to be another person. It can be the person you want to become or an overarching principle or idea you want to pursue. While it isn't a silver bullet, your totem can be your North Star and help you navigate through choppy waters.

Life is short.

In the thick of our professional lives, it can seem like we have plenty of time to reach our goals. If you are earlier in your career, you may be right. Graduating from law school in your mid to late twenties, you have time to explore your interests and develop your craft.

Having said this, it can be surprising how quickly life happens. One moment we're learning how to write a legal brief, and the next moment, we're representing clients in high-stakes complex litigation. One moment we're in our 1L criminal law courses, and the next, we're taking on a new client who faces decades in prison. While our day-to-day lives in law school or legal practice may seem slow, our careers advance at a rapid clip.

Further, nothing in our careers is guaranteed. Even *tomorrow* isn't guaranteed. We assume that we will wake up in the morning and continuously advance toward our long-term career goals, whether those goals are inside or outside the law. Nonetheless, life can get in the way. We think we have plenty of time to achieve those goals, but the reality is that we may have less time than we anticipate.

We need to recognize the finite amount of time we have. As Daron K. Roberts told me, we only have one life. It is up to us to decide what to do with it. When deciding what to do with it, we cannot be passive. We must take ownership of our careers. No one else is living our lives. While others may have strong opinions on how to live our lives, we are the ones that must accept the consequences of our decisions.

As Ayelette Robinson said, the reality is that we have more control than we think. It may seem like we are stuck in a certain position or on a certain career track. It may feel like we have to spend a defined number of years in a role before leaving to pursue what we really want to pursue. But there are always options. Granted, there may be certain situations where a drastic career change *right this second* isn't realistic. You'll have to judge whether you're in that situation. But even if you can't make that dream career move today, there are certainly steps you can take to get closer to that ultimate move.

If you truly want a non-traditional career outside of the law, it helps to think like an entrepreneur. This is true even if you aren't technically starting a new company or venture. Because you are pursuing a non-traditional path, you are almost required to do things differently than the crowd. Adopting an entrepreneurial mindset can help you identify some of those unique routes to get to your goals. There's no guarantee, but by building "the startup of you,"[3] you'll tilt the odds in your favor.

It all comes back to taking action. Seneca is one of the "big three" philosophers in Stoicism.[4] He intimately recognized that humans often overestimate how much time they really have. "You live as if you were destined to live forever," he said in *On the Shortness of Life*. "You squander time as if you drew from a full and abundant supply, though all the while that day which you bestow on some person or thing is perhaps your last."

Time is the most precious commodity on our planet. Simply put, you have choices and opportunities, though they may be hard to see at the moment. The time to pursue them could be right now.

---

3   This is a reference to *The Start-up of You*, a book co-authored by Reid Hoffman. Hoffman was a cofounder of LinkedIn. The book touts the importance of adopting an entrepreneurial mindset to achieve your career goals. While it was published in 2012, many of the lessons still apply today.

4   The other two are Marcus Aurelius and Epictetus.

Acknowledgements

There are so many people to thank in a book like this. For starters, I want to thank Nelly Baksht, Jay Bilas, Diahann Billings-Burford, Sander Daniels, Mia Dell, Tiffany Duong, David Hornik, Richard Hsu, Jessica Medina, Keith Rabois, Daron K. Roberts, Ayelette Robinson, Angela Saverice-Rohan, Anthony Scaramucci, and Melinda Snodgrass for sharing your career experiences with me. I'm immensely thankful for your trust in me and your willingness to share both the good and the bad from your journeys inside and outside the law. Without all of you, this book wouldn't exist.

Compared to other types of books, this book is more logistically challenging. For instance, scheduling interviews takes time. Because of this, I want to thank the many individuals who helped transform this book from an idea into a reality. In no order of rank or importance, I want to specifically thank Pamela Canny, Cristina Cassese, Amy Cusick, Ian Cutler, Samantha Darsie, Mai Davis, Debra L. Hartmann, Jenna Lorenzano, English Player, Marideth Post, Jared Shanker, and Kristine Villasis. Between coordinating interviews to copy editing and designing this book, your assistance was vital.

Finally, I want to thank all the family, friends, and colleagues who stood by me—both on my career journey and in creating this book. While this book was a long time coming, it wouldn't have been possible without your words of encouragement, love, and inspiration. I can't thank you enough for your support.

About the Author

Adam Pascarella is the founder and CEO of Second Order Capital Management, an investment management firm located in New York City. Previously, Adam was a practicing attorney at Baker McKenzie, a Vault 100 law firm one of the world's largest commercial law firms. At the firm, Adam specialized in general commercial litigation.

Adam received his Bachelor of Arts in Political Science from the University of Michigan and his Juris Doctor from the University of Pennsylvania Carey Law School. His work has been published in *ABA for Law Students*, *Law360*, *Lexology*, *The Startup*, and the New York Public Library. Adam lives in New York City with his wife Leah, son Paul, and dog Ruby.

www.adampascarella.com

@apascar

www.ingramcontent.com/pod-product-compliance
Lightning Source LLC
Chambersburg PA
CBHW030450210326
41597CB00013B/616